REMOTE CORNERS

REMOTE CORNERS
A Sierra Leone Memoir

Harry Mitchell

The Radcliffe Press
London · New York

Published in 2002 by The Radcliffe Press
6 Salem Road, London W2 4BU
175 Fifth Avenue, New York NY 10010

In the United States and Canada distributed by
Palgrave Macmillan, a division of St Martin's Press
175 Fifth Avenue, New York NY 10010

ISBN 1–86064–817–7

A full CIP record for this book is available from the British Library
A full CIP record for this book is available from the Library of Congress

Library of Congress Catalog card: available

Typeset in Sabon by Oxford Publishing Services, Oxford
Printed and bound in Great Britain by MPG Books Ltd, Bodmin

Contents

Illustrations

1. The author standing outside his bungalow, number 9, on the Bo Government Reservation.
2. The author with friends in Kambia. Mike Sandercock standing, with his wife Helen and their two sons and Dennis Hedges.
3. A view of the district office (right) and district barri (left) in Kambia.
4. The author's stepdaughter, Kamini, in 1957 with a friend.
5. The author and Dorothy Roberts, wife of Eric Roberts, research scientist at Rokupr, later Professor of Agriculture at Reading University. We were on a launch on the Great Scarcies River, April 1958.
6. Rokupr market, Megan inspecting fruit display.
7. River scene, Rokupr warf.
8. River scene at Rokupr, Kambia District, on the Great Scarcies.
9. Climbing a palm tree to collect the coconuts.
10. Interior of a small store
11. Men playing gbalangis, an African version of the xylophone.
12. African mother and child carried in a lappa in the traditional way.
13. African faces.
14. African faces.
15. Extraordinary headgear.
16. A young Susu woman in Rokupr.

Acronyms and Abbreviations

ADC	assistant district commissioner
CID	Criminal Investigation Department
CMF	Court Messenger Force
CPO	chief police officer
CRO	Commonwealth Relations Office
DC	district commissioner
IDM	illicit diamond mining
LSE	London School of Economics (and Political Science)
MO	medical officer
NCO	non-commissioned officer
PWD	Public Works Department
PZ	Paterson, Zochonis & Company
RSPCA	Royal Society for the Prevention of Cruelty to Animals
RUF	Revolutionary United Front
SLST	Sierra Leone Selection Trust
TA	tribal authority

Glossary

banda	long, low buildings made from local materials, used for drying and smoking fish
barri	open-sided courthouse
beg	an inducement given to obtain a favour
bonga	smoked dried fish
bug bug	white ants or other troublesome insects
chummery	accommodation shared by a group of single men
dash	tip or bribe
fundador	mild Spanish brandy
lappa	cloth worn by African women, wrapped around their bodies
palaver	discussion or dispute
pan	corrugated iron
tie tie	creeper usable as makeshift rope
warri	cattle enclosure
wu hitie	literally to hang heads, to discuss something — a Mende expression

Preface

As is explained in the opening chapter, this book was written originally more than 40 years ago. In anticipation of publication it has been substantially revised during the early part of 2001. Many passages contained general comments on a variety of subjects and, where possible, I have updated them by changing tenses and other such devices. In other cases such a means of updating seemed inappropriate or indeed impossible, and I have identified them by displaying them as indented paragraphs.

I need to make special mention of and thanks for the photographs in this book. I did not own a camera in Sierra Leone, so all the photographs I have were taken by other people, most of them by Bob Knill, an agricultural officer and a contemporary of mine whom I came to know with his wife Megan at the West African Rice Research Station at Rokupr when I was assistant district commissioner at Kambia. He was an enthusiastic and skilled amateur photographer as can be seen from these shots taken more than 40 years ago. Sadly, he was killed in a road accident in Pujehun District in 1959. After I returned to the United Kingdom I met Megan again and married her. We are still happily married.

The map is copied from what must now be a very rare publication, the Report of a Commission of Inquiry into Disturbances in the Provinces between November 1955 and

March 1956, referred to in the text as the Cox Commission report. It shows district boundaries, names of districts, roads and the railway just as they were during the period from 1954 to 1959, which this book covers. The Crown Agents for Overseas Governments and Administrations published the report on behalf of the Government of Sierra Leone in 1956.

I have to apologize for the use in some places of the word 'native', which nowadays has sometimes a pejorative connotation but is unavoidable when writing about the administration of Sierra Leone before independence. Sierra Leone was a colony and protectorate, the colony comprising the Freetown peninsula and a thin strip of coastline, the protectorate being the rest of the country, the interior that came under British protection at the end of the nineteenth century. In legal and government parlance 'native' meant the indigenous inhabitants of the protectorate, to whom a different legal regime applied from that which applied to the 'non-natives'. The latter included Europeans, Lebanese, Syrians and most important of all, the Creoles. The latter were descendants of the freed slaves settled in Freetown after being brought from the West Indies when the colony of Sierra Leone was established by Britain at the end of the eighteenth century for the express purpose of providing a homeland for the resettled former slaves. They are ethnically African, but in culture, names, language and everything else are very different from the indigenous people of the former protectorate. Their ancestors had come from West Africa and in some cases no doubt from Sierra Leone, but they had lost connection with their roots and no longer spoke any African language. The natives of the protectorate, as it was before independence, were subject to the jurisdiction of their own native courts, established in chiefdoms that had a large degree of autonomy and had their own native administrations. These were the expressions used in the laws of Sierra Leone and were in everyday use in government.

Preface

Wherever possible I have avoided using the word, but where it has been retained that is because it is the correct word in the context.

Harry Mitchell
10 March 2002

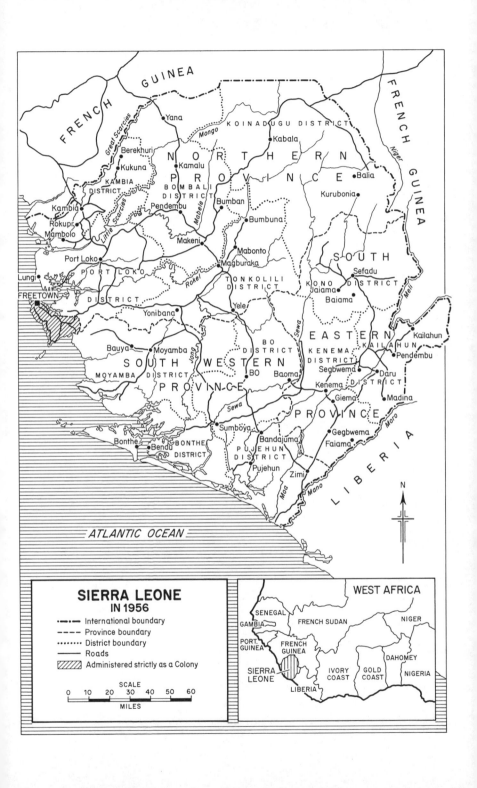

FRENCH GUINEA

FRENCH GUINEA

Yana

KOINADUGU DISTRICT

Mongo

Kabala

NORTHERN

Great Scarcies

Berekhuri

Kukuna

Kamalu

PROVINCE

Balia

KAMBIA
DISTRICT

BOMBALI
DISTRICT

Kurubonia

Kambia

Little Scarcies

Pendembu

Bumban

Mabele

Bumbuna

Rokupr

Mambolo

Makeni

SOUTH

Port Loko

Mabonto

Sefadu

PORT LOKO

Magburaka

KONO
DISTRICT

Rokel

Lungi

FREETOWN

DISTRICT

TONKOLILI
DISTRICT

Jaiama

Baiama

Meli

Yonibana

Yele

Sewa

EASTERN

Kailahun

Bauya

Moyamba

BO
DISTRICT

KENEMA
DISTRICT

KAILAHUN

Pendembu

Jong

SOUTH WESTERN

BO

Baoma

Segbwema

Daru

MOYAMBA

DISTRICT

Kenema

DISTRICT

PROVINCE

Sewa

Giema

Madina

PROVINCE

LIBERIA

Sumboya

Gegbwema

Bonthe

Bendu

BONTHE
DISTRICT

Bandajuma

Faiama

Moro

PUJEHUN
DISTRICT

Pujehun

Zimi

Moa

Mano

ATLANTIC OCEAN

N

SIERRA LEONE
IN 1956
·—·—· International boundary
- - - Province boundary
········· District boundary
——— Roads
▨ Administered strictly as a Colony

SCALE
0   10   20   30   40   50   60
MILES

WEST AFRICA

SENEGAL

GAMBIA

FRENCH SUDAN

NIGER

PORT.
GUINEA

FRENCH
GUINEA

SIERRA
LEONE

IVORY
COAST

GOLD
COAST

DAHOMEY

NIGERIA

LIBERIA

An Updating Chapter

This memoir was written on a portable typewriter a little over 40 years ago in India, mainly on Sunday mornings sitting on the veranda of a bungalow I occupied with my family outside Bombay, where I worked for a British owned company. I left Sierra Leone in October 1959 and have never returned. I arrived in India a little over a year later and decided that it would be a good idea to record my five years in the colonial service in Sierra Leone, particularly as my recollections of those years were still recent and fresh and the way of life I had experienced there was fast disappearing with the granting of independence to Britain's remaining colonies at an ever increasing pace. By the mid-1960s the process was largely complete. I had a complete change of career after leaving Sierra Leone and from the end of 1959 I worked in a succession of companies in industry, first in India and then in the United Kingdom. Shortly before my retirement from full-time employment as company secretary of Wellcome, the pharmaceutical company that is now part of GlaxoSmithKline, I took up an appointment as a part-time immigration adjudicator and have continued to work in that capacity for the past nine years. Adjudicators hear appeals against adverse decisions by the Immigration and Nationality Department of the Home Office, and for the past few years most of the appeals have been against refusals of asylum applications. The appellants come from all over the world but predominantly from Africa, China, the Indian sub-continent, Eastern Europe, Turkey and some Middle Eastern countries. From time to time I have had before me appellants from Sierra Leone and I have always made a point of telling them that I have spent time there, though my experience is from a long time ago. An important part of the work of a district commissioner was judicial, sitting as magistrate with an original jurisdiction mostly in criminal matters or as an administrative officer, dealing with major land disputes or hearing appeals against decisions of the native administration courts. There is a nice symmetry in having started off my career in this way and now concluding it in a comparable fashion, dealing in some instances with people now in the United Kingdom whose fathers or grandfathers might well have been looking to me to dispense justice in Sierra Leone all those years ago.

In recent years, Sierra Leone has been much in the news on account of the horrific events that have taken place there and the general turmoil in which it has been immersed. Over the years since independence there has been a succession of violent changes of government, which has been very much the norm in African countries for the past several decades. Sierra Leone has witnessed a slide into anarchy; in large areas of the country the government's writ no longer runs and control, if any, is exercised by gangs of rebels owing some measure of allegiance to the Revolutionary United Front (RUF). Their control has been exercised by terror, notoriously by wantonly murdering people and mutilating them by cutting off hands and arms. The RUF has recruited large numbers of young children to carry weapons and perpetrate these brutal crimes. Their motivation is greed and the ambition of controlling the large-scale illicit traffic in diamonds. It is generally believed that the president of neighbouring Liberia is an important power behind the RUF.

Problems with illicit mining began in the 1950s when Sierra Leone was still a colony. Much earlier in the twentieth century the Sierra Leone Selection Trust (SLST), a company I believe was a subsidiary of De Beers, bought a concession that gave it exclusive ownership of all diamonds in the country and the right to mine them. The main area of the country where diamonds were found was around Yengema in Kono District in the east. SLST established its mining operation at Yengema on a substantial scale. In the early 1950s, as a result of much activity by prospectors, a lot of local people became aware that diamonds were easy to mine in the alluvial swamps near the major rivers and illicit mining started. It attracted young men from all over the country and from neighbouring countries. All they needed was a shovel, sieve and other simple tools. They dug holes and panned the earth in the hope of finding the precious stones. Lebanese and other traders moved in to facilitate the illicit export of the stones that began to find their way to the diamond market of Antwerp.

The young miners began to make money beyond their previous wildest dreams if they were successful, though most of the rich pickings inevitably went to the middlemen. The mining began to degrade large areas of bush, which came to resemble First World War battlefields pockmarked with shell holes. The diamond rush had major deleterious social effects. The departure of so many young men left large areas of the country with no one to farm the land and there was a drastic reduction in rice production. Rice was a major crop and had been exported, but the drop in production was such that it became necessary for the government to import rice from Italy. One of my first tasks as assistant district commissioner in Bo, my first station, was that of dealing with allocations of imported rice to the large numbers of government employees there, for whom it was otherwise very difficult to buy rice for their families. There was plenty of money about and there was a big rise in the import of consumer goods of all kinds, though the quantity of visible exports was greatly diminished.

The main diamond areas became centres of lawlessness and the concentration of large numbers of people in undeveloped bush areas created health and sanitation problems. In 1956 the government took the first serious steps to try to eradicate the problem by expelling large numbers of Africans who had entered from neighbouring countries. At the same time, by negotiation the monopoly hitherto enjoyed by SLST over the whole country was limited to Kono District and part of another neighbouring district. SLST was compensated out of public funds. Legislation was enacted that allowed the government to issue licences to applicants for areas other than those reserved to SLST. Later attempts were made to control internal migration by setting up diamond protection areas and controlling access to them by people who were not ordinarily resident in them by a system of residential permits. This was not very successful as for political reasons the administration of the permit system was entrusted to the chiefs rather than to the district commissioners, and the obtaining of permits rapidly became a cause of corruption. The last district in which I served was Kono, the main centre for mining and there I spent most of my time sitting as a magistrate, dealing with prosecutions for illicit mining, for which draconian punishments were imposed by special laws. We were obliged to impose a minimum sentence of one year's imprisonment for the offence. Major efforts were made to maintain law and order in the face of the temptations of greed and the making of illicit wealth.

Diamond mining and its accompanying lawlessness were already prevalent on a large scale before independence and the government had to make considerable efforts to keep the situation under control. Success was far from 100 per cent but we were able by and large to keep the peace using the available resources of the local police force, the provincial administration and the courts. Those resources were limited. The police had some European officers at the level of assistant superintendent and above, but ranks below that were entirely staffed by local Africans, who also occupied some of the senior positions. The provincial administration consisted of provincial commissioners, district and assistant district commissioners, mainly European, not more than 20 of us at any one time, covering all the country's 12 districts outside Freetown. All the clerks and other junior staff were African. District and assistant district commissioners were all *ex officio* magistrates and were supplemented in this capacity by a few full time magistrates, mostly African. Apart from these basic forces of law and order there was the Sierra Leone Regiment, a few hundred African soldiers with a small number of expatriate officers and senior NCOs. They would no doubt have been available for internal security duties if needed, but they were not called upon for that purpose during my five years in Sierra Leone.

The Sierra Leone colonial government was able to maintain law and order and protect its citizens with very modest resources. Apart from continuing problems in the diamond areas, there were during 1956 major disturbances in the Northern Province, unconnected with diamond mining, against oppressive and corrupt practices by the paramount chiefs. The police and the provincial administration were stretched to their limits and there were a few deaths and some damage to property.

What a different and terrible picture now presents itself. After years of civil war, violent changes of government, deaths and mutilation and much destruction of property it now requires a force of 11,000 United Nations troops, a battalion of British troops, a substantial naval task force with 800 marines in reserve, what now passes for the Sierra Leone army and a local militia to do a not very successful job of keeping the peace in the face of attacks from the RUF. There was never any necessity to call for the help of the

British armed forces or those of any other country in colonial days and the country was ruled efficiently without any routine resort to the use of firearms or other offensive weapons. Apart from the human cost, the financial cost to the governments of the many countries involved must be enormous, and so far there is very little to show for it. Apart from military expenditure, we learn that the British government has in recent years poured in aid to the value of £60 million to shore up the government of President Kabbah and it cannot be said that we or for that matter the people of Sierra Leone have had value for money.

Those of us who knew Sierra Leone in its last few years as a colony were highly sceptical about its prospects as an independent nation and we all expected that independence would bring problems and a decline in the quality of government, though that was not a message the world's governments and politicians were willing to listen to at the time. Our scepticism has proved well founded, though I do not think any of us could have foreseen the awful chaos into which the country has now descended. The record of what has happened to former African colonies of the European powers since independence is poor. One thinks of the chaos that immediately followed independence in the former Belgian Congo, the current long running war in that country, the dictatorship of Idi Amin in Uganda, the attempted secession of Biafra from Nigeria, civil war in the Sudan, genocide on a massive scale in Rwanda, current events in Zimbabwe, countless coups d'état – the list is endless. Dictators rule and line their own pockets, there is economic mismanagement on a large scale, basic tasks of government are neglected, civil servants and soldiers are not paid. There are one or two bright spots such as Ghana and Uganda, which have had their dark days but now are reported to be on the mend, but overall the description of black Africa on the cover of a recent issue of the *Economist* as 'the hopeless continent' seems apt.

The world is too small a place for the rich nations to be able to ignore the problems of Africa. Apart from other considerations, African countries are now, along with other benighted countries, becoming significant exporters of people, desperately fleeing deteriorating conditions at home and looking for a better life for themselves as economic migrants posing as asylum seekers. In this way the host countries in Europe and North America particularly are finding that Africa imposes extra costs on their domestic social security budgets as well as calling for rising expenditure on military and civil aid to African countries.

It is notorious that in the nineteenth century and earlier, when colonies were being acquired, there was often much reluctance on the part of European governments to take on the additional burdens colonies often represented. But the burdens those same countries and others now have to accept and that are bound to increase with the passage of time must already be far greater than any our forefathers had to shoulder. Furthermore, the donor countries are unable to exert any effective control over the political and economic affairs of Africa and their main interventions are in the form of emergency missions such as those now being undertaken in Sierra Leone, to prop up collapsing regimes. This is a terrible nemesis for the rush on the part of the European colonial powers, under much pressure from the United Nations, to divest themselves of their responsibilities in Africa in the 1960s, without regard for the consequences.

It is not too widely appreciated that the time span between the 'scramble for Africa' in the last 20 years of the nineteenth century and the conferring of statehood on colonies that were created at that time was equivalent to that of only one human life. The starting point was unpromising. The interior of black Africa was peopled by warring tribes of mainly illiterate people. Roads, schools, hospitals and the rest of the infrastructure of a modern society did not exist. The colonial powers did a remarkable job in pacifying the colonies and creating the missing infrastructure, so that by the 1950s it seemed to be possible to accept that conditions were ripe for the Africans to govern themselves. But this assumption was premature. More time was needed to build up a strong and educated middle class, including people in sufficient numbers with the skills and expertise necessary to manage the complex functions of a modern society and, most importantly, time was needed also to build up institutions independent of the state so that after independence there could be some countervailing force against future abuses of power by governments. But time was not allowed; the transition to independent statehood had to be achieved as quickly as possible and we now have to live with the results of that undue haste.

There have been tentative suggestions in recent years that one way to begin to solve Africa's problems would be for countries to surrender their sovereignty and become once again colonies. Such suggestions are no doubt anathema still to many people, but I suspect that they may now find a greater measure of acceptance than would have been the case a few years ago. There are good grounds for believing that large numbers of the people most affected by the current growing chaos, the ordinary people of the African states, would welcome the change. To take recent evidence from Sierra Leone, Mr Penfold, the British high commissioner there during the country's most desperate crisis, was the object of hero worship in Freetown because of his efforts to restore democratic rule and to assist in defeating the RUF. How unthinkable is the idea?

There would of course be political problems to be overcome. Dictators who have come to power by ruthless means and who use such means to hang on to power are unlikely to be too amenable to abdicating, but the Western world is not without powerful means of persuasion in the form of denial of further aid and refusal to consider any forgiveness of the huge accumulated debts of African nations. A more serious

8

obstacle would be the unwillingness of European or other countries to take on the huge responsibility of trying to create order out of the chaos and near anarchy into which so many African countries have declined.

Their task would be formidable and far more hazardous than the one they faced when the African colonies were originally created in the last years of the nineteenth century. There would be opposition from many quarters, not least from European and North American taxpayers. But it ought to be possible to persuade the objectors that this was a far more sensible course of action than continuing to pour financial and other resources into a bottomless pit, which is what the richer countries have been doing for years.

I do not offer here any blueprint for the salvation of Africa, but I do propose tentatively a solution for the continent's appalling problems, which is worthy of serious consideration. Some sort of formula might be found that would involve the United Nations becoming the trustee for the African countries concerned and handing over responsibility for particular countries to ex-colonial powers who were willing to take it. This was the formula devised for dealing with the former German colonies in Africa after the First World War. The League of Nations took them over and gave mandates to France and Britain to govern them, so that for example Tanganyika, now part of Tanzania, was administered by Britain, and Cameroon was partitioned between the two European powers. In due course the United Nations took over and the same arrangement continued, the former colonies concerned becoming trusteeship territories. I accept, however, that the likelihood of any solution of this kind being found to be politically acceptable around the world is very remote. There may not be any alternative to accepting Africa's continuing slide into increasing anarchy, bringing suffering and despair to its people.

1
Prelude

It was suggested to me by friends some time ago that I should write a book based on my experiences over five years between 1954 and 1959 as an administrative officer in Sierra Leone. The material is there if I do but care to apply myself to the physical task of writing, though I do not aspire to emulate the achievement of Arthur Grimble, whose account of life in Pacific islands, *A Pattern of Islands*, published in 1952, must surely outclass all colonial civil servants' memoirs that ever were or ever will be written. A former member of the Colonial Service — or Overseas Civil Service as it was officially called from 1954 — is in a particularly good position to write a book about the country in which he has served, for he knows it, or should know it, better than any other expatriate living there, better indeed than many of the indigenous people.

Why then do so few of us write, leaving the task of presenting to the world the territories we love to journalists and other professional travellers who seldom stay more than a few weeks? Some of the reasons are obvious: most have no inclination to write or may feel, as I have sometimes felt, that years of writing official reports, memoranda and judgments in court cases are bound to stultify any innate creative ability; there are declarations under the Official Secrets Act to be observed as well as any restraints on publication the *General Orders* of any colony may have imposed on a serving officer: there may also be a feeling that writing is something best left to professionals, even if it means a degree of misrepresentation resulting from inadequate knowledge. And yet this is a pity, for the servants of the former British Empire were usually privileged to enjoy a wide, varied and colourful experience such as is vouchsafed to few others.

But colonial administrators are no different from anyone else, and once they have become accustomed to their initially exotic surroundings after taking up their posts, begin to take them for granted. This is a natural and necessary adjustment that anyone must make to a new environment. The poet or the mystic may regard each new day that dawns, each fresh glimpse of a familiar scene as something to be marvelled at, a manifestation of the infinite wonder and variety of the universe; to most of us, such revelations come but rarely. We are content to divide our time between earning a living and spending an agreeable leisure in the company of family or friends. Not only are we content, but also we would not for long be happy with any other pattern of life, and no matter how new and exciting our surroundings we eventually make them fit into such a pattern.

The expatriate newly arrived in West Africa soon learns to regard palm trees, black faces and villages of mud, wattle and thatch houses as part of the daily scene. Strange sounds and sights assail him and quickly become as familiar to him as those he has left behind. Unless he is of a marked literary bent he is unlikely to have felt at any time during his previous home life disposed to write about it. When he first goes to West Africa he may, like a schoolboy visiting Europe for the first time, try to keep a diary in which to record the myriad new impressions crowding in on him daily. But the flesh is weak, resolution atrophies, work and the building of a new social life become the main calls on one's waking hours and daily life soon ceases to seem so remarkable as to make the effort of recording it worthwhile.

In my own case it is only now, knowing that I shall probably never return to West Africa, that I begin to realize what a wealth of experience I had there. It is as much for my own benefit as with a view to possible publication that I am now attempting to set down some part of this, so that in later years something more substantial than a hazy collection of memories will remain.

How did I come to join the overseas civil service? Far be it from me to deceive anyone into thinking that this was a career about which I dreamed from the days of early adolescence, longing for the moment to arrive on which I would actually pick up the 'white man's burden'. No, I had thoughts of a much softer life in more congenial surroundings than those of the African bush. But at the end of three years at Cambridge, having failed to be accepted for the foreign service, the one career on which I had set my sights, I found myself with no certain prospects for the future, no positive desire to do anything in particular and a degree, which, though far from academically shameful, did not immediately fit me for any specific work. I was in the same position as thousands of young men, products of the welfare state and recipients of government grants to fund higher education, with no substance and no professional, middle-class background to bolster them during the awkward period of transition from the world of education to that of employment. Contrary to the belief fostered at that time by the 'angry young men' of the 1950s, bewildered and frustrated graduates were never a monopoly of the redbrick universities, nor are Oxford and Cambridge strongholds of aristocratic and bourgeois privilege to the extent that is widely believed.

I was feeling lost and helpless when my director of studies, a barrister as well as a fellow of my college, took a hand and gave me guidance I would otherwise have lacked. 'Do not take anything unless you positively want it,' was his advice. But the door to the one career I had ever positively wanted was now closed, and there seemed nothing left except to become a schoolteacher, a career that I had always been determined to avoid. 'I think you should try for the colonial service,' said my director. At that time this career attracted me even less than teaching, and I said so. The prospect of spending the rest of my life marooned in a remote corner of some unspeakably dreadful colony, cut off from more than a minimum of civilized contacts, appalled me. I did not hesitate to speak my mind. 'I am sure you will like the service,' was the reply.

A few days later I nonchalantly and cynically completed an application form sent me by the Colonial Office; I was at this time filling in so many forms of this kind from potential employers that another one meant very little. I was required to give all the details of education, experience and interests and also to state whether I had any preference for a posting to particular colonial territories. At that time the colonial empire in Africa and Southeast Asia was still intact, so in theory there was a reasonable choice and I entered 'Cyprus and East Africa' in the blank space.

I was called for interview a few weeks later when I had already come down from Cambridge and was beginning to feel the chill winds of the unfriendly outside world. I was lost and felt I had reached a dead end. My situation was not helped by the break up of my home. My parents had split up a few months before in great acrimony; this had clouded my last few months at Cambridge and exacerbated the feelings of despair I experienced. All my life I had lived with short-term aims in view — school, punctuated during the last few years by public examinations, 18 months' national service and then Cambridge. Three years seem a long time at the outset and a university degree can easily be regarded as an end in itself. The realization after these hurdles have been cleared that two-thirds of one's active life still lie ahead and that somehow during that time one has to earn a living can come as a shock. I returned to my hometown in the North of England and worked for a few weeks as a clerk on what I hoped was a temporary basis. I had of course taken temporary jobs before when I was an undergraduate, delivering Christmas mail, working in offices and once working as a swimming pool attendant at a seaside resort during the summer. This time, as I sat day by day calculating invoices, I had the uncomfortable feeling that there was nothing to stop this from becoming a permanent job, which certainly did not come up to even my most modest expectations of what life might have in store for me. Fortunately, no such thing happened, but the feeling was a nasty one while it lasted.

I was called twice to the Colonial Office, once to meet the director of recruitment and his assistant and once to be interviewed by a selection board. One remark made by the director of recruitment in the course of my interview with him stands out in my recollection; this was to the effect that most countries in the world were not governed at all by the standards to which we were accustomed in the United Kingdom. It was only some years later that I came to appreciate the truth of this and it is even truer now than it was in 1953. When I came before the selection board I was asked whether there were any territories in which I would not wish to serve. I replied that I had no strong views on the matter, though I added in an offhand way that I did not think I would like to go to Aden. This was unfortunate, as one member of the board had at one time served in Aden and was offended that I should think so ill of that colony. A few years later I visited Aden when the ship on which my family and I were returning by sea from India called there. A few hours ashore confirmed the impression I had always had of a barren, arid country in one of the most inhospitable regions of the world.

A week or so later I received a telegram (now an obsolete form of communication but then much used, particularly for urgent messages) to inform me that I had been accepted for the colonial service and was offered an appointment as a cadet administrative officer in Sierra Leone. The Secretary of State sent me his congratulations, or so the telegram said. I had heard of Sierra Leone but would have been at a loss to say exactly where it was, what was the name of its capital or to say anything else about it. Reference to an encyclopaedia gave me a far from encouraging picture. I noted that the country had a rainfall of 150 to 200 inches annually, concentrated within six months of the year, that daytime temperatures were normally in the eighties and nineties and that the European population was no more than 500. Apart from what the encyclopaedia told me, I had a general impression of the west coast of Africa as a backward and very much underdeveloped part of the world, where the few and scattered European expatriates sweated out a lonely and seedy existence with the help of the gin bottle. I hesitated for some days before replying to the letter that followed the telegram, wondering whether West Africa was the region where I would care to bury myself for many years. Since, however, no other job was in the offing and the possibility of entering industry or commerce as a trainee had in any case little appeal for me at the time, I took a deep breath and replied, accepting the offer. Whether wisely or not, I had settled my future and this was a source of relief.

I had one appointment with a prospective employer outstanding, and decided to keep it. I was invited for a preliminary interview with the store manager of Marks & Spencer in Preston, not far from my hometown Darwen. He presumably had to make an initial assessment of my potential management abilities and made it obvious that he had reached the conclusion before he met me that I was hopelessly unsuitable. From the start he described me as 'the academic type — no use to us'. He asked me whether I had visited any of the company's stores, talked to buyers and acquired some idea of their sales policy. I answered 'no'.

'Have you any experience of handling female labour?'

'No'.

What a stupid question this was to put to a new graduate with no experience of any kind of employment other than vacation jobs. My interviewer had evidently come up the hard way after a limited education and had little patience with the newer generation who expected a management cadetship as their birthright and reward for passing university examinations. At this point, feeling with some justification that the interview was getting me nowhere, I picked up my coat and walked out of the office without even a good morning. I have often thought since that day that I could well have ended the interview by saying, 'If your company has many managers like you then I would not thank you for the offer of a job.' Matching rudeness with rudeness in this way might have produced a more favourable reaction. Another course of action I could very reasonably have taken would have been to write to the head office of Marks & Spencer, complain that I had not been fairly treated in interview and ask for another interview with some manager less prone to bias against graduates. I did not do anything further and have never had any regrets about deciding that Marks & Spencer would have to manage without me. I am sure that I would never have had any enthusiasm for selling ladies' underwear. I enjoyed the feeling of security that came from knowing that I was already assured of employment and that enabled me to walk defiantly and not very politely out of the store manager's office without a qualm.

Before I could take up my appointment in Sierra Leone there was a course to be undergone in London, known as the Devonshire Course. These courses were organized in London, Oxford and Cambridge for newly recruited colonial cadets, the choice of university being dependent on the local language that had to be studied as part of the course.

In my case the language was Mende, one of the two main languages of Sierra Leone, and a course was available at the School of Oriental and African Studies. The course overall was organized by the London School of Economics and lasted one academic year. It was intended to give us a smattering of knowledge of the many and varied aspects of the work that would fall to us in our respective territories. Apart from the language, we had to learn something of anthropology, economics, law, tropical agriculture and colonial administration, with lectures on such subjects as tropical hygiene and medicine and field engineering thrown in for good measure.

My main criticism of the course, when experience enabled me to evaluate its usefulness, was that it was insufficiently practical, though by the same token it was congenial to men (all the administrators on the course were men, though there were a few women destined for various colonies who were doing a specialist course in education) who had just completed intensive degree courses and now had the opportunity to dabble in a variety of interesting subjects without being subjected to any pressure to complete an unwieldy examination syllabus. Examinations there were at the end of the year, but no great effort was needed to pass them; failure, which was rare, possibly an unknown event, would certainly not have meant termination of a man's appointment, though it would have been a black mark against him at the beginning of his career.

The course could well have been more concentrated and less academic. I often had occasion to wish when I was in Sierra Leone that I had had a thorough training in the care and maintenance of motor vehicles. Like many others in West Africa, I was usually dependent on my own car, and in a country where garages are non-existent and the few mechanics mostly incompetent, an intimate understanding of the workings of a car, coupled with the ability to diagnose the many faults that develop in it after it has been driven on some of the most appalling roads in the world, would have been a boon.

A better understanding of cooking would also have been useful. Throughout my service I remained a bachelor, running my own household, and however conscientious a cook I had I always felt that it would have been to my advantage to have had a closer practical knowledge of this most necessary art, with a reasonable range of recipes at my disposal to supplement the cook's limited repertoire. As it was, sheer necessity compelled me to learn something of vehicle maintenance, but indolence and an unwillingness to face having to work in a small kitchen over a primitive wood burning stove with temperatures even outside the kitchen in the nineties and very high humidity inhibited me from pursuing culinary studies. I passed these comments to my director of studies in a letter. He passed them on to the Colonial Office, where he had some contacts and I believe that in consequence subsequent courses were improved by the introduction of these two subjects.

These criticisms apart, I shall always count my year in London on the Devonshire Course as one of the most pleasant in my life. London can be all things to all men and in later years I returned to find it a cold and indifferent city. But anyone who is young and leading a more or less carefree life there in the company of his coevals and equals can be as enthusiastic about it as Dr Johnson or any other devoted Londoner. All of us cadets had work to do, but the thought was ever in our minds that this was to be our last period of uninterrupted contact with Britain for possibly many years, and we exploited it to the utmost in our various ways.

Marriage was a very popular way. Nearly all of us were going to territories where we would never meet eligible women and where bachelors tended to stay bachelors, so the incidence of marriage was high and increased as the end of the year and sailing dates drew nearer. My own efforts in this direction were sadly unsuccessful.

We managed to find time for many other activities, among them organizing a choir to sing Christmas carols at Guy's Hospital. This is the only occasion in my life when I have conducted a choir. The former Oxford and Cambridge oarsmen, myself among them, made up an eight, which performed respectably under LSE colours in the Head of the

River race. The Devonshire Course itself afforded us one enjoyable diversion in the form of ten days during the Easter vacation at London University's College of Agriculture at Wye in Kent. I doubt whether any of us learned very much about agriculture, but we all enjoyed the fresh air and good food after the boarding house or students' hostel fare of London. In addition to lectures we were given the opportunity of dabbling in all manner of techniques, which could, I suppose, be shown to have some link with the work we were destined to do. It was possible to appreciate the relevance of a morning spent learning the rudiments of surveying, but it was difficult to see in what way we were going to be helped by odd half hours spent on bricklaying, welding or driving different makes of tractors across open fields with gay abandon. But it was spring, the sun shone; we were all enjoying ourselves and did not pause to ask such questions. After this there came one more term of London, ending with examinations and farewell parties. All of us received our sailing instructions and dispersed to spend a last few weeks with our families.

One necessary practical chore we all had to undertake was the purchase of the kit we would need to take with us. We each had a kit allowance of £60, not over-generous even at 1954 prices, but without it we would simply not have been able to equip ourselves. Our custom went to one or other of the firms of tropical outfitters, now I assume long an extinct trade. I visited Lawn & Alder in Golden Square. Houses provided for civil servants in the colonies had only basic furniture and we had to buy everything else we needed, crockery, cutlery, pots and pans, bed linen, towels, mosquito nets, camp bed, tropical suit, dinner jacket, mosquito boots to protect ankles against being bitten in the evening — the list was not endless but long. A major item I bought, and which I still possess, was a huge zinc-lined and very heavy airtight trunk for storing linen and protecting it against the ravages of a humid climate. It resides in my garage and is still used for its original purpose. Part of the service provided by the tropical outfitter was to pack all the items purchased and arrange for them to be dispatched to the ship on which I was sailing.

And so, on 12 August 1954, I found myself at the Prince's Landing Stage in Liverpool, boarding the Elder Dempster mail boat *Aureol* for the nine-day journey to Freetown, capital and main seaport of Sierra Leone. Six other members of the Devonshire Course were on the same ship, one for Gambia, our first port of call, and the rest of us for Sierra Leone. For me, as for most of the others, it was the first taste of a sea voyage longer than a channel crossing and therefore an exciting new experience.

In the course of the trip we were able to gain our first impressions of 'coasters', as Europeans on the west coast of Africa were generally known. Mine was an unfavourable one of men who lived for drink and whose conversation was limited. I came later to realize that a coaster was back in West Africa as soon as he stepped on board the ship, having perhaps some slight regrets at leaving Britain again after a pleasant few weeks or months of lotus eating, but otherwise glad to be back in the company of men who spoke the same language and to whom he did not have to explain that Lagos is nowhere near Nairobi or that the inhabitants of tropical Africa are not all naked savages sporting the heads of their slain enemies around their waists. Thus, the seven of us, on our way to Africa for the first time, were immediately transported into a strange world. Not the least strange feature of it was the custom of opening the ship's bars at 7.30 a.m. until 8.00 a.m. for serving brandy and ginger ale to hardened topers who wished to clear their heads before breakfast.

After a week at sea we reached Bathurst — renamed Banjul after independence — the tiny capital of what were then the colony and protectorate of Gambia, named after one of Africa's great rivers. Here we had our first sight of

Africa. The country is sausage-shaped, two strips of land along the north and south banks of the river, making a 300-mile-long excision from the former French colony of Senegal. A glance at the map makes it clear that it must have been created merely to spite the French. The river is broad and navigable for a long way inland and is an important trade route. At its mouth it is two or three miles wide and the colonial capital, a small collection of trading companies' stores, warehouses and government buildings, was on the south bank there. At this time there was no quay at which a ship the size of *Aureol* could tie up, so we anchored in the stream and offloaded passengers and cargo into lighters and small boats. It was an unexciting introduction to Africa. Apart from the town, all we could see were the distant banks, long flat strips of green. We were surprised to feel cold. This was, however, August, and the height of the rainy season. There was a light drizzle, the sky was overcast and the atmosphere was damp and muggy. We watched without envy the one member of our group destined for the Gambia going ashore in a police launch. The cheerful crowd of African stevedores who had swarmed aboard when we anchored now left us, many of them wearing paper hats, the remains of the previous night's carnival celebrations among the first-class passengers. Towards evening the ship weighed anchor and headed out to sea again, now only 30 hours' sailing time from Freetown.

2

Freetown

Early on the morning of 21 August 1954, nine days after leaving Liverpool, we went on deck to have our first glimpse of Sierra Leone. We were some way offshore, and I imagine that we had probably arrived at the entrance of the harbour some hours earlier and waited for the tide, for the pilot, for daylight and for the scheduled time for tying up. The view was impressive, very different from our Gambian landfall. There was a dense heat haze over the sea and through it we could see the hills of the colony peninsula, seeming at first glance to rise straight out of the sea, though in fact between Aberdeen Point, where the lighthouse stood at the end of a long spit of land, and the beginning of the hills there was a large area of flat, swampy land.

A little later *Aureol* began to move past the Aberdeen lighthouse into the harbour and we had an opportunity to appreciate Freetown at our leisure. Of the buildings there is little one can say. At this time the only building worthy of comment was Government House, the governor's official home, a monstrous and expensive-looking block of concrete with a flat roof, looking from the distance like a 1950s' cinema and built on the remains of an old Portuguese fort. Apart from this the town was a jumble of houses, stores, warehouses, government offices and other buildings, all with corrugated-iron roofs.

Freetown's lack of architectural distinction is, however,

more than compensated for by the magnificence of its setting at the foot of green-forested hills, rising to a height of 3000 feet. This range of hills, running the length and breadth of the 20-mile-long peninsula from Freetown to the village of Waterloo, makes Sierra Leone unique on this otherwise flat, featureless and surf bound coast. So also does the excellent natural harbour of Freetown where, it has been said, it would be possible to anchor the entire British navy — and this was said at a time when the navy was far bigger than it is now.

In both world wars Freetown was an important convoy station, where ships carrying troops and military supplies to and from the east, or other ships bringing precious food supplies from South America to Britain used to meet, having to go round the Cape of Good Hope because of the closure of the Mediterranean and Suez Canal. I often met people who visited Freetown in this way, and it was most important for the town's reputation that troops and other passengers and crew on ships calling there were seldom allowed ashore, even though they might be anchored there for several weeks. Freetown is hot at most times of the year and does not cool down at night; sleeping on ships in the harbour, long before the days of air conditioning, cannot have been pleasant.

The west coast of Africa was for a long time a source of slaves, most of whom were shipped across the Atlantic to work in the plantations of the West Indies. In the second half of the eighteenth century the anti-slavery movement became influential and was strengthened by a famous judgment of Lord Mansfield, which declared that the laws of England did not recognize the status of slavery. As a result of this judgment some 15,000 slaves then in Britain became free and the government of the day was faced with the problem of resettling them. With the assistance of the anti-slavery campaigners, notably Granville Sharp, it was arranged that the ex-slaves should be taken to Sierra Leone (the name had been given to the peninsula by the Portuguese long before), the territory that later became the crown colony being acquired for this purpose from a Timne chieftain.

The first shipment, which included a number of white Plymouth prostitutes, reached Freetown in 1787. Here they gathered as soon as they landed under the shade of a great cotton tree, which still stands — or at least still stood in my time — outside the law courts in Freetown, at the junction of Pademba Road and Westmoreland Street and was classed as an historic monument. The early settlers underwent many vicissitudes, not the least of which was the heavy toll taken by malaria. Freetown was an unhealthy place in the eighteenth and nineteenth centuries. The administration of the colony was left to the abolitionists until 1808, when the British government, with much reluctance, took it over as a crown colony.

In this and following paragraphs about the Creoles I have retained the text of my 1960s' manuscript unaltered.

> The descendants of the settlers, known as the Creoles, still form an important part of modern Freetown's society. They are different from and consider themselves very superior to the tribes of the protectorate, to whom they habitually refer as the aborigines. Many of their ancestors were themselves the descendants of slaves who had never seen Africa in their lives, and the founders of Freetown had nothing in common with the African peoples by whom they were surrounded. Few of them knew any language other than a dialect of English; they mostly had English names, usually taken from their former slave masters and were ill adapted to the struggle that was forced on them by resettlement.
>
> They later proved their usefulness as British influence spread along the west coast and their services were needed in clerical and administrative posts by colonial governments and commercial firms. The Creoles have always been a Christian community and

firm believers in the value of education. Their language, a derivative of English and recognizable as such after a brief acquaintance, has become the lingua franca of the whole of Sierra Leone and is widely used by all sophisticated Africans, particularly when they do not understand each other's tribal languages, by the Lebanese traders and by Europeans in their dealings with Africans. Creole children learn English quickly when they go to school, and in the more aristocratic households the patois is frowned on and only standard English is spoken.

The ascendancy of the Creoles is now over, though they are still prominent in all ranks of the civil service, in the judiciary and in the professions. Over the years they have married people from the protectorate who have settled in Freetown in large numbers, to such an extent that it is hard to say nowadays which Africans in Freetown are Creoles and which are not. The number of genuine Creoles is now estimated to be around 30,000 and it is only necessary to see a few of them around Freetown to realize that their way of life is in many respects unchanged from that inherited from Europe via the West Indies a century and a half ago. Their women wear cloche hats and other fashions that would have been thought outmoded in the days of our grandmothers; on a hot Sunday afternoon, when the thoughts of expatriates are turning either towards bed after a heavy lunch or towards a lazy dip in the sea at Lumley Beach, it is not uncommon to see a distinguished looking Creole gentleman on his way to Sunday school, dressed in a heavy black jacket, striped trousers, winged collar and tie and a bowler or top hat. In the better class families, a strict discipline is imposed on the children, which is best described as Victorian. And marriage outside a narrow circle of families would never be countenanced.

Nowadays the Creoles are a worried race. They are and always have been a small minority, comparable in some ways to the Eurasians of India. They have little European blood in them and for practical purposes may be considered as purely of African stock. Nevertheless, their culture and history give them strong feelings of affinity with Europeans. So long as the colony's Legislative Council had a majority of seats reserved for nominated officials they had no cause to worry and were in a privileged position. But with the political developments of recent years, which have led to the introduction of universal male suffrage throughout the country, the protectorate with its population of 2,000,000 as against fewer than 200,000 in the colony has inevitably come to dominate the scene.

By the time these words are being read, Sierra Leone will have been an independent member of the Commonwealth for over two years and the fate of the Creoles will have been decided. I am sure it has been a less catastrophic one than many of them envisaged. In the last months before independence in April 1961 a group of Creoles brought a case before the Judicial Committee of the Privy Council, seeking an injunction restraining the British government from granting independence to Sierra Leone on the grounds that such a grant would infringe their old-established rights as settlers and subjects of the crown. Their petition had no hope of success, but the pride in British citizenship, which is partly the motive behind it, is surely moving.

Many Creoles have for years now lived in apprehension about the future and some have taken steps to identify themselves with the people of the protectorate by intermarrying, adopting native names and native dress. It is more than likely that they will achieve an amiable *modus vivendi* with the protectorate-

26

dominated government if they have accepted that they no longer hold their former ascendancy. If, however, they insist on continuing to hold themselves aloof from the 'aborigines' and to regard themselves as a superior race of African aristocrats, they will find it difficult to adjust to the new society.

I must continue to speak of the colony and protectorate of Sierra Leone, though this division obviously disappeared with the coming of independence. Before independence, however, it was legally and in other ways a significant division of which one could never fail to be aware. The colony consisted of Freetown and its peninsula, plus most of the rest of the country's coastline. Apart from the peninsula, however, the only other part of Sierra Leone administered as a colony was the small town of Bonthe, a decaying port and trading centre on an island off the coast, where Creoles are also much in evidence. The rest of the coastal areas, though formally annexed to the crown at different times during the nineteenth century, were for long administered as part of the protectorate as a matter of convenience.

It was not until the end of the nineteenth century that the British government began to take an active interest in Freetown's hinterland, and it was only in the interests of protection of trade and of preventing the French from acquiring too much territory that we began to extend our sphere of influence most reluctantly by sending round travelling commissioners who concluded treaties in the name of the Queen with the paramount chiefs of the Mende, Timne, Susu, Koranko and other tribes.

In the 1890s and in the early years of the twentieth century a railway was built to link Freetown with the protectorate. Freetown was the main port and headquarters of government and grew in importance.

An increase in government responsibilities meant a corresponding increase in civil service strength, and at this time the government became alarmed at the heavy death rate from malaria and other diseases among officers sent out from the United Kingdom. Thus grew the legend of the 'white man's grave', a name that West Africa and Sierra Leone in particular have still not managed altogether to shake off.

It was decided to build quarters for European officers on top of one of the hills above the town. This was undertaken as an emergency measure and pre-fabricated houses were shipped out from Britain in sections to be erected on the site, anticipating by more than 50 years, this modern building technique. The houses were meant to be temporary structures only, but most of them are still standing today. To serve Hill Station, as this new suburb came to be called, the railway was extended from Government Wharf on the harbour by a winding route to the top of the hill and European officers were thus able to commute daily to and from the secretariat. This stretch of line was reputed to be the steepest friction railway, having no assistance from rack and pinion. It was closed in 1929 after a road had been built to Hill Station and officers were able to travel to and from Freetown by car.

Aureol moved slowly up the Sierra Leone River and stood off the quay for a while to allow its sister ship the *Accra* to clear the quay and get under way before we tied up. The Queen Elizabeth II Quay was Freetown's latest pride, having been opened only the previous year. Until then all ships had had to anchor in the stream off Government Wharf and offload cargo and passengers into lighters and launches. This was often a hazardous business in rough weather.

We all went ashore nervously, treading on African soil or at least African concrete for the first time. We had decided to wear suits, not being sure what kind of formal greeting might await us. My own tropical suit, bought ready made from Lawn & Alder, had proved to be a failure, being of some inferior material of a quality comparable to potato sacking, which would not hold a crease for more than a few minutes. I had had it pressed once on the ship, but this was an expensive service, so I compromised and wore a pair of dark flannel trousers with the cream coloured jacket of the suit. As we were about to step onto the gangway one of my colleagues looked me up and down and asked, 'What's the matter? Couldn't you afford the trousers?' It was a flippant and irrelevant remark for the occasion, but it afforded welcome light relief on an occasion when we were all nervous and a little apprehensive.

Two administrative officers, one African and one European, welcomed us and, after clearing immigration and customs, we went out to waiting cars. We now saw what Freetown looked like at close quarters — a large collection of uninspired buildings, mostly with roofs of corrugated iron or 'pan', to use the local vocabulary, narrow streets and crowded pavements. The African women's dresses and head ties provided an occasional splash of colour. I confess that I have no vivid memories of my first drive through Freetown.

We were all being posted to different stations in the protectorate, but would be spending a day or two in Freetown first to engage servants, do essential shopping and meet some of our superiors. In the normal way, on first arrival, we might have expected hospitality in the form of accommodation in bungalows occupied by administrative officers, but as there were six of us, the staff of the secretariat among themselves had decided that this was not feasible, so we were all lodged in what was known officially as the government rest house and unofficially as the transit camp. The latter name suited the place much better. We had all met one or two officers on leave while we were in London and had been warned about its shortcomings.

The transit camp was just as bad as they had led us to expect. It had been built during the war as a refuge for ship-wrecked seamen and others who had the misfortune to find themselves stranded in Freetown. It was a collection of single-storeyed wooden huts divided into bedrooms, each with two beds. Another hut served as the restaurant and an annexe to this as the bar. The bedrooms were dark and not very clean, the bed linen was grey, the mosquito nets over the beds had large holes in them and the towels were filthy. The food was tolerable, but it was disconcerting to see ugly-looking vultures with their red, scraggy necks scavenging for their meals from scraps thrown into the drainage gutters and even on the kitchen tables on which food was prepared.

Apart from the transit camp, the only place where people visiting Freetown could stay was the City Hotel. This was a seedy establishment in the centre of Freetown near the secretariat, and the standard of accommodation was if anything worse than that at the transit camp. Readers who are familiar with Graham Greene's *The Heart of the Matter*, which was based on the author's long sojourn in Freetown during the war, may recall how two of the characters stayed at the City Hotel and vied with each other as to the number of cockroaches they could kill in their respective rooms.

All of us had invitations to lunch with various officials on our first day. Two of us were invited to the house of an officer, Derek Hughes, whom we had already met in London. He had been in Sierra Leone for 13 years, had spent much time as a district commissioner in the Mende speaking parts of the protectorate and could speak fluent Mende himself. He had thoughtfully arranged to engage servants for us both, or at least to offer us servants whom he could recommend himself. I knew by now that I was going to Bo, administrative headquarters of the protectorate and of South-Western Province, in the heart of Mende country, so I engaged a Mende servant, one Musa Kemokai. He was a handsome man of about 30 and had been trained as a

cook by our host. He went back to the transit camp with me
and later produced another man, Solomon Jusu, whom he
described as his brother. 'Brother' is an elastic term in
African parlance and is often used to describe a cousin with
whom there are close family ties. In this case, however, there
was no blood relationship at all and the word was used only
in a figurative sense.

I was persuaded of the need to employ two servants, a
cook and a steward. Later I realized that this was not necessary and that it would have been more economical to insist
on having a cook who would also carry out most of the
duties otherwise carried out by a steward and to engage a
'small boy' (this term had nothing to do with size or age, as
many small boys were over 20) to do the more menial jobs
such as washing dishes, sweeping floors, cleaning shoes and
laundering clothes. Wages of servants were rising all the
time I was in Sierra Leone, well-trained and reliable ones
were hard to come by and I would without doubt have
saved money if I had adopted this arrangement. Having a
fully-fledged cook and steward was an indulgence, particularly for a bachelor on a lowly salary, but it meant a
more smoothly functioning household.

My hiring of Solomon proved to be an expensive mistake;
I was warned before I left Freetown that he had a bad
reputation and that I was taking a risk with him. He had
dark, intelligent looking eyes and lips that even for an
African were unusually thick. He had spent a long time in
Freetown and it was part of the accepted mythology of
Sierra Leone that a long stay in the capital inevitably corrupted a servant. Solomon was good supporting evidence for
this theory. Musa had never spent long in Freetown and
stayed longer with me than Solomon did. I doubt whether
there was any strong friendship between the two of them
and suspect that Solomon secured an introduction to me as
an employer by dashing Musa a sum of money. The dash is
the normal concomitant of all forms of social intercourse in

West Africa; it is the condition precedent for the obtaining of jobs, for interviews with chiefs and other important people and any other kind of favour.

Our various lunch parties over, we were left to our own devices for the rest of the weekend (we had arrived on Saturday morning), and felt not a little neglected, these being our first few days in the country to which we had come to take up our careers. On Sunday evening we were entertained to drinks by the acting colonial secretary and on Monday were received by the acting governor at Government House. We sat on a veranda several floors up, looking out over the waterfront and harbour. The conversation turned to the topic of how long a career the six of us could expect to enjoy in Sierra Leone, in view of the developments towards self-government then already under way in the then Gold Coast and Nigeria and which had begun in 1953 in Sierra Leone with the appointment of several ministers, including a chief minister, to whom departmental portfolios were assigned. His Excellency assured us that we could look forward to a secure career of at least another 20 years. Looking back I wonder how even then he could have been so confident. In the event, he was certainly mistaken.

There was much else for us to do in Freetown, shopping for essential stores, clearing heavy baggage through customs and opening bank accounts. It did not take us long to realize that this was an expensive country in which to live and that our salaries, which had seemed reasonably generous when we were first told what they were going to be, were going to be barely adequate. The opening of local bank accounts was most significant. We were all short of cash and started with overdrafts of £10 each; among the advantages enjoyed by Europeans in Sierra Leone was the dubious one of being able to obtain credit easily. The local manager of Barclays Dominion, Colonial & Overseas — to give the bank the full title by which it was then known — had no qualms about lending us money, although he knew that we had arrived only three days previously and were not known to anyone.

Early on Wednesday morning, four days after our arrival in Freetown, the three of us who were initially bound for Bo, left the transit camp to catch the train from Water Street station. It was a stopping train, whose scheduled time for the journey of 136 miles was about 12 hours. (There now follows another passage written 40 years ago but long ago made obsolete by the complete closure of Sierra Leone's railway.)

I have already mentioned the railway in connection with the opening of Hill Station. Its main purpose was to develop the trade between the coast and the protectorate. It had to be built out of limited funds and the whole of the mileage is single track, except for passing loops at stations. The line was built without any proper survey, so it follows the contours and in consequence twists and turns continually like some of the worst of English country roads. In addition, the gauge is only two foot six inches, which seriously limits the size and weight of loads that can be carried. In spite of these limitations it is a remarkable achievement, considering the difficult conditions under which it was built, especially the section between Freetown and Waterloo. It runs at the foot of the peninsula hills and frequently has to cross deep gorges of awesome depth and precipitous sides on spectacular bridges of which no modern railway engineer would feel ashamed.

There are plans for extensive reconstruction of the line so as to give it a better alignment and easier gradients, cutting out many of the bends, shortening the length of the route and reducing operating costs. These improvements will be expensive, and since the railway's substantial annual deficit is already a heavy charge on the budget, it is almost certain that whatever money might be available would be better spent on improving the country's roads. One school of thought holds that the railway ought to be closed down altogether. This is an attractive idea for which there is considerable economic justification, but politically it would be impossible because of the large numbers of people who would be thrown out of work. At the other extreme are some who hold that the railway ought to have its gauge increased to three foot six inches and its track doubled. This amounts to building a new railway and is ruled out on financial grounds.

It would be unfair to overlook the railway's former importance. In the days when Sierra Leone depended on the export of palm kernels and other cash crops to earn its livelihood the railway provided the only means other than the rivers of transporting produce from the protectorate down to the coast. In recent years it has become inadequate for dealing with the tremendously increased demands for imported goods of all kinds upcountry and there has been much more emphasis on the development of road transport.

Our train pulled out of Water Street station no more than a few minutes late. The first part of its journey, as far as Cline Town, took us through the streets of Freetown and through the middle of a market whose stalls were on both sides of the track. Once clear of the town we ran along the edge of the colony peninsula, the hills rising steeply on our right, the ground falling away to distant mangrove swamps and the estuary of the Sierra Leone River on our left. We stopped at the sleepy villages of Kissy, Hastings and Waterloo, miniature versions of Freetown with their clapboard houses and rusty tin roofs. At Songo, 32 miles from Freetown, we crossed from the colony into the protectorate. We were now clear of the hills and the character of the vegetation began to change.

> The slopes of the colony hills are mostly covered with high grass, scattered bushes and palm trees; some thickly wooded hills remain, thanks to the efforts of the forestry department in creating a forest reserve.

As we went further into the protectorate we found ourselves hemmed in on both sides by dense bush, of the kind that covers vast areas of West Africa, consisting mainly of an abundance of palm trees, trees of other varieties, low bushes and an inextricable tangle of creepers. This is the 'impenetrable jungle' beloved of writers who visit Africa, which I have seen described more aptly as 'green hell'. Occasional villages and rice farms afforded the only relief to the monotony.

The villages were clusters of mud huts, mostly round with steeply sloping roofs made either of palm fronds or of high grass. The traditional African hut in Sierra Leone is of the simplest pattern, having but one room, an opening in lieu of a door and no windows. In the middle of the room, on the mud floor, a wood fire may be lit for cooking, for warmth on cold days and for drying the thatch of the roof to keep it weatherproof. The framework of the walls is an elaborate criss-cross arrangement of wattle sticks on which wet mud is plastered during the dry season. The roof timbers consist of poles cut from the bush and the thatch of palm fronds is secured to these by 'tie tie' or creepers. Thus a simple, habitable house is built out of materials available on the spot.

Nowadays the more sophisticated will build something more pretentious, a square or rectangular house with two or more rooms, a veranda and windows with wooden shutters made by a local carpenter. In the towns, native materials have largely been discarded and houses built of mud or concrete blocks, with sawn timber and pan roofs are increasingly in evidence. They are less picturesque, but more durable and cheaper to maintain. A mud hut needs to have its walls replastered and its thatch renewed every year; so long as wives and other members of the family are at hand, this is no problem, but when labour has to be paid for it becomes expensive and permanent materials are to be preferred.

Mud houses have the advantage of being cool. From this point of view there is no worse combination of building materials for the tropics than concrete walls and pan roofs, yet it is from these that most permanent houses are nowadays being built. On days of heavy downpours such as are commonly experienced in this part of Africa in July and August, however, a sound roof is something for which to be thankful. Also, concrete walls and floors are immune from the white ants or 'bug bug', to use the local expression. These termites will soon consume any woodwork that has not been treated with creosote beforehand or is not too tough for them to eat. An army of them will make short work of doorframes, window frames and roof timbers. I well remember inspecting one government rest house, which had recently been repaired and rebuilt but whose roof timbers had not received any protective treatment. Standing inside the building I could hear the white ants in their thousands swarming joyfully over the joists and purlins and feasting on them; the noise was like that of a constantly crackling fire of twigs.

From time to time we stopped at a station, which usually consisted of a stationmaster's office and little else. Here vendors with trays or head pans of food or drink would besiege the train, crying in singsong Creole, 'stout deh', 'cigarette deh', 'kola deh', 'fine bread', or whatever else they were selling. The officially scheduled duration of the stop would generally be only a few minutes, but we often stayed half an hour or more while the crew of the train had a meal or passed the time of day with their friends. These were normal delays and we were fortunate in being spared some of the worst hold-ups for which the Sierra Leone Railway was notorious and which on occasion could make the train 24 or more hours late. On one occasion when I was using the train, the locomotive parted company with its coaches because of a broken coupling and we had to wait until a new one was brought and fitted. Derailments were frequent on account of the sharp bends and the steep gradients on some of the sections created their own problems. I heard of one train that made several unsuccessful attempts to climb a particular hill. Eventually the driver divided the train in the middle, took the leading coaches on to the next station and came back for the rest.

It was a cold, wet and cheerless day and the landscape was to our unaccustomed eyes unfriendly, monotonous and chaotic. The towns through which we passed all looked alike, single-storeyed shacks and stores of corrugated-iron sheets and the inevitable mud huts, all bedraggled and forlorn in the middle of the relentless bush on a grey day. On top of that, we had had no cooked meal all day and since a very early breakfast had been surviving on sandwiches and tea from thermos flasks. The Sierra Leone Railway did not run to restaurant cars and the food on sale at stations did not look appealing.

One small incident served to brighten the gloom. We were drawing out of a station when a woman passenger in a coach in front realized that she had left her umbrella behind — obviously important in the middle of the rainy season — and shouted to some people who had come to see her off at the station. A young African woman, wearing only a *lappa* or cloth wrapped once round her, tied at the hip and leaving her breasts bare, began to run after the train with the umbrella. The *lappa* was tied tightly and hindered her movements at first, but after she had run a few yards it worked itself loose and slipped. Thereafter, to preserve her modesty she had to run with one hand holding the *lappa* and the other the umbrella, which cannot have been easy and slowed her pace. She had to run perhaps a quarter of a mile before she caught up with the woman and was able to give her the umbrella. Fortunately, the train was moving so slowly that she was never in danger of not reaching the woman. It was a charming illustration of how African women, though they may often expose more of their bodies than other races would consider respectable, have nevertheless to observe their own canons of what is considered decent and will try to do so even in the most difficult circumstances.

We reached Bo at 8.00 p.m., by which time it was dark. The train went no further, and when we got out onto the platform we found ourselves in the midst of a mob of people struggling off the train with their boxes and bundles. A lorry had come to meet us at the station, but there was no sign of the district commissioner or his assistant, who we had thought might be there. Our loads were taken care of by a number of labourers who had come with the lorry, but as there was no other transport, we ourselves got into the back of the lorry for the journey to the assistant district commissioner's house. Bo had electricity, but as yet no street lighting, so from the lorry we could see only a few scattered lights on buildings. The district commissioner, Jack Wann, and his assistant DC Howard Bamforth, were surprised to see us. They had intended to come to the station to meet us in their cars but had not expected the train to be on time and were relaxing with drinks. They had assumed that a whistle they heard was that of a goods train and had carried on drinking. The next hour was embarrassing for everyone. We three cadets were dazed at being thrown into the midst of such alien surroundings, and our hosts were not as communicative as we would have liked. Howard's wife Enid made a greater contribution than anyone by telling us about a visit they had both made to Pujehun, the headquarters town of an adjacent district, 50 miles south of Bo, to which John Cook, one of our number, would be travelling to take up his post there the following day. Later I discovered that Howard had reprimanded Enid for talking too much. After a while Jack Wann took me off to his house where I was to stay the night. My two colleagues were staying at Howard's bungalow and were leaving for their respective postings to other districts the following morning. I did not see them again before I left Bo. It was after nine o'clock and I was glad of a hot bath. I apologized to my host for keeping him from his dinner. I later discover that this apology was superfluous, as he rarely ate before ten o'clock.

3
Bo

Next morning I saw Bo in daylight for the first time. The DC's house was in a government reservation on the edge of the town of Bo. This was a normal arrangement at stations in Sierra Leone and I would imagine in many other colonies. The reservation covered several hundred acres of mostly hilly or undulating land. Much of it was still dense, uncleared bush, but around the houses large areas of bush had been cut back, giving the trees a chance to grow and making most attractive parkland. The DC's house stood on top of a hill, with a view across a valley towards a colony of junior staff quarters. A view of any kind is rare in this part of Sierra Leone; thick bush and forest abound and hide the shape of the landscape, giving any journey the impression of travelling through a continuous green cutting. An occasional glimpse of distant hills or of the banks of a river was as exhilarating as a cold drink on a hot day. From the air the country looks exciting and one realizes the wildness of so much of tropical Africa. A first glance shows nothing but a mass of tall trees and tangled vegetation, a confused turmoil of greenery, relieved here and there by a tiny village, though the practised eye soon learns to pick out bush paths and patches of land cleared for cultivation.

Jack Wann had gone to the office before me and sent a messenger to show me the way there. The footpath to the office ran down into the valley and up the other side, crossing on the way a broad open stretch of parkland including a drained swamp. Jack Wann had hopes of using this parkland as a golf course of sorts and in the course of the very limited conversation on our arrival the previous night he had asked whether any of us played golf, which of course none of us did. The parkland also served as a fire belt, an important protection, as it was the custom of local farmers to burn the bush when they wished to plant their seeds at the height of the dry season. They seldom troubled to consider which way the wind would carry the flames and disaster was not uncommon. In the course of my service I came across one village whose inhabitants burned the bush on the windward side of their village and destroyed all their own houses. They did not feel that this was an error of judgement on their part from which they ought to learn wisdom for the future, but accepted it in a fatalistic manner, just as they would accept the death of a relative or a bad harvest — that is, as the will of a vaguely defined power bearing perhaps some resemblance to the Christian or Muslim deity or to the medicine of a malevolent enemy. The doctrine of free will has no place in traditional African philosophy.

The district commissioner's office was one of a number of unimposing buildings grouped spaciously round a flagstaff in the middle of an open space. It consisted of one long single-storeyed building with the inevitable veranda and corrugated-iron roof, occupied by clerks and the assistant district commissioner. The DC's own office was in a small separate building. In the same compound were the offices of the provincial commissioner for the South-Western Province, the DC's immediate superior, the magistrate, provincial conservator of forests and education officer. Behind the office buildings were the local prison and court *barri*. This building and others like it will figure often in these pages, so it will be as well to explain what is meant by a *barri*. It is a courthouse well suited to the climate, a roof supported by pillars and open sides with just a dwarf wall, admitting cooling breezes. It is a pleasant forum for holding court on hot days but has the disadvantage that heavy rains, which are normal in season, are usually blown in by a strong wind, making the *barri* unusable. The traditional *barri* was circular, but those built in the 1950s were rectangular, their dimensions depending on the affluence of the chiefdom or government department that caused them to be built and upon the numbers of people they were intended to hold. At one *barri* there was a dais to be occupied by the magistrate, DC or whoever else was presiding over the proceedings. There might also be a minimum amount of crudely constructed court furniture.

I did not stay long at the office, but went to the station to collect my heavy baggage, which had been left there overnight. Bo by daylight had something of the appearance of a shantytown, though subsequently, after my sense of values had become suitably adjusted, I came to regard it as a metropolis. The buildings in the centre of Bo were of concrete blocks and corrugated iron. It was an important trading centre and its streets had an abundance of shops and stores along them. All the main European trading companies, United Africa Company, Paterson Zochonis and others, had branches close to the station and their own private sidings. There were also many stores owned by Lebanese and African traders.

Trade in Sierra Leone as in other parts of Africa always followed a simple two-way pattern. Originally the trading companies set up branches in the protectorate in order to buy produce from the local farmers — in particular palm kernels, though groundnuts, coffee and piassava also figured. They also sold a range of imported goods, so as to give the farmers an incentive to raise cash by bringing in their produce. By 1954, however, the trade in produce had shrunk to almost negligible proportions because of the vast growth in illicit diamond mining and dealing, which had taken young men away from farming and at the same time resulted in the circulation of large sums of easy money in a country where imported goods were in short supply.

In consequence, the companies found the volume of their import trade multiplied and were faced with an insatiable demand for luxury goods such as bicycles, radio sets, cars, not to mention tinned corned beef, sardines, beer and stout, in addition to cloth, an important staple of West African trade, The tenuous road and rail communications of the protectorate were incapable of bringing up the necessary quantities of goods from Freetown to satisfy the demand; in any event the demand for goods was even greater in Freetown and companies with their local headquarters there would naturally try to satisfy that demand first. Imported goods in the protectorate were always more expensive than in Freetown, because of the addition of freight charges, and scarcity caused inflation, with the result that the respectable citizen with a fixed income or the farmer with almost no income found life very difficult.

Basically, the pattern of trade was the same as it had always been, except that the volume was much greater and illicitly mined and smuggled diamonds had taken the place of farm produce as exports. A country such as Sierra Leone needs to import almost everything it needs for the maintenance of a sophisticated way of life, down to pins and needles. At this time there was nothing at all manufactured in the country, though a few years later there was talk of making cigarettes and brewing beer. Secondary industries of this kind are the easiest to set up when industrialization is first started in a hitherto underdeveloped country, but no country as small as Sierra Leone can ever become self-sufficient in manufactured goods and its economy is therefore particularly susceptible to fluctuations in the prices of raw materials, which it has to export in order to earn a living.

One other feature of West African trade that deserves some comment is the abundance of middlemen. The large European trading companies are the main importers and formerly were also the main exporters of produce, though since the war exporting has been in the hands of government run marketing boards, to which they are obliged to sell the produce they buy. The companies do not deal with their customers or with their primary suppliers directly, but function as wholesalers in both buying and selling. The retailers are mostly Lebanese or Syrians who have settled throughout West Africa. [References in the text to Syrians alone may be taken as referring to Syrians and Lebanese.]

At one extreme are near millionaires who control large organizations, compete with European companies in securing agencies abroad, own or lease large areas of commercially valuable land and hold many of the less affluent Syrians in the palm of their hands by giving credit and taking mortgages on their land. At the other end, poor Syrians do business from one room in small towns in the protectorate, making a modest living. Some of these are thriftless, but others are younger sons who have never had the capital needed to set up in business in a larger or more prosperous town. Most Syrians and Lebanese run one-man businesses, which they like to keep within the family. They are capable businessmen who have spent most of their lives in Sierra Leone and in some cases were born there.

They have a more intimate knowledge of Africa than most Europeans can ever hope to acquire, and invariably speak one or two of the vernacular languages, as well as Creole and Arabic. Many of them have had little education and some are illiterate, but they are nevertheless able to keep complex accounts in their heads. Some of the younger men are better educated and may even be graduates of the University of Beirut. As government officers we were expected to be wary of close friendships with Syrians and to observe the maxim '*timeo Lebanos et dona ferentes*'. Many of them were generous to a point that was embarrassing. Some would go to the lengths of supplying food and drink to government officers visiting their towns or would supply goods from their shops without taking payment. I have myself often appreciated a bottle of cold beer from a Syrian trader's refrigerator when visiting some out-of-the-way town on a hot day.

The Syrians did not always represent the end of the line of middlemen, even though their trading activities took them to the most out-of-the-way parts of the protectorate and brought them into close contact with individual Africans. Large numbers of African women earned a meagre living by petty trading. The commonest forms this took were the selling of rice and other foodstuffs in small measures in the markets and the sale of fruit and other refreshments to travellers at ferries, railway stations and busy road junctions. It was usual for a woman to buy a tin of 20 or 50 cigarettes and sell them separately at tuppence each; another would go to the nearest town, buy a dozen bottles of Guinness (a very popular brew), a packet of matches, a few bars of soap and other oddments and with this small stock in trade set up a stall on the veranda of her house when she returned to her village. It was a form of trade with small outlay and small profit, but though it may have seemed uneconomic — it has been described by one economist as a form of disguised unemployment — its very ubiquitousness showed that it had a necessary part to play in the country's economy.

Bo owed its importance to being a halfway halt on the railway. Not until after the Second World War did a train officially described with pardonable exaggeration as 'The Express' began to run three times a week doing the whole journey from Freetown to Pendembu, the terminus of the line, perhaps 250 miles away near the Liberian border, on one day, returning the following day. Bo at 136 miles was just over halfway and passengers previously had to spend the night there before continuing their journey in either direction. The town was not far from the geographical centre of the protectorate and it was inevitable that it should become an important centre, even though it had no river or other good source of water close at hand, and large areas of swampy ground restricted building and caused the town to sprawl much further than would otherwise have been necessary.

After 1945 Bo grew steadily and became important as a trading centre and as the headquarters of government in the protectorate. In 1948 an electricity supply was installed, the first in the country outside Freetown. The first secondary school in the protectorate, originally set up to educate the sons of paramount chiefs, had long been established there. By 1954 the illicit diamond mining rush, much of it within the boundaries of Bo District, had created boom conditions in the town and many of the small Syrian traders found themselves rich men overnight. New stores, houses and government buildings were being put up at a tremendous pace, but Bo was still unmistakably a 'bush' town. Even in the centre there were still one or two mud huts occupying potentially valuable sites, though these were destined soon to disappear. One did not have to look far to find patches of ground still being farmed in traditional fashion, and banana trees with their enormous fronds, symbolic of many Sierra Leone villages, were everywhere in evidence. Many of the main streets had been tarred but others were still earth roads with bumpy and irregular surfaces and full of potholes. Few houses were connected to the electricity supply and most of them depended on kerosene lamps for lighting. Much remained to be done to convert Bo into the twentieth century idea of a town, and this alone made it an exciting place in which to live.

I collected my loads at Bo station and went with them to the house in the government reservation that had been allocated to me and where Musa and Solomon were waiting. It was a roomy T-shaped house, single storeyed and built of mud blocks with the usual corrugated-iron roof. A long room with a spacious veranda at one end served as dining and sitting room. There were two bedrooms and bathrooms, one on each side of the main room. Separate from the rest of the house, but joined to it by a covered passageway open at the sides, were the outhouses. These consisted of a kitchen, storeroom and servants' quarters. Further away from the house was a garage, which during my tenancy was used only for storing firewood.

Behind the house were parkland and trees, while in the front the ground fell away towards a swamp. Here the land immediately next to the house had been cleared to form a lawn of sorts, dominated by a tall flamboyant tree. Around the back and sides of the house shrubs had been planted to shield the windows from prying eyes — though it was seldom that anyone other than servants or invited guests entered the compound. Bo had as yet no piped water supply and my house, in common with others on the reservation, was fed by several 44-gallon drums mounted on pillars of concrete blocks outside the bathrooms and kitchen. In the dry season a water gang would top these up daily by bringing buckets from a well half a mile away and in the rainy season water from the roof was fed into them by gutters.

It was a daunting task that now faced me. I had to unpack the boxes and crates brought from Britain containing crockery, household and bed linen, camping equipment, clothing and books and try to create from these, plus the sparse and austere furniture supplied by government, something resembling a functioning home. Running a house presented totally unfamiliar problems for me. Hitherto I had always lived at home or in the communal surroundings provided first by the Royal Air Force during national service, then by a Cambridge college and latterly by the British Council hostel in London where I had lived during my time on the Devonshire Course. Controlling servants, buying food, planning meals, checking expenditure and other necessary tasks of domestic administration represented an unknown world. Add to this the strangeness and newness of my environment and the reader will perhaps sympathize with me when I say that I felt lost and lonely. I soon realized, however, that I was not so lonely after all: Enid, the assistant district commissioner's wife, sent me a shopping list, recommending the stores in town where I would get the best bargains in such essentials as cooking fat, cleaning materials and potatoes and Howard took me shopping in his car.

Money was beginning to worry me. My servants were costing me more than they need have done and were taking advantage of my being green and unused to the ways of the country. I had to spend a lot on stores and soon realized that there were many deficiencies in the kit I had brought from Britain, which would need to be made good before my household could function properly and before I was equipped to go on trek. I had for example no pressure or kerosene lamps. So long as I stayed in Bo, where there was an electricity supply, that was of no consequence but I would need lamps when I went out around the district. I had bought a very good dinner service, but it would have been very foolish to take it on trek with me, so I had to buy a collection of cheap crockery for this purpose. Government had given each of us a kit allowance of £60 to buy kit, but this sum had not changed for over 20 years and was inadequate. I had already spent this and more in London and still needed more kit, which I had to buy in Sierra Leone.

It was a boon to anyone in my predicament that credit was easy to obtain. All the trading companies and Syrian traders were liberal with Europeans, many of whom never managed to clear their debts from one tour of duty to the next. This meant that one need never go short of the necessities or, indeed, of the more modest luxuries of life. In my own case, within a week of my arrival I had opened two accounts with trading companies in Freetown and one in Bo and had an overdraft at the bank. Although I never became prosperous, I was subsequently able to extricate myself from debt and live in reasonable comfort within my income, but the first few months in the country were a trying and anxious time.

My house was over a mile from the district office and I had to walk this distance four times a day. We had no official transport and individual officers, who might have to travel hundreds of miles a month on some of the worst roads to be found anywhere in the world, were required and expected to buy cars for themselves. Few officers had the capital to make such an investment and government would lend them the money free of interest and recover it from their salaries over a period of up to five years. This might mean a monthly deduction of £15 or more from a salary of less than £100. In return the officer received an allowance of between £7 and £11 depending on engine capacity, plus a mileage allowance for official journeys. Out of this he had to buy petrol and meet all running costs. Government kept the rates for standing and mileage allowances as low as possible with the result that officers were subsidizing government transport from their own pockets.

On the low salary I was earning during my first tour I could not possibly afford a car, and I did not buy one until my first leave in 1956. I could perhaps have afforded a second-hand vehicle, but the effective life of a car was seldom more than three years, facilities for proper maintenance did not exist; add to these drawbacks my own lack of familiarity with the internal combustion engine and it was obvious that such a purchase would have been unwise. In spite of the inconvenience, I never regretted my abstention from buying a car, for I was spared the need of having to make my financial position even more precarious and was able to enjoy the luxury of taking delivery of a new car on my first leave.

For some time I walked between house and office along the road, but this became embarrassing, as other European officers on their way to and from work always stopped and gave me lifts, which often took them out of their way. I discovered short cuts along bush paths that mostly avoided the road. The route I eventually adopted took me across a stream by a washing place frequented by people from the town who went there to bathe and wash their clothes.

Here it was not uncommon to see young women bathing naked, though usually taking care to hide their private parts with an appropriate show of modesty. There are no tribes in Sierra Leone who customarily go around naked, as used to be the case with some of the people of northern Ghana or of the Jos Plateau in Nigeria. However, it was never considered immodest for a woman to show her breasts, though in more sophisticated towns women would cover themselves in public. At public washing places it was accepted that men and women could strip off all their clothes and there were no taboos against mixed bathing. It was the custom that the private parts must always be concealed, either by putting a hand over them or by turning one's back. I soon came to take for granted the daily scene at the bathing place and before long was exchanging greetings with men and women in all stages of dress and undress. A studied avoidance of them when I had to pass them four times a day would have been thought just as offensive as a display of prurient curiosity. My aim always had to be to treat meetings in these circumstances as part of the daily routine, calling for no special comment from either side.

4

Starting Work

In every sense Sierra Leone was a new venture for me: a new country, new people and a way of life very different from that of the average city or suburban dweller in Britain. It was also a new experience in that for the first time in my life, at the age of 24, I was settling down to work. National service, Cambridge and the Devonshire Course in London had postponed this fate. Although I had long devoted myself to academic learning, I was a child in every-day practical matters and had everything to learn.

I had to share an office with Howard, the assistant district commissioner who was already in post, a man in his second tour and who therefore seemed to me immensely learned and widely experienced, in much the same way that a third former seems a veritable giant to a small boy starting secondary school in his first few days. Pursuing this simile, Jack Wann, the DC, who had been in the country for ten years, seemed like the headmaster, having a degree of wisdom I could never hope to achieve.

I was told on my first day in the office by Jack Wann that I could not expect any formal tuition as he and Howard were much too busy, that I must learn things as best I could by reading files and in any other way I thought fit, and that I was welcome to ask questions whenever I was in doubt. This

was intimidating to someone like myself, accustomed hitherto to attending courses of lectures and reading prescribed
books, but in the end I found this to be a most stimulating
way of learning.

Initially it was difficult for me to find anything definite to
do and my first allotted task was the humdrum one of sort-
ing out the secret correspondence. This was a purely clerical
job, but clerks were not entrusted with the handling of secret
and confidential papers, which were normally kept in a special cupboard to which only the DC had a key. Filing these
papers was a task that tended to be neglected for months at
a time and was a useful occupation for a new cadet. It was
also instructive, as it gave me a chance to find out the kinds
of matters with which DCs had to deal. The papers related
to chiefdom problems, security and impending constitutional
changes as well as more domestic concerns such as confidential reports on clerical and other subordinate staff.

For purposes of administration, the protectorate was
divided into 12 districts, each the responsibility of a district
commissioner. These districts were grouped into three provinces, southwest, southeast, and northern, each of which had
a provincial commissioner. Bo was the headquarters of the
South-Western Province commissioner, and also of the chief
commissioner for the protectorate, at the apex of the administrative pyramid. The chief commissioner was responsible
to the governor for the good government of the protectorate
and was a member of the Executive and Legislative Councils. When constitutional changes took place in 1958, which
resulted in more responsibility being assigned to elected
ministers, the post of chief commissioner was abolished. But
at the time when I first went to Bo it was the nerve centre of
the protectorate and a major government centre.

The duties of a DC were infinitely varied and the amount
of work he did and the matters on which he concentrated
were in large measure a matter of personal choice. With

improvements in communications and changes in the political structure of government, an increasing volume of legislation and directives from the centre restricted his discretion, but even so he was still largely a free agent in the way in which he managed his district.

His main task was, as it had always been since the establishment of the protectorate, the handling of native affairs. He was the link between government and the chiefs, charged with seeing that the latter kept within the bounds of their authority and helping them to administer their chiefdoms in as enlightened a manner as could reasonably be expected. This meant in particular supervising the working of the native courts, which had a fairly wide jurisdiction in settling such cases between Africans as fell within the ambit of customary law.

Traditionally, courts were held and justice dispensed in a very rough-and-ready manner, but gradually the administration had introduced improvements such as the keeping of proper court records, payment of fixed court fees and holding regular court sessions. Any African could appeal to the DC if he was aggrieved by a decision of the native court, and the DC had power to review the case and vary the decision in any way he thought fit. The DC could also, if he considered it desirable, transfer any case from the native to the magistrate's court. These were important safeguards against the ever-present danger of oppression by the chiefs.

Attempts were also made to improve chiefdom administration by setting up treasuries into which all taxes and other revenues were paid and from which salaries and other expenses were met. A well-run chiefdom could have a surplus which could be spent on such improvements as wells, schools, roads and similar amenities designed to bring a little light into the general darkness.

The DC was also a magistrate with powers of punishment, varying with the particular offence up to a maximum of two years' imprisonment. Much of the court work was being taken over by full-time legally qualified magistrates covering several districts, but the DC still needed and frequently used magisterial powers. For long he had also been in charge of the police force of the protectorate, known as the Court Messenger Force. A very sad event, which took place within a week of my arrival in Bo, was the abolition of this force and the taking over of most of its duties by a professional police force that was not controlled by the DC.

The DC was the father figure of his district for Africans and everyone else. He was in constant contact with the various government departments operating within the district and was regularly consulted by them about matters affecting the district. Any disputes arising between these departments and native authorities, such as an argument about setting aside land within a particular chiefdom as protected forest, would be referred to him for informal arbitration. Any Syrian or European company in need of land for business purposes had to negotiate a lease with the local chiefs that must be approved and signed by the DC. He was president of the district council, an assembly of all the paramount chiefs of his district and other representatives of each chiefdom, which was responsible for constructing and maintaining minor roads and providing other local services. If he was enthusiastic about roads he might encourage the people in the chiefdoms to turn out and build their own, supervising the surveying and construction himself and carrying out the whole project with little or no money.

If he was interested in education there was ample scope for encouraging missions and African administrations to set up elementary schools in the chiefdoms. He would supervise tax collection, lay out football pitches, build rest houses in the outlying parts of the district and function as coroner, commissioner for oaths and registrar of marriages. In the years immediately preceding independence an increasing amount of time was taken up with organizing elections to local district councils and the House of Representatives, Sierra Leone's first elected parliament. The elections were organized in British style with ballot boxes, polling booths, voters' lists and all the other paraphernalia of democracy.

His basic task has always been the maintenance of law, order and good government within the district under his charge, but his other duties are widely varied, giving him endless scope to follow whatever line of development he thinks best for the benefit of his district. It is a job that in recent years has become increasingly frustrating, and district commissioners have inevitably found themselves under fire from politicians who are jealous of their power and influence and of the great respect in which they are held by the population. Even in these difficult conditions, however, it still remained a fascinating job, and it is a pity that the empire is coming to an end so rapidly and depriving future young men of an opportunity to perform a magnificent service.

President Kennedy's Peace Corps and similar bodies can never be a substitute for the overseas civil service and its French equivalent. The servants of international bodies in Third World countries can never be more than pale imitations of their full-blooded colonial forerunners. I doubt whether the United Nations flag is capable of arousing the same emotions as purely national allegiances in a worthy cause; furthermore, the successors to the departed imperialists are just birds of passage, seldom spending more than a few years in any one country and never acquiring for it the same sense of attachment and belonging that was common among the servants of the British and French empires.

The men who governed Sierra Leone and our other colonies were no supermen, nor should they be thought of as secular missionaries spreading the gospel of good government and democracy among the heathen. They were men of intelligence and of some breadth of understanding. Some of them in the course of their careers made contributions to learning in the shape of grammars of the little known African languages they studied, handbooks of customary law and articles on the customs of the people whom they administered or on the flora and fauna of their territories. But it would be wrong to think of the average DC as a scholar. In fact there never was such an animal as the average DC. Some were religious but most were as worldly as the rest of humanity; some were bookish; others were addicted to field sports and shooting; many worked with fiendish enthusiasm; others were content to let affairs in their districts take their normal course with the minimum of interference.

Possibly the only common denominator among administrative officers in the protectorate was their affectionate contempt for their poor benighted brethren who worked in the secretariat in Freetown. This friendly antagonism between administrators in the bush and those in the secretariat — divided into various ministries in the preparations for independence — was a long tradition. It was common for each side to accuse the other of not knowing what was going on in the country. There was some truth in this, as the officials in Freetown were often out of touch with popular feeling in the protectorate and tended to forget the reality of conditions there, while their colleagues upcountry were not aware of the subtle machinations of Freetown politics and hence found many of the directives issuing from there incomprehensible. To some extent the two categories were interchangeable, but no sooner had a man gone from bush to secretariat or vice versa than he immediately changed his allegiance to the ideology prevalent in his new surroundings.

I have in the past, before the days of New Labour, heard it said of Labour members of parliament in the United Kingdom who were elevated to the peerage that once in the House of Lords they became crusted Tories. I once saw a comparable transformation in a DC who for a short time acted as permanent secretary to one of the ministries. He very quickly became critical of his colleagues of a few weeks before and openly opined that his erstwhile superiors, the provincial commissioners, were idle and incompetent, were not doing the job they ought to be doing and would have only themselves to blame if government decided to abolish their positions. It would appear to be a remarkable volte-face for a man who had spent many years in the protectorate and knew at first hand all the problems of the provincial administration, but it was not unusual. The same officer later went back, against his will, to take charge of a district. I would have liked to hear how he fared and particularly how he made his peace with the provincial commissioner.

The politicians, some of whom assumed responsibility for ministerial portfolios for the first time in 1953, were jealous of the power and influence the district commissioners had in the protectorate and were ready to go to great lengths to undermine it, without regard for the consequences to the country. The disastrous effects of this became dramatically apparent in the wave of violence that spread through Northern Province in 1955 and early 1956.

Almost the first action for which African ministers can be held responsible after assuming office was the abolition of the Court Messenger Force, to which I have earlier referred. The force was under the control of the provincial administration. All the NCOs and privates were African, many of them ex-servicemen who had seen fighting in Burma with the West African Frontier Force in the Second World War. The function of the force was to assist the provincial commissioners and DCs in the efficient discharge of their duties.

Districts were big and DCs could not be everywhere, so court messengers were sent out to make initial investigations into complaints. With disputes over farming land, or 'bush disputes' they would first go to inspect the land at the instance of the aggrieved party to the dispute and if the matter called for the DC's intervention they would take steps to see that no one farmed the land until the DC had visited the area and brought about a settlement. In court cases not concerned with land they would ensure that judgments were enforced. They supervised the building of local roads and rest houses, escorted the DC on his treks, acted as interpreters and office messengers and gathered information about matters of political interest in the district. They carried out normal police duties of investigating and prosecuting crime, but this was not usually a major part of their activities.

Court messengers were vital to the proper functioning of the provincial administration. Chiefs who might otherwise be tempted to levy unlawful taxes and otherwise oppress Africans within their jurisdiction were restrained by the knowledge that anything they did was likely to be reported back to the DC, who promptly would intervene to put an end to malpractices. The system was of course never perfect; there were cases of oppression and misrule and the agents of government were not present in sufficient numbers to eradicate them completely, but at least they were kept within reasonable bounds, and from the earliest days the protectorate of Sierra Leone had a remarkably trouble-free history.

The Court Messenger Force was an obvious target for African politicians who regarded the expatriate officers of the provincial administration as the principal agents of the imperial system they were trying to shake off and refused to appreciate that they were simply underpaid civil servants with a difficult job to do, who had no objection to working under their new masters provided the latter showed some evidence of willingness to cooperate and to try to understand the problems with which these officers had to contend.

In 1953 there was trouble in the diamond-mining district of Kono in South-Eastern Province, where illicit miners posed a constant threat to security. The Court Messenger Force in the district was too small in numbers to cope and a contingent of police had to be sent from Freetown to help them. This gave the politicians the pretext they wanted to bring in legislation applying the Police Ordinance to the protectorate and repealing the Court Messenger Force Ordinance. The legislation was rushed through with hardly any debate and 1 September 1954 was fixed as the date on which the CMF would be disbanded and the police would take over responsibility for the maintenance of law and order in the protectorate. Even at the time when the legislation was passed, it was realized that the police would have insufficient numbers of trained men to take over properly on that date, but such was the eagerness of the politicians that this consideration was brushed aside.

The change was not made without strong opposition from the provincial administration, particularly from the chief commissioner for the protectorate, Hubert Childs, who gave solemn warnings about the potentially disastrous effects of abolishing an important executive arm of government in the protectorate and putting in its place a new and untried substitute. He argued that it was fallacious to think of the Court Messenger Force as an inchoate police force and that the proposed change made no provision for the performance of the manifold administrative and intelligence duties the court messengers had always performed. He drew attention to the danger of letting these functions go by default. Members of the Executive Council, Sierra Leone's precursor of a cabinet, dismissed his warnings as the protests of vested interests.

Thus the CMF, which had been the mainstay of the provincial administration for over 60 years, was swept away almost overnight and its place taken by an inexperienced police force, largely ignorant of the protectorate and inadequate in numbers. Some of the effects of the change became immediately apparent in the lack of proper messengers attached to district offices and the entire dependence from then on of the provincial administration on the police for trek escorts and administrative investigations — a most unsatisfactory arrangement — not to mention the arrogance of expatriate police officers who went about openly saying that they were now in charge of affairs in the protectorate and that the days of the DC were over. The effects showed up less than 18 months after abolition in the riots of 1955–56 in the Northern Province, the worst and most widespread outbreak of violence the country had ever known.

I am anticipating events and assuming a degree of wisdom that obviously did not become mine immediately. For the present I had everything to learn. I spent much time browsing among files whose contents appeared to be of no comprehensible significance. I received a warrant from the chief justice authorizing me to act as a magistrate, and began to exercise my authority by signing charge sheets, summonses, arrest warrants and bail bonds. Not for some time did I begin to hear cases. There was much to learn about how government worked and I was given copies of *General Orders* and *Financial Orders* to study, in addition to several bulky bound volumes containing the laws of Sierra Leone.

For my first three years I would be a cadet and during that time I was expected to take examinations on the contents of these publications. I was also instructed to learn Mende, one of the two main languages of the protectorate, in which I had the advantage of having made a start in London. A cadet who passed all examinations (which were not difficult) and showed himself reasonably proficient in his duties would in due course be confirmed in his appointment by a notice published in the *Official Gazette*. This meant that he was thereafter a permanent member of the service, entitled to a pension on retirement, and could not be summarily dismissed.

Within a few weeks I was given my first taste of responsibility. One result of the migration of the country's young men to the diamond fields in large numbers was a severe shortage of rice, the staple food, since there was no one left to do the bush clearing, planting and harvesting. This shortage became so serious that government was forced to import shiploads of rice from Italy and Burma. This was an outrageous state of affairs for a country with large areas of upland and riverine swamp and ample rainfall, far from over populated, certainly capable of feeding itself and even, with a little effort, of exporting food. What made the situation tenable was that the government was able to sell the imported rice at a profit, which was used to subsidize the price paid to the African farmers for locally grown rice.

The rice was mainly intended to supply Freetown and other urban areas where local rice had become almost unobtainable. Bo had a government rice mill, originally built for milling and storing rice grown in the surrounding districts before it was shipped to Freetown. Now it was being used as a distribution centre for rice brought up by rail from Freetown. I have already described the inadequacies of the railway, which was unable to bring up enough imported goods to meet the insatiable demand in the protectorate and was likewise unable to bring up enough rice. In any event, Freetown had first call on the rice and the protectorate had to make do with what was left. The rice that reached Bo had to be rationed so that the demands of government departments and commercial companies for their employees as well as of schools and traders could be met as fairly as possible. The rice mill was looked after by a manager who was a fairly junior official, and in the absence of anyone more senior from the Department of Commerce and Industry, the task of supervising rationing fell on the DC, who had general responsibility for coordinating the work of all departments in the district and retained residuary responsibility for managing any activity that a junior official otherwise managed.

I began to pay daily visits to the mill, which was near the railway station and had its own siding. It meant a long walk, as I had no car, but I accepted walking as a regular necessity, which though inconvenient and time-consuming was no hardship. Each day the mill compound was full of a mob of government employees, mostly labourers from the Public Works Department, brandishing pieces of paper and demanding bags of rice. A dozen or more policemen had to be stationed in and around the mill to prevent assaults on the manager or other serious disorders. It did not take me long to realize that the first step towards a more orderly system of distribution was to limit the number of people having access to the compound. It would therefore be necessary for each government department or other organization whose employees were buying rice to estimate their needs for all their employees each month and collect the rice in bulk. To this end I issued a circular to all concerned and asked for their cooperation. This was my first executive decision and I felt proud of it, as well as of the modest success I achieved in restoring order around the mill. Thereafter, my task was mainly to ration out what supplies we received in the fairest possible manner.

Another slightly unpleasant task I was given in my first few weeks was that of paying out money for monkeys' heads. Monkeys were responsible for much damage to crops, and although the farmers were all well aware of this, it was difficult to make them shake off their habitual lethargy and set about trying to shoot these pests. To encourage them, the district councils organized annual monkey drives and sixpence (in pre-decimal currency) was paid for every head of a monkey produced. This kind of job was suitable for a cadet who was not yet experienced enough to do more responsible work on his own but who could at least be trusted not to embezzle the large sums of cash he was given to distribute.

This was my first chance since my arrival to see something of Bo District outside the town. I borrowed the provincial commissioner's lorry, a vehicle I frequently had to use when I was in Bo, in the absence of anything smaller and more comfortable, and to which I became very attached. I took with me sandwiches and a flask of coffee, plus a briefcase containing large sums in sixpences and shillings. I had a good day for travelling: it had rained the day before, so there was no dust thrown up from the laterite roads, and an overcast sky kept the temperature down.

Bo had an estimated population of 10,000 at the time and was counted as a big town in Sierra Leone, but the actual size of it can be judged from the fact that one could start from the government reservation on the north, drive through the middle of it out to the road on the south side and be in the bush again with no building in sight within a few minutes. Soon we were going down the Tikonko road, bumping over potholes and sliding over muddy patches with nothing but low forest and dense, featureless bush on both sides. We passed Tikonko, a chiefdom headquarters town seven miles from Bo with a population of about 2000. A few miles further on we came to the Sewa River, which was crossed by a ferry, and here we had to take our place at the end of the queue of lorries already waiting.

Sierra Leone is a well-watered country drained by many major rivers cutting across all lines of communication between the interior and the coast. All the main roads were interrupted at intervals by ferries on which vehicles were taken across one at a time on wooden pontoons attached by a pulley to a steel cable suspended over the river between pillars on each bank and moved by a gang of men pulling on the cable. In the rainy season the strong current, which did most of the work, helped them, but in the dry season, with a lower water level and slack current, the crossing would be slow and laborious. At the height of the rains, ferries had to be closed because of the danger that the pontoons might capsize in the powerful currents. They were also closed at night, though it was common practice for drivers who wished to cross at night to dash the ferrymen for this special service. Normally there was no charge for the use of public ferries.

Ferries aggravated the difficulties of opening up the protectorate and keeping it supplied. Lorries were regularly held up several hours or even days waiting for their turn to cross. The problem had been becoming steadily more acute for years and the government had received a substantial sum from colonial development and welfare funds provided by the United Kingdom government to replace nine ferries with bridges. The Sewa ferry south of Bo was the most congested in the country and priority was being given to building a bridge some miles upstream. Work on this was already well advanced when I arrived in Bo.

Ferry crossings provided agreeable interludes on otherwise monotonous and uncomfortable journeys by road. A brief halt gave one a chance to stretch one's limbs, walk around, chat to lorry drivers and others, and view the stalls of petty traders who were invariably found at ferries. Sometimes one might meet there other European government officials or African ministers and have the opportunity to exchange gossip and learn something of what was going on in Freetown or in other parts of the protectorate. They could charitably be regarded as one of the hallmarks of an unhurried way of life, but as the queues of lorries lengthened and delays and exasperation increased, they became an increasing hindrance to the business of travellers, whatever that might be. The opening of the new bridges from 1955 onwards to replace ferries was welcomed with relief all round.

In the course of my day out I visited several towns in which the farmers from the surrounding areas had congregated, bringing with them an unsavoury collection of severed monkeys' heads. These were laid out for my inspection and after I had counted them and paid for them at sixpence each I ordered them to be thrown into the bush, where the driver ants would soon dispose of them. It was a nauseating task, but I managed to complete it without letting my disgust become too obvious. Some of the farmers tried to raise other complaints and matters with me, the visit of an administrative officer being regarded as a time for bringing to his attention any matter in which they thought government might be able to help them. I felt too unsure of myself to do more than ask them to wait for the next time the DC came on a more formal visit.

The roads along which I travelled were narrow, unsurfaced and muddy, but at least motorable. To visit one of the towns on the day's itinerary I had to go for some miles along a road built and maintained by the district council and from this got some idea of just how bad roads in the country could be. It had probably been built along a former bush path without any serious attempt at surveying for a better alignment. It wound and twisted in a crazy manner and went straight up and down hills regardless of gradients. Pipe culverts carrying streams under the road had only a thin covering of earth on top of them and thus made a distinct bump in the surface of the road. At one point the road was completely waterlogged and the maintenance gang had put down bundles of sticks in the mud so as to give the wheels of vehicles something on which to grip.

The day over, the last sixpences paid out, I returned to Bo, once more crossing by the ferry. I was tired from the endless jolting of the lorry, but I had the satisfaction of knowing that I had started to see the district.

5

On Trek

On trek. The phrase conjures up a picture of some Saunders of the River, complete with topi and spine pad, accompanied by his faithful African porters. One imagines him wading through a crocodile infested swamp, seeking out the haunts of tribes with outlandish names, holding parleys with ferocious warriors dressed in little more than their war paint. The reality nowadays is more prosaic, but the colour and excitement are not yet entirely lost.

Trekking or touring is an essential part of an administrative officer's work. It is a temptation nowadays, with the increasing amount of paper requiring attention, to spend more time in the office. Contact with the people he is governing is as necessary as it ever was, and the best way of making contact is by moving round the district, spending two or three days in each place. Now that roads are making places more easily accessible — notwithstanding their poor quality— there is a tendency to do business on day trips by car. But to find out what is happening in a particular chiefdom it is necessary to sit down there (to use the Sierra Leone idiom) and have the opportunity of talking to people other than chiefs.

For my first trek I was to accompany Jack Wann on a tour

of four chiefdoms in the northeast of the district, taking a fortnight. The main purpose of the visit was the preparation of each chiefdom's estimates of revenue and expenditure for the next financial year. Time was also allowed for dealing with complaints, court appeals and any other business outstanding in the chiefdom.

I lacked some essentials of kit needed for going on trek, having already stretched my resources to the limit to provide myself with the bare minimum of things needed to set up house. I had a camp bed, a tin bath and little else. Fortunately, this did not matter so long as I was accompanying the DC, who was well supplied with camp chairs, pressure lamps and boxes and was able to meet most of my needs as well as his own. I had the chance to gain some idea of what I would need for a reasonable degree of comfort on trek.

We left Bo early on Monday morning on the passenger train going east to Pendembu. There was no first-class compartment, so we had the privilege of travelling in the guard's van. We got off the train at Yamandu, a station 20 miles from Bo. From here we walked. Our party consisted of Jack Wann, myself, an interpreter, three policemen acting as escorts and three personal servants, two of Jack's and one of mine. Between us we had about 30 loads and had sent instructions in advance for that number of carriers to meet us. We found them waiting at the station and sent them on ahead with the servants and two of the policemen, so that we would arrive at the rest house to find everything unpacked and ready.

The local paramount chief had come to meet us from his own town of Baoma, the next town up the line. We stayed at Yamandu an hour or more, discussing chiefdom matters in what was still to me an incomprehensible version of English, its comprehensibility not helped for me by the still mysterious nature of much of the subject matter. We also inspected a recently completed local gaol or lockup built for the African administration, and after exchanging final courtesies with the chief started on our walk to Benduma, eight miles to the north.

The road led out of Yamandu up a hill, through an assortment of thatched and pan-roofed houses. There were dozens of small traders at improvised stalls on each side of the road, selling shirts, lengths of cloth, beer, corned beef, cheap combs, cowboy hats and all manner of goods to suit the colourful tastes of the newly rich diamond diggers who thronged the area. Yamandu was not far from the Sewa River, which with its tributaries and nearby swamps was a fruitful area for alluvial diamond mining. The government had so far failed to frame any definite policy for dealing with the illicit miners and, in the face of such widespread and unchecked lawlessness, the government itself was becoming an object of contempt.

We walked most of the time through high bush over undulating ground. Occasionally the country opened out when we were crossing swamps, but for most of the way we could see nothing but the vegetation enclosing us on both sides. This was monotonous, but at least we were cooler than we would have been in the open. I soon realized that I was not appropriately dressed for this kind of travelling. I was wearing a pair of ordinary leather shoes and long khaki stockings, such as I normally wore to go to the office. We often had to ford streams or wade for a short way across swamps, and my shoes filled up with water and became uncomfortable. Jack Wann was much more sensibly shod in a pair of plimsolls and short socks. Even the short socks were not strictly necessary, and on later walking treks I took to wearing plimsolls without socks.

Walking along bush tracks can be trying. Apart from the hazards of streams and swamps, every track is littered with stones and irregularly ribbed with tree roots. Usually any government officer who was undertaking a walking trek would give advance notice of the route he intended to follow, so that the local chief could arrange to turn out the local young men to clear the vegetation growing over the track, a process known as brushing, and could repair bridges. At other times the roads were neglected and people using them had to push their way through high grass and wade across swamps and streams.

Our arrival at Benduma, headquarters of Bagbwe chiefdom, was heralded with old-fashioned ceremony such as might at one time have been normal protocol but was now confined to occasions when distinguished visitors arriving on foot had to be greeted. One of the chief's messengers was posted at a vantage point half a mile from the town and raced back to the town when he saw us. Another messenger fired a gun into the air as a signal to the paramount chief and all the elders to gather on the road near the rest house to greet us. As we approached this gathering the chief's horn was blown and the entire messenger force of the chiefdom — a sergeant, corporal and five messengers — came to attention.

The paramount chief was a woman, Madame Mabaja. It was not unusual among the Mende and Sherbro for a woman to hold this office, though I never heard of it among any of the other tribes of Sierra Leone, nor did I ever hear of a woman holding any other office in a chiefdom. Women chiefs were usually figureheads, content to leave the administration of their chiefdoms to some man who found favour with them. Madame Mabaja was no exception and her eldest son Bobo Samai, an educated man who became a friend of mine, ran Bagbwe chiefdom.

We exchanged greetings with the chief and her elders and it was agreed that as we had had a long walk and it was now already the middle of the afternoon, we would leave formal business until the following morning. The elders returned to the town while Jack Wann and I walked to the rest house. Our servants had already unpacked our boxes, set out chairs and put up our camp beds before we arrived. The rest house was a simple building with mud walls and floors and a thatched roof. There was no furniture in it apart from a table lent by the chief.

I had already concluded that a walking trek, though arduous, had its compensations, not least of which was the close contact it gave with the simple people who lived in the many scattered villages in the bush. On our walk from Yamandu we had greeted everyone who passed us with a few words in Mende and had paused briefly in the villages, where the town chief and his villagers had come out to meet us. I was most impressed with the respectful ceremony that marked our arrival in Benduma. We had to put up with the simplest of living conditions, and the only comforts were those we carried with us, but at least in the rest house we were not cramped for space and had ample privacy.

We had not been long there when our interpreter came from the town, accompanied by an elder and by a young boy carrying on his head a large bowl of rice and eggs and in his hand two chickens with their legs tethered. This was the traditional 'dash' or present from the chief. By custom, distinguished strangers visiting the chiefdom must always be given presents, which usually took the form of food. On special occasions a cow or a hand-woven country cloth might be presented. In the more sophisticated world of the 1950s crates of beer or bottles of whisky sometimes took the place of more traditional presents.

General Orders, the civil servant's guide to official correct behaviour, decreed that where such presents were given to officers and could not be refused without causing offence to the donors, the officers must give something in return, in cash or in kind, to the equivalent of the market value of the present received. On a short trek this was reasonable, as chickens, rice and eggs could be had more cheaply in this way than in the markets of Bo or other major towns. On a long trek, however, in the course of which many towns and villages might be visited, the quantity of gifts became an embarrassment and was far more than was consumable.

If a visiting officer followed *General Orders* strictly he might find himself out of pocket because he was neither allowed to claim the value of his return presents as a travelling expense nor had the option of handing over to government the actual dashes received. Most officers would have been very glad to dispose of surplus rice and other food in this way, but this would have placed on government the onus of paying for suitable return presents and did not therefore find favour. This particular regulation may be regarded as the epitome of British colonial policy, enshrining three basic principles: respect for native law and custom, maintenance of the dignity and incorruptibility of the colonial service and the avoidance of any expenditure that was not absolutely essential. The hardship it might cause to underpaid officers was either ignored or regarded as one of the features of life in the service that toughened men. There were certain senior officials, usually bachelors, who believed in the value of poverty as an instrument of discipline.

For reasons the framers of it could never have foreseen, this general order failed to achieve its intended result, that of making sure that government officers were not beholden in any way to private individuals as the result of hospitality and gifts they received. In many chiefdoms, especially in the Northern Province, the visit of the DC was made an excuse for a general levy of chickens and rice throughout the chiefdom, each village being required to supply its quota. Large quantities would be collected in this way, far larger than the DC would ever see, and most of it was divided among the chiefs. The fiction was maintained that the present came from the paramount chief and the DC had therefore to slip his return dash into the chief's hand just before leaving.

It is most unlikely that any share of the cash ever found its way to the people who had provided the rice. To begin with, when I started touring on my own, I tried scrupulously to comply with the general order, but I soon found it ruinous, particularly in my parlous financial condition, so I simply ceased giving return dashes, though I gratefully accepted the presents. I have never felt guilty about this. The general order was a mean and iniquitous imposition on ill paid albeit hard-working and conscientious officers. I did not particularly want the supplies of food of which the dashes consisted, and I was very conscious of the futility and unfairness of giving a return dash to the paramount chief.

In earlier days it was not uncommon for the chief to send a young woman to the rest house to serve the DC's pleasure. This charming custom had, however, fallen into desuetude, particularly as so many officers had their wives with them and partly also because improved communications caused details of the private lives of both bachelors and married men to become common knowledge throughout the country. That said, I do not imply that sexual liaisons between European officers and African women no longer occurred — they most certainly did.

Soon it was dark on the evening of our first day on trek, and after we had bathed we sat on the rest house veranda talking and drinking at our leisure until it was time to eat. After supper I brought out a pack of cards, but we soon discovered that there are no satisfactory card games for two people. Connoisseurs of Hoyle may be able to correct me in this, but that learned author's treatise was not to hand, and we gave up the idea of playing cards. Jack Wann was a keen chess player, but this was a game of which I knew little, so that too was out. The pattern of our leisure time on trek settled down to a routine of reading, writing letters and talking. I had everything to learn about Africa and about my work, and I could not have wanted a better teacher.

Next morning when we woke the Union Jack was already

flying from a tall bamboo pole stuck into the ground outside the rest house. It was part of the ritual of the DC's travels in his own district that the flag was flown from morning to sunset, and one of the duties of our escort policemen was to see that we took a flag with us and that it was raised and lowered daily at the appropriate times. The DC was the representative of the Governor and of the Queen, and it was fitting that he should show the flag in this way. Such sentiments may nowadays seem quaint and old-fashioned, but I felt a great pride in the privilege of being able to fly the Union Jack at the rest house wherever I went.

Later we met the assembled members of the tribal authority in the *barri*. Here again I was struck by the necessarily unhurried pace of life and business in these surroundings. Bagbwe chiefdom was smaller than most, but it had no communications other than bush paths and some of the town and village chiefs had to walk 15 miles or more daily in each direction to attend meetings at Benduma. This they considered no hardship, but it meant that meetings could not begin until fairly late in the morning and had to finish no later than 4.00 p.m. to give the members time to reach their villages in the remaining hours of daylight. If the paramount chief was hospitable, the visiting members might be fed during the day, but often they would have to go without food all day.

At about 10.00 a.m. the interpreter came to tell us that the people were ready. A small boy was sent on ahead carrying a box of the files to which we might need to refer, and we followed. The ordinary members of the tribal authority (TA) were sitting in the body of the *barri*, while various curious onlookers sat on the walls or stood round the sides. On the dais were Madame Mabaja, Bobo Samai, and the section chiefs; I think five in all. Everyone except the section chief stood up as we entered and took our places on the dais at the table that had been reserved for us. Jack Wann, speaking through the interpreter, opened the proceedings by greeting the assembled body in the customary way and introduced me to them as a newly appointed officer who was seeing Sierra Leone for the first time.

These formalities over, he began with the first important item of business, the preparation of the chiefdom estimates for the next financial year. To me, unfamiliar as I was with accounting of any description, this was a baffling exercise, but one at which I would have to become competent. I will not bore the reader with details, except that total revenue and expenditure had first to be estimated. If there was a reasonable surplus after normal recurrent expenses such as salaries had been covered, then provision might be made for minor improvements such as putting a corrugated-iron roof on the rest house, digging a few wells or building a small lockup for prisoners held on the order of the native court. All too often there was no surplus and, as a result, the people saw nothing for their annual taxes and came to the conclusion that the money had been misused.

In theory, the tribal authorities were supposed to prepare their own estimates for government's approval, but since most of the members of these bodies were illiterate this was impracticable. It was also beyond the ability of the average native administration clerk, invariably a man of little education. In some of the better-run chiefdoms, particularly those that had educated paramount chiefs, draft estimates might be prepared by the chief and some of his educated advisers, but in these cases the total expenditure figure at which they arrived was often far in excess of the estimated revenue and no helpful suggestions would be forthcoming as to how the budget deficit could be made up. Most of the work inevitably fell on the DC, though the pretence was maintained that the estimates were the work of the TA.

At this time the Colonial Office was still star struck with the idea that it was necessary to develop local government at the district, chiefdom or other appropriate level in the colonies as a training ground and preparation for self-government at the national level. This was the burden of a celebrated and ill-conceived directive put out by the then secretary of state for the colonies in 1948. In Sierra Leone, native administrations had already been established in a number of chiefdoms from 1937. This expression meant a tribal authority that had a proper system of recording its revenue and expenditure, including the employment of a clerk. After the war native administrations were introduced in many more chiefdoms and, by 1954, there were no more than three out of 150 chiefdoms in the country that were not organized in this way.

However, the impression officials in Freetown or London might have had of self-contained units looking after their own affairs was illusory. The impetus for efficient tax collection, keeping accounts and spending money on the items for which it was allocated, still had to come from the DC. Without his constant and detailed supervision the whole edifice would have collapsed. The same was true of other attempts at developing local government in Sierra Leone. The outcome was the imposition of extra labours on the provincial administration, with no increase in local self-sufficiency.

We completed the estimates with the uncomprehending acquiescence of the tribal authority members, who showed signs of interest only when we were discussing their own remuneration, which was paid in the form of a rebate on each tax they collected from individual taxpayers under their jurisdiction. We passed on to other business. Bagbwe chiefdom was deeply divided as the result of a feud between the two ruling houses, meaning families from which at some time in the course of recent history paramount chiefs had been appointed. It was common to have two such houses within a chiefdom, and where the chiefdom was the result of an amalgamation the number was multiplied.

A paramount chief, once elected, held office for life. He

could be removed for misconduct by government after an inquiry, but the procedure for this was cumbersome, so in practice his tenure was secure, much more so than it would have been under traditional African law and custom, because of the protection of the colonial government. One consequence of this was that the ruling house that was in opposition would frequently do what it could to discredit the regime in power, hoping thereby to get the chief removed or to have the chiefdom carved up.

In Bagbwe, the *casus belli* had been provided by a proposal to build with voluntary labour a motor road to link the chiefdom with the rest of the district. The road was to come through Niawa Lenga chiefdom to the northwest, from where it was already possible to reach Bo by road. It would run through Galu, Madame Mabaja's home town and from there on to Benduma, some miles to the south, ending at Yamandu as a convenient point on the railway. It was a sensible scheme that would have done much to improve the prosperity of the chiefdom by giving easier access to markets for palm kernels and other produce. Roads were often built by the free labour of all the young men of a chiefdom given by consent in the common interest. Sierra Leone was a poor country unable to find large sums to pay contractors to construct roads, and in this way the country's greatest unused asset, idle or underemployed hands, was put to work. Many hundreds of miles of road had been built in this way, with no help from the government apart from the supervision and advice of the DC.

Work had already started on building the first stretch from Niawa Lenga chiefdom when Madame Mabaja's rivals intervened and began to create trouble. They commanded the support of two of the chiefdom's five sections. Benduma was in one of the two sections and, as the previous paramount chief had belonged to the rival house, he had had the chiefdom headquarters moved from Galu, where it had previously been, to Benduma, although this was in the south of the chiefdom and much less convenient. Young men from all sections had turned out to work on the road. We in Bo knew that a Mr Gbenga, a member of the rival house, was a trade union organizer. He went among the men working on the road and told them that they were being made to do unlawful forced labour and that they should demand payment for the work they were doing. He also issued union cards to some of them and collected union dues. He was able to play strongly on the allegiance of the men from his own two sections, who downed tools and thereafter refused to help further. The young men from the other sections were not willing to continue on their own and work came to a stop. Visits by the DC and provincial commissioner failed to get it restarted.

Our aim on this occasion was to attempt to reconcile the two houses, which had now not been on speaking terms for several years. There was a case pending between them in the Supreme Court. The DC scolded all the assembled members of the TA with hard words, telling them that in the short time he had been in the district he had heard nothing good of the chiefdom and that it was time they tried to work together instead of perpetuating their quarrels, which in the end brought no benefit to anyone. He made no mention of restarting work on the road, as hope of this had already been abandoned.

Officers dealing with 'palavers' of this kind regularly enlisted the help of assessor chiefs, namely competent paramount chiefs from other chiefdoms who would be able to command the respect of the warring factions. A chief from Pujehun District, our immediate neighbour to the south of Bo District, came to help on this occasion. His name was Alimami Jai Kai Kai, an educated man held in high esteem among the Mende, who had for several years been a member of the Legislative Council. He was a tall, lean and distinguished looking man. Although his family had been in

Pujehun for some generations and were accepted as Mende, it was generally believed that he was of Foulah ancestry, the Foulah being a race of cattle owners, known in Northern Nigeria as the Fulani and found all over West Africa. They were usually tall men with light skins and finely drawn Hamitic features, in contrast with the Mende and other tribes along the coast who were short, stocky and with distinctly Negroid features.

After Jack Wann had finished haranguing the gathering he handed over to Chief Jai Kai Kai, who spent a day in the *barri* talking to the Bagbwe elders, while Jack and I sat in the rest house awaiting results. Our assessor's aim was to persuade the opposition party to offer a 'beg' in the form of a sum of money, a number of cows or some other substantial sacrifice in order to make their peace with Madame Mabaja's supporters, and to persuade the latter to accept this. The attempt at conciliation was, however, unsuccessful, so embittered were the relations between the two parties, and we were obliged to leave the feud unresolved.

We spent another day disposing of miscellaneous complaints and appeals; these formed an important part of the business on any visit to a chiefdom. There were appeals from dissatisfied litigants before the chiefdom's own court, complaints that decisions of the court had not been enforced, requests for shotgun licences, applications from young men wanting to join the army and requests from some people for refunds of tax paid earlier in the year on the grounds that their houses had been burned down. The DC paid each chiefdom two routine visits in the course of a year, one to collect tax and one to prepare estimates. For the ordinary African these visits were his only contact with the government for whose protection and help he was entitled to ask and it was important to deal with all complaints and other matters on the spot as far as possible, making a record of them at the same time. Even this contact might well involve the complainant in a long walk to the chiefdom headquarters town to put his case to the DC, but the alternative was an even longer journey to district headquarters.

A chiefdom's political condition could often be judged from the nature and volume of complaints. A large number of petty ones would perhaps indicate a weak and ineffective chief who was struggling against much intrigue and opposition within the chiefdom. More serious allegations could be taken as a symptom of bad administration and victimization of members of rival factions. A small number of complaints on any visit was healthy and normal, but a total absence of them might be a sign of danger, meaning that the chief had too strong a grip on his chiefdom and that his people were afraid to speak out openly against him because of the punishment they might suffer after the DC had left.

Complaints were dealt with in the *barri*, though people often came to see the DC covertly at the rest house if they feared for any reason to put their case in public. In the *barri* the complainant would stand in front of the DC's table and speak through an interpreter, often with great eloquence, a talent highly esteemed among Africans. If the case were an appeal against a decision of the native court, the DC would call upon the clerk to produce the court record. By reading this and asking questions of court members present he would elucidate the background. If he was satisfied that all was in order he would confirm the native court's decision and make a note to that effect on the record. If necessary, he might call all the witnesses and rehear the case, making whatever finding he thought fit. Sometimes the case would be a new one and the complainant would then be advised to take out a summons in the native court and let the matter be dealt with there first before any further remedy was sought. Whatever the case and no matter how trivial it might be, some definite reply must be given, some final or interim order made to satisfy the complainants that their cases were being given a proper hearing and that justice was being done.

At the end of the day the DC thanked the members of the tribal authority for attending the meeting and they dispersed to their villages. The following morning we moved on to the next chiefdom, Baja, even smaller than Bagbwe and further from any motor road. Again we sent the carriers on in advance. The distance was short, but we were not ourselves going by the direct road. Instead we followed a trace, which had been cut for a prospective motor road that was intended to link Baja with the northern part of Bagbwe. This meant a long and exhausting detour. It was soon evident even to my unpractised eye that the trace was not a good one, for it went across swamps that would need causeways to carry the road and over some very steep hills, rocky in places, where a lot of blasting would be needed. We had 16 miles of difficult walking and it was in the middle of the afternoon that we reached Ngelehun, the headquarters town. Jack Wann, a much more hardened walker than I, as well as being taller, left me behind on the last stages of the journey and was waiting for me at the rest house when I arrived.

The rest house was similar to the one we had left at Benduma, but attractively sited on top of a hill on the far side of a river from the town, which was reached from there by a stick bridge. We could see the river below and hear the soft music of its rapids all day long. It was a tributary of the Sewa, which dominated so much of Bo District. We also had views of other hills in the distance, which was a relief after the monotonous absence of views on bush paths. The town itself, though small, was neatly planned, with straight footpaths and houses on properly spaced out building plots instead of the higgledy-piggledy chaos so typical of an African village. Between the *barri* and the river was a pleasant open space, shaded by two enormous breadfruit trees.

Baja chiefdom consisted of three sections and had just over

1000 taxpayers. By the empirical formula we normally applied in the absence of any population statistics, this meant a population of about 4000. A taxpayer meant an adult male over the age of 21 and the addition of three others took care of women and children. Our business there was soon finished and we moved on to the next chiefdom, Komboya, with its headquarters at Njala, ten miles to the northeast of Ngelehun.

Njala was still further from motor roads but had, however, well-made streets and a good layout. It also boasted a primary school and church run by the Roman Catholics, in the care of two Irish fathers. Theirs was an unenviable life in such surroundings, cut off from any regular contact with the rest of the world and working among people on whom the message of their faith made little impression. On this occasion the fathers were away and we did not meet them, but I met them on subsequent visits. They were two very cheerful men, well informed about everything that was going on around them, as are Roman Catholic priests everywhere; one of them had already spent seven years at Njala. They had no illusions about working among people whose lives were dominated by belief in magic and the power of African medicines, and realized that adoption of a Christian faith by Africans was often no more than a superficial conversion.

Roman Catholic missions in Sierra Leone followed a realistic policy of concentrating on the secular aspects of their work, most notably running schools and hospitals. They had a more comprehensive coverage of the country than any other mission and were content to go on digging themselves in more securely in the expectation that eventually they would win adherents to their faith. I am not a Roman Catholic, but while I was in Sierra Leone I came to have the greatest admiration for the fathers, whose practical ability in worldly matters and singleness of purpose were unequalled.

Jack Wann had arranged a special show for our visit to this chiefdom. On our second day there we were joined by a young assistant superintendent of police from Bo, who was to prosecute two members of the tribal authority for holding illegal courts; Jack was to hear the cases as magistrate. The holding of private or illegal courts was a common practice everywhere in the protectorate, and one it was impossible to eradicate. If there was a minor dispute about land or women between people in an out-of-the-way village it was much easier for all concerned to ask the local headman to 'cut' the case on the veranda of his house than to begin proceedings in the properly constituted native court, which usually meant a long journey to the chiefdom headquarters in order to take out a summons issued by the chiefdom clerk, followed by much expense and many delays and adjournments before the case was disposed of.

Nevertheless, if cases were heard in this way it meant that the authority of the native court was being flouted and that revenue was being lost to the chiefdom. This marks an interesting contrast with the attitude to litigation in England and many other European countries. It is regarded as something to be indulged in only as a last resort when all other means of settlement of a dispute have failed or for one reason or another are regarded as impractical. Arbitration and other less formal and quicker — though not necessarily cheaper — ways of settling arguments are encouraged. It could be contended that the headman was providing a cheap local arbitration service that was satisfactory to the parties, but there were good local reasons for taking a different view.

News of the impending trial had travelled widely and many people walked miles to be present at Njala on the day. Over 1000 were there to witness the proceedings. We heard evidence of how an aggrieved husband had made a complaint regarding the infidelity of his wife to the headmen who were now on trial for holding an illegal court. She, when questioned, had confessed the name of another man as her lover and this man was called by the headmen and fined 30

82

shillings (£1.50) plus the headmen's fee, the 30 shillings being given to the husband as compensation.

'Woman damage' cases of this kind were common in the native court and 30 shillings was the standard award of compensation. They could be a regular source of income to more prosperous men who by African custom might have several wives. The headmen did not raise any serious defence to the charges, so they were convicted, fined £5 each and ordered to refund the amounts collected as fees. It may be that the convictions made an impression and cut the incidence of illegal courts in Komboya chiefdom, but it is unlikely that the impression lasted long.

The trial over, we went on to hear complaints, of which there were many. The paramount chief had many enemies. The integrity of some of the elders and members of the native court was dubious and some of the decisions the DC was asked to review were curious. In one case of woman damage the court had awarded compensation to a husband for infidelity admitted to have occurred before the woman concerned had become his wife. The chiefdom speaker, deputy to the paramount chief, had presided over the court when this case was heard and gave the excuse that he had probably been suffering an attack of fever when he arrived at this decision. On this and subsequent visits I found many instances of maladministration and it was obvious that drastic steps were needed to bring to an end the inefficiency and corruption that prevailed. The construction of a road, making closer and more regular supervision possible, was a most desirable improvement.

The last stage of our walking trek took us from Njala Komboya to Negbema, capital of Niawa Lenga chiefdom, a distance of almost 20 miles, our longest day's walk. Our route lay through Bagbwe chiefdom to the north of Benduma. The first stage of our journey, from Njala to Galu, was over a plateau of mostly savannah grass. It had poor soil, unfit for farming, but it had the advantage of letting us see the country around us, mostly hills with large areas of bare rock exposed, the effects of erosion. The soil on the plateau formed only a thin layer on top of the rock, held together tenuously by the savannah. Often we walked over bare rock from which all the soil had been washed away.

Galu was in Bagbwe chiefdom and when we came down from the plateau and halted there, Madame Mabaja and some of her elders were waiting to greet us. The full journey was too far for one lot of carriers, so we paid off those who had come with us from Njala and gave the loads to a fresh relay.

With ten miles still to go my feet were already sore and my heels were badly blistered and bleeding. I was suffering from the cumulative effect of these unaccustomed marches. Jack Wann sent me on with the carriers to give me a start, but he overtook me at Galu and reached Negbema long before I did. I found the last part of the walk very trying and fell behind the rest of the party. Our interpreter, Alfred Tucker, and one policeman stayed with me. It was now the middle of the day and very hot. We were walking along a half-built motor road that was to link Galu and Negbema, the same road that had given rise to the feud in Bagbwe chiefdom and that was now being finished by Bo District Council. All vegetation and trees had been cleared to the usual width of 20 feet and there was no shade to give us any relief from the blazing sun. To get cool I immersed myself in several of the streams we crossed, pausing only to take off the gumboots I had decided were the most comfortable wear in the present state of my feet. I was also wearing three pairs of woollen stockings for extra protection. I have seldom felt so thankful or relieved as I did when I reached Negbema at 4.00 p.m. and knew that the ordeal was over. That evening I appreciated the luxury of a bath and the other simple comforts of the rest house as much as if I had been staying at a five star hotel. Alfred Tucker told me some months later that he had felt very sorry for me when he saw how I was suffering.

From Negbema Jack Wann was called to Bo and I was left to prepare the estimates myself. I was by now familiar with the routine and was able to produce a draft of sorts. Fortunately, Jack returned before I presented the estimates to the tribal authority in their final form and was able to correct some of my more obvious mistakes. Niawa Lenga was a well-governed chiefdom with a young and educated paramount chief, and once the estimates were completed there was little other business for us. After three nights there we walked to the end of the motorable part of the road, 200 yards from the rest house. Jack Wann had brought his car back with him and we had a comfortable ride back to Bo, 20 miles away, while our loads, servants, policemen and interpreter followed us in a lorry.

Arriving back in Bo after over a fortnight in the bush was like being taken to London from the heart of the countryside. Cars and lorries, busy streets, big buildings and signs of thriving commerce gave it the air of a big city by comparison with the small villages that were the only human settlements we had seen in the course of our trek. It was a joy to return to the modest comforts my house in the government reservation afforded.

I could not have wished for a better introduction to trekking than this fortnight had given me.

Walking is no longer such a regular way of visiting chiefdoms, now that so many are accessible by road. Even so, it will be many years before the necessity for walking disappears. A chiefdom headquarters may be served by road, but administrative officers often have occasion to visit other parts of the chiefdom, particularly for the purpose of adjudicating on major boundary disputes between chiefdoms.

Walking gives one a greater feeling of intimacy with the country than any form of mechanized travel. There is a pleasure to be had in exchanging greetings with passers-by on bush paths or with people working on their farms. On this trek we had often stopped in villages for a rest and immediately became the objects of curiosity on the part of the locals, who gathered round to look at us while we sucked oranges on the village headman's veranda. People in such remote areas rarely saw any government official and were always unaffectedly pleased to see anyone as important as the DC. It gave them the satisfaction of knowing that they were not forgotten and the excitement of vicarious contact with big towns and motor roads.

On this and later treks I often passed through villages where no white man had been seen for many years and even through some where a white man had never been seen at all before. The passage of the DC caused a flattering stir among the population, which turned out *en masse* to look at this rare creature. Such moments made the sweat and the blisters worthwhile. I enjoyed this trek partly because it was my first one, but also because it was a companionable one. The company of another European on trek was something a bachelor could not normally expect, and lively or intelligent conversation was a pleasure one had to learn to live without for long periods. I became accustomed to having no other company in the evenings, after the day's work was finished, than a book and a bottle of beer or glass of whisky.

The only justification for the two of us going together on this occasion was that it was a necessary part of my training. Jack Wann and I spent the long evenings talking of Africa and of Europe. He loved winter sports and always took a winter leave so that he could ski in Switzerland, Norway or Austria. I talked of Cambridge and of the Devonshire Course, my most recent experiences before I had come to Sierra Leone. Such conversations seemed absurdly and nostalgically unreal as we sat on the veranda of a mud and wattle house in the bush by the light of a hissing pressure lamp. I felt a sense of coming back to earth when the talk turned, as inevitably it must, to Africa and our immediate surroundings.

6

More of Bo

As the months passed I began to feel at home and to tackle work with increased confidence. Gradually I took on more responsibility. Rice distribution was a continuing headache, for supplies from Freetown were never enough to cope with the insatiable demands of Bo and neighbouring districts. I also took charge of the station upkeep gang. These were the labourers who kept the government reservation trimmed or 'brushed' and who supplied wood and water to the houses. On most stations this gang would consist of no more than a dozen men and the responsibility was a nominal one. Bo, however, with a large reservation, over 40 senior quarters plus many more for junior staff and numerous office buildings, needed more than 100 men working over a large area in small gangs. I ought to have inspected them every day, but with so many other duties this was impossible. A full tour of inspection meant a morning's work and much walking, even if I was able to borrow the provincial commissioner's lorry to help me on my way. It was, however, an excuse to leave the office and I availed myself of it whenever I felt energetic and tired of files.

I learned by hard experience in the course of doing this part of my job that it was unwise to put too much trust in subordinates. I had an African timekeeper in overall charge of the gangs and felt myself able to leave him to run things on his own for some time. At the end of each month the timesheets were presented to me to sign before the wages were paid. The total wage bill was usually about £700 and one month I found to my horror that this figure shot up to £1100. I checked the timesheets in detail and found there many names of men whose engagements I had not authorized. I called in the timekeeper and questioned him about the names. Cringing in a most abject manner and almost in tears he confessed that he had taken on the men on his own authority. Although he did not admit this, he had of course demanded a substantial dash of two or three pounds from each of them and was probably levying a contribution from them each month. He begged to be forgiven and promised to reform his ways, but there could be no second chance for a man capable of such turpitude and I dismissed him immediately. I also had to dismiss the surplus labourers and cut down the regular gangs so as to avoid overspending the allocation of money for station upkeep.

Peculation by dishonest clerks and other junior employees was a constant source of worry to most people in managerial positions in West Africa and to prevent or discourage it entailed a lot of detailed supervision of their work, which distracted one from more important tasks. My own inexperience and gullibility were mainly to blame for this unfortunate incident, but I have to say in self-exculpation that in common with most other expatriates, administrative officers in particular, I was carrying far more responsibility than I could hope to cope with satisfactorily and it was not surprising if things went awry from time to time.

The district prison was also in my care. This consisted of a long block of cells with a thatched roof and small office for the prison keeper. It was too small for the steadily increasing prison population of Bo. While I was in the district the thatch was replaced by corrugated iron and an extra block of cells was built. Each morning the keeper brought me his 'daily state' register showing how many prisoners of various categories he had in his charge and how many admissions and discharges there had been the previous day. Sometimes I would check this to make sure that there had not been any premature releases. I also had to inspect the prison cells and compound regularly, see that they were being kept clean and ensure that proper diet was being supplied to the prisoners. Occasionally I made a surprise visit at night to see that all the prisoners were locked in and that the warder on duty was awake.

Convicted prisoners were employed on woodcutting and other menial tasks, forming a useful supplement to the station upkeep gang. It would have been easy for any of them to escape if they wished, as one warder had to look after a working party of seven or eight, none of whom were under any form of physical restraint. Some occasionally did, but most had no incentive, as prison life gave them a roof over their heads, regular meals and a degree of security they had never known before. I would not wish to appear to say that the prisoners were ideally happy, as they all had to endure restrictions on freedom, separation from family and denial of access to women, the common lot of prisoners anywhere. On the other hand a prison sentence did not carry the same social stigma in Sierra Leone as it might in the United Kingdom, nor did the wearing of prison uniform suggest any degradation. Prisoners bore their lot with the good humour and cheerful acceptance that characterize the African attitude to any situation short of catastrophe.

I was now considered sufficiently experienced to be sent on trek alone. Before Christmas 1954 I visited two chiefdoms to prepare estimates and deal with general complaints. I felt apprehensive at hearing court appeals as my knowledge of native customary law was so far scanty and the finer points of cases relating to woman damage or dowry were not yet fully intelligible to me. I expressed these doubts to Jack Wann before starting off, but he assured me that there was no cause to worry. 'For the most part, appeals from native courts are a matter of common sense. Do your best and don't worry about any mistakes you may have made; the Africans will forgive you these, you are a white man and do not understand their customs'. This was valuable advice that reflected one important truth; ordinary Africans realized that Europeans were as fallible as any other race, but considered that their impartiality and incorruptibility outweighed any disadvantages resulting from their lack of deep understanding of African ways and customs. While they might have great admiration for the technical prowess and ability of Europeans generally, this did not prevent them from being shrewd and discerning in their assessments of individuals. They were quick to sense if anyone did not like them and were understandably hesitant about accepting guidance from administrative officers in their early twenties; their custom taught them to respect the wisdom of age.

I realized early on that the important thing was to give at least the impression of self-assurance, no matter how much in doubt I might be about the correctness of my decisions. I am sure that I must have made some mistakes in the course of dealing with the appeals that came before me in the course of my first trek, but I managed to maintain the appearance of confidence and all went well. Perhaps the members of the tribal authorities whom I met in their *barri*s might have had misgivings about my ability and have questioned the wisdom of government in sending me alone to deal with their affairs, but they were too polite to allow any such misgivings to show, and I was always accorded the same respect a more experienced officer could expect on a tour of his district.

On the last night of this trek there occurred an incident that well illustrates the type of domestic hazard we had to accept as normal. At about 9.00 p.m. I was sitting on the veranda of the rest house, the usual mud and wattle building with a thatched roof. I was alternately reading and pausing to listen to the ceaseless chorus of chirping cicadas, which at night in the bush is equivalent to silence. I happened to look round and suddenly realized that all was not well. Driver ants had invaded the rest house. On its whitewashed walls there was a pullulating pattern of thick black lines, converging and diverging to form a complex pattern of streams and tributaries, spreading in sinuous lines across the uneven surface of the walls like fungus across a cheese.

To see a drive of these ants can be a terrifying experience, a vision of a totalitarian world in miniature. They live in enormous mounds built of earth, honeycombed with an elaborate network of tunnels. From time to time they venture out in search of food, blindly following their leaders and devouring anything edible that comes in their way. A big drive may be miles in length and take days to pass any given spot on its route. Anyone who happens to stand near them will find himself attacked by the stragglers who become separated from the main stream. It is possible to be covered by them in no time at all and to be painfully bitten many times before one gets rid of them. Any food in the house has to be protected from their depredations by such measures as putting the legs of food cupboards into empty tins filled with water. I have even known them penetrate the supposedly airtight insulation of a refrigerator door and eat the food inside. A house with walls of mud and wattle or mud block had the disadvantage that the ants could easily bore their way through.

This was a double rest house with a set of rooms on each side of the veranda. A quick inspection by torchlight showed that the ants had taken possession of the veranda and of the side of the rest house I was occupying. I had two of the chief's messengers as night watchmen and called them in to help me move all my belongings to the other side, which had not so far been invaded. Once this was done the messengers collected handfuls of dry grass, twigs and anything else inflammable, set fire to them and with them attacked the marching columns. Fire is an effective weapon against ants, possibly the only one, and the messengers succeeded in killing large numbers of them and driving the rest away. I was afraid that in their enthusiasm they might set fire to the rest house, which with its thatched roof would have been gutted very quickly, but all that happened was that the building became filled with acrid smoke, causing my eyes to smart. I felt that the zeal of the messengers deserved some reward and gave them two shillings each. Afterwards I felt thankful at being able to sleep in my camp bed unmolested by these pillaging insects.

Insects are the most obnoxious form of animal life in Africa. Snakes, leopards, alligators and other large animals that are a menace to human beings are sometimes encountered, but insects are the most ubiquitous and irritating in every way. Termites destroy the wooden beams, door and window frames of houses, ants eat the sugar, flies of all varieties are drawn by the light of a pressure lamp in the bush at night, making it impossible to sit as near to it as is necessary to be able to read without straining one's eyes; flying beetles with coverings like armour plating collide with the wall and drop unconscious into one's evening tot of whisky; flying ants come in swarms at the beginning and end of the rains as soon as darkness falls, shed their wings and crawl in hundreds over the snooker table, making further play impossible; eggs of tumbu flies are laid in clothes and will cause a painful swelling under the skin when the clothes are next worn, unless the clothes have been carefully ironed after washing to destroy the eggs.

Most deadly by far is the anopheles mosquito, carrier of malarial parasites, whose breeding ground is the swamp or any pool of stagnant water. Shortly before Christmas I had my first attack of malaria. I had taken the prescribed prophylactic pills regularly but even so fell victim to this scourge of life in the tropics. Malaria is comparable in its effects to a severe dose of influenza. I was in the grip of a high fever on two separate days, with an interval of three days in between. On the first of these days I was hot and sweated, while on the second I shivered with cold and had to have blankets piled on me. I was admitted to a private ward in Bo Government Hospital and stayed there for just over a week. In between the bouts of fever I enjoyed my stay. There was nothing for me to do except relax on the veranda, sleep, read and chat with the young and friendly African nurses. The hospital was able to provide me with the kind of food to which I was accustomed, even though a lady in the next ward and I were the only European in-patients. Friends, colleagues and my servants came every day; this was fortunate as there appeared to be no arrangement for laundering patients' clothes and I was able to hand over my dirty clothes to Solomon.

Treatment consisted mainly of giving me an initial injection, followed by daily doses of quinine, the bitter tasting drug that used to be the regular prophylactic for malaria, but, as I wrote at the time, 'is now used only by those who are actually suffering from the disease'. Had I been married I could have been treated at home, but the medical officer felt that servants could not be expected to look after a sick man with the same loving care as a wife, hence his insistence on keeping me in hospital until the fever had worked itself out. I confess that when I was discharged I left the hospital with some regret at changing the friendly bustle of the ward for a lonely bungalow.

For Christmas 1954 one of my contemporaries, Donald Mackay, invited me to Makeni, headquarters of Northern Province, where he was stationed. I made arrangements to travel on a lorry on 24 December and was collected from the bungalow in the early morning. Being a European and a government officer I was given the privilege of travelling in the passenger seat in the driver's cab. Makeni was only 80 miles away but three ferries interrupted the road. At the first one, Mongheri, there were already more than 12 lorries in front of us, and we had a long and tedious wait of over two hours before we were able to cross. There was the same hold-up at Matotaka ferry, where the driver arranged for me to transfer to a lorry at the front of the queue. I reached Makeni at about 3.00 p.m.

'Mammie lorries' were the lifeblood of protectorate trade and intercourse. I have written elsewhere of the inadequacies of the railway, which in any event served only a limited number of towns. Lorries carried a considerable volume of freight and also provided the only form of public transport in the protectorate apart from the railway. Goods and passengers were loaded indiscriminately into the back and it was a very rough form of travel. There were seldom any seats for the passengers, who at ferries got out and shook off the clouds of dust from the road, which had settled on them. Cabs and chassis were imported and wooden bodies were built locally. As a result they were lethal vehicles for the passengers in serious accidents. The passengers simply sat on the floor or on top of sacks of whatever the cargo was and had nothing onto which they could hang if they were thrown around in a collision. If the vehicle turned over on its side the wooden body would be smashed to pieces by the impact and passengers were seriously injured or killed.

The lorries usually belonged to Syrian or African traders and every morning one could see them in the main streets of Bo and other major towns, outside their owners' stores waiting for passengers before starting their journeys. Every driver had at least one 'apprentice' or 'lorry boy' who would stand beside the vehicle crying 'Freetown, Freetown' or

'Kenema, Kenema' according to where it was going. The other duties of these apprentices included cranking the engine when the battery was flat, filling the petrol tank from the spare drum that most lorries carried, signalling the driver to stop and go by whistle, loading and unloading, and sweeping out the lorry. The ambition of every 'lorry boy' was to become a driver himself, a lordly aristocrat who drove and collected fares, not deigning to stoop to more menial tasks apart from undertaking running repairs, which sometimes became necessary on a journey. The most common of these was clearing petrol blockages, an endemic complaint. The first step was to clean out the quantities of dust that had accumulated inside the carburettor. If the blockage were still not cleared, the lorry boy would take the cap off the petrol tank and blow vigorously into it while the driver primed the petrol pump by hand. These rough-and-ready methods worked wonders and it was always a heartening relief after an anxious quarter of an hour of waiting on the roadside to hear the engine burst into life again with a throaty roar.

Around Makeni were much open grassland and tall hills and less of the luxuriant vegetation that abounded in Bo District. The government reservation was on a steep hill on the edge of the town, from which in the rainy season there was a panoramic view of distant ranges of hills. Unfortunately, there was no such view in December, this being the dry season and the time of the harmattan, a dry wind blowing in from the Sahara, bringing with it clouds of dust which reduced visibility. We could, however, see the valley below us and nearer hills on the opposite side of the town.

A third member of the band of cadets of our year, Eric Fisher, came to join us from Port Loko, a district headquarters 60 miles to the west, and we spent a quiet Christmas together. The provincial commissioner, Northern Province and local DC were both away and the only other people in residence on the station were the German medical officer and his wife. None of the three of us had a car, so we were unable to see anything of the district. We played tennis, ate our Christmas dinner and took long walks. On one of these we went into the town and called on Monsignor Azzolini, Bishop of the Northern Province see of the Roman Catholic Church of Sierra Leone, which was run by Italian priests. He was a polite, friendly and saintly man, clearly dedicated to his life in the church. He opened a bottle of chianti for us and talked of the work of his church, of the schools they were building in different parts of the province and of the new pro-cathedral some of the lay brethren of his order had just finished building at Makeni. I know little of architecture and ask to be forgiven for omitting to provide a detailed description of this building. I can say only that it was spacious and airy with a high vaulted roof, neo-Gothic windows, a tiled floor and a most ornate altar. What made it memorable was that it had any architectural pretensions at all in a country where the design of buildings was almost wholly utilitarian.

At New Year I was back in Bo for an annual social event of some importance. This was a cricket match between Northern Province and the two other provinces and was held on the sports field of the government secondary school. Both teams were made up of senior government officers and the cricket was not regarded as of any great significance, though for form's sake the match was played to its finish. The main justification for the event was that it was an opportunity for a reunion of people who had known each other for years but who, being scattered around the various government stations in the protectorate, rarely saw each other.

On New Year's Eve there was a party in Bo Club. It was little different from the routine monthly club supper, but there were many more people there than usual and dress was formal. We danced on a rough concrete floor to a haphazard collection of gramophone records and at midnight went onto the tennis court, formed a circle and sang *Auld Lang Syne*. Social occasions such as this were a gallant attempt to infuse some gaiety and warmth into otherwise unexciting leisure hours, but they always suffered from one sad and irremediable defect — the men far outnumbered the women. European communities in West Africa invariably had a depressingly high proportion of bachelors and grass widowers among them. Children had to be sent home for their education at an early age and wives often had to go with them; in some cases men had to spend a whole tour of 18 months without seeing their families. For bachelors there were no single women and they perforce had to find solace in each other's company and in secret envy of the presumed marital bliss of other men who had their wives with them.

By New Year's Eve 1954 my DC Jack Wann had moved on elsewhere and his successor Dickie Blake held a party for 25 guests, of which I was one. Before lunch Dickie called me aside and told me that I was to go on trek the following morning. The police were carrying out an operation to drive out illicit diamond miners from the upper reaches of the Sewa River. It was to take the form of a pincer movement, the police from South-Western Province pushing the miners eastward towards the river and those from South-Eastern Province waiting on the opposite bank to arrest anyone who tried to escape in that direction. The centre of operations on our side was to be Ngelehun–Baja, which I had visited on the estimates trek three months before. It was in the middle of the area, near the river, and miners were known to be active in that and neighbouring chiefdoms. The chief police officer (CPO) of the province was taking charge and I was to accompany him to guide him and explain the purpose of the mission to the paramount chief.

The following morning we left Bo by railcar at 4.00 a.m. while it was still dark. The railcar was a small, four-wheeled vehicle, able to seat half a dozen passengers, and was normally used by railway engineers and others whose duties required them to travel frequently up and down the line. It was powered by a petrol engine and capable of much greater speeds than any train. The CPO and myself and two escort policemen travelled in it with our personal loads, while the main body of police followed in a special coach attached to the early morning train. At Baoma we got down and our escort soon rounded up carriers to take our loads to Ngelehun. We had expected difficulty in getting carriers without coercion, as the young men in these parts had much easier ways of making money by illegally digging for diamonds, and we were surprised at how easy it was. The routine of warning the chief to have carriers ready for us had not been followed, as this was to be a surprise operation.

A friendly European missionary who lived near the station at Baoma gave us breakfast before we started on our 12-mile walk. We covered the distance in a little over three hours and descended on an astonished paramount chief, who had not had any warning of our coming and whom we met entertaining his cronies on the veranda of his house. I explained the purpose of our visit and the chief, in the best traditions of African hospitality, went to great trouble to make us comfortable. The rest house was cleaned out, a table and some chairs were sent there and one very good house in the town was made available to the police as temporary police station and barracks.

Notwithstanding the elaborate cloak and dagger preparations, the operation was an uneventful one. Plain clothes police were sent out to gather news, but it seemed that the miners had had some warning of our coming, as they had disappeared or gone into hiding, leaving only their pits as evidence of their activities. The paramount chief, as we had expected, expressed complete ignorance of any such lawlessness in his chiefdom and assured us of his readiness to cooperate with government in ensuring that law and order were maintained. The main value of the operation for the police, and for the CPO in particular, was to give them some idea of the difficulties with which they would have to contend in policing those parts of the protectorate that were remote from roads and the railway. One problem that came to light was that of feeding the constables. Each received a small allowance for every day he spent away from his regular station, and in theory this should have been spent on paying for his food and meeting other living expenses. What actually happened, however, was that the police were fed free of charge and the cost was borne by the African administration. All government officials and their camp followers were entertained in this way and the cost of feeding large numbers could be burdensome to a small chiefdom such as Baja. The police preferred for obvious reasons not to be unduly dependent on local generosity and later developed their own arrangements for supplying units engaged on operations of this kind.

My disappointment at the lack of excitement on this trek was compensated for by the events of the following month. Negotiations had been taking place in Freetown between representatives of employers and trade unions regarding increases in wages for labour. These broke down and the unions called a general strike. For the next few days Freetown was in turmoil. Public buildings and stores were attacked, some set on fire, streets were torn up and barricaded and government services and commerce were brought to a standstill. The army had to be called in to help the police in coping with the disorders. There was much shooting and several people were killed, including a European police officer who was brutally kicked to death by a gang, which attacked him when he was trying to quell a disturbance. One police station was attacked and surrounded by a mob that tried to take it by storm. The superintendent in charge of the station was forced to fire point blank with his revolver at the frenzied Africans rushing in through the main entrance.

It was clear from the start that the disorders did not spring from any serious unrest. It was unrealistic to talk of industrial unrest in a country that had no manufacturing industry and very little in the way of service industry, where the majority of labourers were employed by government departments and employed labourers formed a small minority of the community. Furthermore, most of the rioters were not working men at all, but belonged to the unemployed riff-raff that formed the Freetown underworld. The true causes of the riots never became known, but it was widely believed that they were intended as an attempt to discredit and oust the African ministers who had first assumed their portfolios in 1953, organized by opposition parties.

The strike spread to Bo and to one or two other major centres of population in the protectorate. My station upkeep gang, Public Works Department labourers, people who worked on the railway and many other privately and publicly employed labourers joined the strike. Domestic servants also joined their numbers, having been threatened with beatings if they failed to do so. Emergency measures had to be taken immediately to see that the power station, hospital and other essential services continued to function.

A force of special constables, comprising all male Europeans and many middle-class Africans was hurriedly sworn in and assigned to routine security duties such as guarding government buildings and patrolling the government reservation, relieving regular police to look after security in the town and answer calls from trouble spots. A large pool of government and private vehicles was assembled at the police station and arrangements were made with one of the trading companies to keep a stock of petrol there and issue it as necessary. The provincial commissioner's office was like a command headquarters, with the DC, chief police officer, divisional engineer, medical officer and others rushing in and out, making their reports and receiving instructions. It was a period of tension, but I cannot deny that I found it exhilarating, a break from the peaceful routine of district administration, and I think many others would have agreed after it was over.

I was given the task of patrolling the reservation, where 40 or more African and European families lived, to see that servants were not molested or threatened by strikers. My own servants were afraid to come to work, as were those of other bachelors, but those of married men felt able to carry on so long as the wives were around the house. John Malcolm, the provincial commissioner, considered that confidence would be boosted and there would be less likelihood of the servants running away if someone patrolled continuously from house to house, ensuring that there was no attempt at interference. Accordingly, another European and I, in a PWD car, started patrolling and calling at houses scattered around the sprawling reservation. We felt that without being accused of dereliction of duty we could stop from time to time when invited in for a cup of tea or bottle of beer, and we found our allotted duty congenial.

It was a point of honour among the Europeans that life should go on as normal in spite of difficulties, and one result of this was that the club, which on midweek nights would usually be thinly patronized, had a big boost in its custom. The staff had disappeared, so the members had to run it themselves. The general commotion and tension imparted an unwonted liveliness to conversation, with the result that the drink flowed freely and made the gatherings still more exuberant. In the course of the evening, groups of special constables, complete with red armbands and truncheons, would call for refreshments in the middle of their patrols and add to the general hubbub with their reports of the latest alarms. The atmosphere was that of a beleaguered garrison in the early stages of a siege, before the beer has run out and while there are strong hopes that the relief column will arrive in a few days.

I was without servants and arranged with married friends to have them provide my meals. I bathed irregularly and my house was neither swept nor dusted for several days, but to the amazement of Musa and Solomon, who considered themselves indispensable, I survived and was cheerful. They both made a token appearance each morning but would not stay to work.

Partly because none of the strikers really knew why they were striking and partly because of the energetic steps taken to forestall disorder, there were no serious or violent incidents in Bo. There were some noisy demonstrations, a few stones were thrown and a few stalls overturned in the market, but there were no clashes and the police never needed to use either batons or firearms. Ted Eates, the CPO, felt the need to strengthen his forces at a more senior level and called in an additional assistant superintendent, Dale Smith, from Moyamba, the neighbouring district to the west of Bo. Dale soon arrived prominently sporting a revolver on his belt and was amazed to find how quiet everything seemed to be. I came to know him later in Kambia and always found him entertaining, with a sense of the dramatic and amusing. He had obviously been given the impression that the situation in Bo was very serious and, as he later put it in melodramatic fashion, 'I was prepared to abandon my car outside Bo and fight my way in inch by inch.' I have no doubt that he did a useful job but he must have been very disappointed at the absence of major troubles. News eventually came that the strike had been called off in Freetown and the union representatives in Bo gave instructions for everyone to go back to work. As soon as all was peaceful again the special constabulary was disbanded and the members returned to their normal work.

No doubt many of them treasured wistful memories of those few days during which they enjoyed the satisfaction of performing an important public service, the comradeship of a semi-disciplined force and the excitement of an emergency without having to face any real danger. To the African junior clerks especially it must have been a stimulating experience of a kind they could never expect to find in their regular humdrum tasks.

7

Trouble in the North

No colonial work of fiction or autobiography would be complete without its riots, but it must be appreciated that riots are not an everyday occurrence and most administrative officers were never called upon to quell one in the whole of their careers. During my first few months in Sierra Leone, my provincial commissioner John Malcolm told me that it was a very peaceful country and that serious disturbances were unknown. I had this conversation because one of my regular chores was to type the monthly intelligence report for Bo District. This was classified as secret and was not left to junior clerks to type, so the job had to be done by someone of senior rank. Each month the comment appeared, 'the general situation is quiet,' so I asked what sort of event would result in a different statement being made and this was his reply.

Internal troubles resulting from dynastic disputes in individual chiefdoms were common, but chiefdoms were small and feuds between rival families had no external repercussions. There had not been a rebellion against the government since the late 1890s, when protests against the imposition of a house tax had led to a major rising by the tribes of the protectorate against the British. In the long run one can govern a country only by consent, and Sierra Leone had been governed by a mixture of consent and bluff for almost 60 years. The country had in that time a remarkably trouble-free history and to all appearances justified the commissioner's statement.

However, his statement was made before the 'industrial' problems described in the previous chapter, which had led to serious violence in Freetown and the threat of violence in Bo and elsewhere. It was something of an irony that John Malcolm, having delivered this rather complacent assessment of the general security situation, some months later found himself in the thick of serious disturbances in Bo. His statement also ignored the serious possibility of lawlessness on a large scale, which was posed by illicit diamond mining, a threat to security that the government had so far failed to tackle in earnest. The events of late 1955 and early 1956, however, brought this supposedly halcyon period to an end.

In October 1955 I was sent to Dambara, the capital of Selenga chiefdom, 12 miles from Bo, to prepare estimates for the following year. By now I had been on many treks on my own and felt capable of dealing with any problem that might arise. I had also learned the art of trekking in comfort and had provided myself with lamps, a tin bath and a locally made deckchair in which to relax in the rest house.

The paramount chief of Selenga, Moriba Kargobai, was one of the oldest and most respected chiefs in the protectorate. He was illiterate and had been in office for over 30 years. He was an assessor chief who had helped officers of the administration when they were conducting elections for the post of paramount chief in other chiefdoms and who had regularly attended sessions of the Supreme Court held in Bo to assist the judge in trying Africans for criminal offences. His wisdom and knowledge of customary law were widely respected among the Mende. He was the first president of Bo District Council and held that office until changes in the law made it mandatory for the council to appoint an educated person to that office. His chiefdom was a small one of not more than 1000 taxpayers and was regarded as a model of good government and orderliness. No officer visiting it had ever had any major complaints made to him before my arrival there. I had already had news before leaving Bo that the young men of the chiefdom were up in arms and I found a big crowd waiting for me at Dambara. Clearly they had something pressing on their minds and I decided that the estimates would have to wait.

Their complaints were directed against the chiefdom clerk, who was an African of the chiefdom and related to the chief. He was alleged to be responsible for extorting money and for unlawful levies of all kinds. Changes that came into effect at the beginning of 1955 had been made in the tax laws applicable to the protectorate. Among other things, the new ordinance required that the tribal authority of a chiefdom should each year appoint a tax assessment committee, consisting of the clerk and two members of the TA whose task it was to tour the whole chiefdom and make lists in all the villages of adult males who were liable to pay tax.

One complaint made to me was that the assessment committee of Selenga levied taxes of their own in kind in the course of their tour by calling on the headman of each village to feed them at his own expense and to provide presents of chickens, eggs and rice for them to carry on their way. The headman in his turn collected the required tribute from his villagers and probably managed to keep part of it for himself. The clerk was also said to have refused to omit from the tax lists the names of young men who had left the chiefdom unless a fine in cash was paid to him personally. At the end of the tour the assessment committee returned to Dambara with the spoils, which they divided among themselves. There was a large volume of such complaints and I soon had overwhelming evidence to establish that malpractices of this kind had continued for many years. The plea of long usage was the only substantial one the clerk raised when he came to speak for himself, which he did most eloquently. I had to admire his courage in doing so in public before an angry crowd, from whom he had been forced to hide in the bush for a day or two before I arrived.

It was apparent that the complaints were really directed against the paramount chief, who if he had not profited from these misdeeds, had at least knowingly condoned them. He was, however, a powerful man, known to command the respect of government, and it would have taken a fearless opponent to raise any serious opposition to him. The clerk was a close relative and his right-hand man, but held no traditional office in the chiefdom and hence made an easy scapegoat. He was clearly *persona non grata* with the young men and I made the only order that was practical, namely that he should be transferred to another chiefdom at the end of the month and be replaced by someone else. This satisfied the young men, who went off to their villages elated at having won a victory.

In the course of my visit I had two long discussions with Moriba Kargobai on his own, my interpreter being the only other person present. He was a fair-minded man, ready to admit the error of his ways, or at least of the ways of some of his subchiefs. He had known about the collections of tribute from the villages, but I had no reason to doubt him when he told me that he took no share in the spoils himself, leaving them to be divided among the members of the assessment committee. He told me that for several years now he had not toured the chiefdom, for he knew what a burden such tours were on the ordinary people who had to provide hospitality and suitable presents for the chief and his entourage. He had been incensed by the gathering of young men before my visit to complain about the clerk and had purported to impose a collective fine of £50 on them for conspiracy. He was not happy when I told him that he did not have the power on his own to impose such a fine without bringing any case before the native court and that he would have to forget about the fine, but he accepted this from me with a good grace.

I felt chastened and conscious of the heavy responsibility that lay on me, a 24-year-old cadet, who found himself having to reprimand, however mildly, such a wise and experienced old man who had been governing this chiefdom several years before I was born. He had a great respect for the fairness and impartiality of officers of the provincial administration and did not object to my removing his clerk in the way a haughtier and more headstrong man might have done. When we were alone he talked to me at great length of the benefit British rule had brought to Sierra Leone, of the end that had been put to inter-chiefdom wars, of the roads, railways, hospitals and schools. He pleaded most vigorously that the British should never leave the country and abandon its people to African rulers, who would be too readily swayed by sectional and tribal interests and would be incapable of just administration.

I was often treated to harangues of this kind, especially from older chiefs who had grown up under British rule, and it was always difficult to know how much store one should set by them. In great measure they were intended as a polite form of flattery of the listener, but I am sure it would be wrong to treat them as wholly insincere. Many older people had serious apprehensions as to the serious deterioration in standards of government that might follow independence and, sadly as events in Sierra Leone in recent years have shown, there were good grounds for those apprehensions.

I felt much sympathy for chief Moriba Kargobai, whose power and prestige I had been obliged to trim in the interests of justice and security in the chiefdom. He was accustomed to traditional ways and bewildered by the rapid changes taking place around him. I became so emotionally involved in the 'palaver' that I felt incapable of sympathy for the young men who had engineered it and regretted a little that the chief's wish to fine them for conspiracy had to be thwarted. I realized objectively that there had been some oppression and that I must prescribe the fitting remedies, but I found myself imposing the solutions in a grudging manner as a result of seeing the damage done to the chief's dignity. I recorded all these sentiments in a long report, which so far as I recall never went outside the DC's office and for all I know — though I doubt it — may still lie in some archive of old files in Sierra Leone.

I would be flattering myself if I could say that this inquiry made me aware of strong undercurrents of discontent in the protectorate generally among young men who felt oppressed by their traditional chiefs, but I had no reason to attribute any wider significance to a palaver in a small chiefdom. I can fairly add that my DC at the time, an officer who had obviously had many more years' experience than I, did not see it as a major portent either. At the end of my inquiry, after the young men had returned to their villages and I was left with just the chief and the members of his tribal authority, I went on to discuss and prepare the chiefdom estimates. The local tax for 1955 had been 30 shillings per head, the highest ever figure, but in view of the many new demands on the tribal authority, including the payment of a heavy contribution to the revenue of Bo District Council, it was impossible to make the estimates balance without raising the tax. We agreed that this should be set for the coming year at 42 shillings. No one realized the implications of this decision at the time. Events in the Northern Province showed in dramatic fashion that increased taxes along with an oppressive and illegal regime of extortion by the chiefs could lead to major riots.

This was October 1955. The next month saw the outbreak of a series of disturbances in the Northern Province, the most serious since the hut tax riots of 60 years earlier and a turning point in the history of the protectorate.

The starting point was a proposal to raise the tax the tribal authority of Maforki chiefdom in Port Loko District imposed. The tax had already been set at 32 shillings and 6 pence per head and the DC was asked to get government approval for an increase of a further five shillings, to be used specifically to construct a house for the paramount chief. The provincial commissioner approved the extra levy on condition it was made once only and that it should be earmarked for this particular purpose. There was a stormy reaction in the chiefdom and some of the young men held protest meetings called by one Peter Kamara. I should explain that in the context of chiefdom politics the expression 'young man' bore no reference to age but simply meant a commoner as opposed to a chief or member of the tribal authority. A large crowd headed by Peter Kamara put its complaint to the DC and later to the provincial commissioner. The proposed extra levy was wisely withdrawn — this being the only sensible course of action — but the meetings served as a spark to touch off a conflagration.

During the next three months there were protests throughout the Northern Province against high taxation and oppression of the people, which took many forms. There were clashes with the police in which people were killed and injured; houses and other property belonging to members of tribal authorities were destroyed. In Kambia District in particular, where oppression had been worse than anywhere else, there was an immediate outbreak of violence, not preceded by the putting of complaints to the DC.

The proposals for steep increases in lawfully imposed taxes were a relatively minor complaint and it was almost accidental that these should have been the starting point of the disturbances. The main cause of grievance was the vast and ever increasing number of illegal fines and levies in many forms, which were not paid into the African administration but were used for the private benefit of the chiefs who

111

collected them. Many complaints were made against assessment committees, similar to those that had been made to me
in Selenga chiefdom. Many paramount chiefs had grossly
abused their residual right to forced labour on the building
of their houses and some had gone so far as to revive the
practice of compelling the young men to work on their
farms, a right that had been abolished many years before.
All kinds of illegal fines and fees were collected in the course
of dealing with cases brought before the native courts and
the figures of court revenue that appeared in native administration accounts represented only a fraction of the actual
costs litigants had to meet.

Many misdeeds that now came to light had been regularly
perpetrated for years, but so long as the provincial administration had the Court Messenger Force to keep a knowing
and watchful eye on what went on in the chiefdoms, the
worst abuses were kept in check. With the abolition of this
force it was assumed that the district commissioner lost his
power over chiefs, an impression some of the chiefs sought
to reinforce by their own pronouncements and autocratic
behaviour. Oppression and extortion reached levels never
before known. The attempt by government to hand over to
the district councils many functions connected with the
development of the districts further strengthened the feeling
that the chiefs were no longer subject to any form of
restraint. The councils were at this time made up entirely of
the paramount chiefs of each district, plus certain nominated
members, with the DC as president. With ministerial encour-
agement, several councils during 1955 elected educated men
from among their own members to replace DCs as presi-
dents. These were usually educated paramount chiefs and it
was widely held that they were 'black DCs'.

The ordinary peasants and fishermen of the protectorate
were bewildered and frightened at so many rapid changes
working to their detriment and protested in the only way

they thought would be effective. They were told afterwards that they need not have used violence and destroyed property, that if they had put their complaints in a proper manner, government would have listened to them sympathetically and put matters right. It is my regretful conclusion, however, that the people of the protectorate had no choice but to fight to draw attention to their sufferings. It is unlikely that the Executive Council, where the majority of African ministers believed in the prerogatives of chiefs (one of them was a paramount chief himself) would have been amenable to any reforms that meant restricting those prerogatives.

Two features of these riots are worthy of special note. First, it was a rebellion against chiefs, mainly among the Timne, the largest single tribe in Northern Province, among whom the tradition of strong and respected paramount chiefs was firmly established. The temper of the rioters can be gauged from such incidents as the sacking of one chief's house in a Susu chiefdom in Kambia District. The frenzied mob destroyed everything but the walls and roof; the chief's refrigerator and radio set were thrown into a well and bundles of banknotes found in the house were burned. The people would not have anything to do with tainted property or money; they were in a mood of righteous anger and refused to sully their cause by looting.

Chiefdom palavers arising out of complaints and intrigues against the paramount chief had long been a common occurrence in the two southern provinces, particularly among the Mende, and over the years several paramount chiefs had been deposed following government inquiries into their misconduct. By comparison, among the Timne, Susu and other tribes of the Northern Province, the office of chief had always seemed unassailable and sacrosanct. The revulsion against the feudal customs of chieftaincy, whereby ordinary people were treated as little better than serfs, came late in the north and with devastating suddenness.

The second remarkable feature of the riots is that they constituted a reactionary revolution, if the oxymoron may be permitted. In other territories colonial riots often meant disorders in which Europeans were attacked and brutally murdered, government buildings were stoned and angry mobs expressed their animosity against the alien ruling power. These were different. The anger of the crowds of rioters was directed wholly against their own traditional rulers, whose greed and oppression had driven their subjects beyond endurance. At no time were European lives in any danger. Stones were sometimes thrown at police officers who were trying to quell the disturbances and one European officer was injured; this, however, was because the police were perceived as obstructing the people from taking their revenge on the chiefs and on those who were assumed to be taking sides with the chiefs. The idea that the police force had a duty to protect the lives and property of all citizens regardless of position or politics was not appreciated.

In the beginning, the leaders of the rioters were anxious to see that their just cause was not corrupted in any way and that innocent people did not suffer. In one town some of the more irresponsible 'strikers', as the rebels came to be known, levied contributions from all the traders. When their leaders came to know of this, they insisted the money be paid back and made sure that their order was promptly obeyed. In another town the strikers entered a store a Syrian was renting from the paramount chief and they told him that he would have to leave because they wished to destroy the building. He was given a few hours in which to pack and, before setting fire to the store, the strikers helped him load his stock and personal belongings into a launch that took him to Freetown.

The cry of the people was not for self-government, ever at this time the main preoccupation of the Colonial Office and of local politicians, but for a return to the system of

1. ABOVE. The author standing outside his bungalow, number 9, on the Bo Government Reservation.

2. RIGHT. The author with friends in Kambia. Mike Sandercock standing, with his wife Helen and their two sons and Dennis Hedges.

3. ABOVE. A view of the district office (right) and district *barri* (left) in Kambia.

4. LEFT. The author's stepdaughter Kamini with a friend, in 1957.

5. ABOVE. The author and Dorothy Roberts, wife of Eric Roberts, research scientist at Rokupr, later Professor of Agriculture at Reading University. We were on a launch on the Great Scarcies River, April 1958.

6. RIGHT. Rokupr market, Megan inspecting fruit display.

7. ABOVE. River scene, Rokupr wharf.

8. BELOW. River scene at Rokupr, Kambia District, on the Great Scarcies.

9. ABOVE. Climbing a palm tree to collect the coconuts.

10. RIGHT. Interior of a small store.

11. ABOVE. Men playing *gbalangis,* an African version of the xylophone.

12. LEFT. African mother and child carried in a lappa in the traditional way.

13 and 14. ABOVE AND LEFT. African faces.

15. RIGHT.
Extraordinary
headgear.

16. LEFT. A young
Susu woman, Rokupr.

benevolent autocracy they had known not so long before, under which the chiefs were subject to a stricter surveillance than had been the case since the abolition of the Court Messenger Force and they were able to take their grievances to the DC knowing that these would be impartially investigated and justice would be done.

The Colonial Office appointed an independent commission of inquiry that came to Sierra Leone in April 1956 and submitted its report on the disturbances in July of the same year. This became known as the Cox Report after the name of the commission's chairman. It gives an account of the course of the riots, a comprehensive study of the developments leading to them and many recommendations for what changes in government policy were needed if the manifest ills that had come to light were to be remedied. I greatly treasure my own personal copy of this now rare publication, a masterly document, which future historians of Sierra Leone or of the British colonial empire will find invaluable.

The northern part of Bo District bordered on the Timne chiefdoms of the Northern Province and it was inevitable that the disorders there should spread some of their contagion into the adjoining Mende chiefdoms, where there were similar causes of discontent. The situation was tense for some time but there was no major outbreak of violence in any of our chiefdoms. This may have been partly because the Mende had long been in the habit of airing their grievances against their chiefs and had not been inhibited by the same awe and adulation of chieftaincy that had prevailed among their neighbours. Furthermore, illicit diamond mining brought prosperity to the Mende chiefdoms along the Sewa River and made their inhabitants both more ready to acquiesce in any unlawful levies imposed by their chiefs and better able to meet them.

Demonstrations did, however, take place, and in some of the more important towns there were gatherings of several thousand young men to protest against the iniquities of their rulers. In some instances this may have been little more than a desire to be in the fashion, but there was without doubt much discontent not far below the surface and some justification for it. Once the riots had started and some of the causes of them had become apparent, government gave instructions that district commissioners should investigate the working of the local taxation system in at least one of their respective district's chiefdoms.

I was sent to Bagbwe chiefdom for this purpose, for I had now made several visits there since my first trek over a year previously and was familiar with its personalities and problems. Ostensibly, this was a routine visit for the purpose of holding elections to vacancies in the tribal authority and dealing with court cases. My instructions were not to invite comment on the operation of the tax system, since such an investigation might in itself lead to trouble, but to read between the lines of any complaints that might be made to me and to pursue the inquiry by discreet means.

To hold these elections, it was necessary to visit all five of the section towns, in each of which the taxpayers were to gather and choose the new members of the tribal authority for their section. As soon as the first meeting started it was apparent that the order to exercise discretion was superfluous. Without any prompting the young men began to put forward general complaints about the malpractices of the tax assessment committee, the forced labour they were obliged to give the paramount chief, Madame Mabaja, on her farms and in building her house at Galu, and about other matters that were now the staple fare of visits by administrative officers to chiefdoms throughout the protectorate. One unusual complaint was about the Bundu Society, a women's society common among the Mende, whose officials were responsible for the circumcision by clitoridectomy of all young girls at an early age and who prescribed the rules to be observed in respect of pregnancy and childbirth. It was the practice of the society in Bagbwe to impose a fine on the family of any woman who died in labour, as this was regarded as an occurrence that must bring bad luck to the whole community. Madame Mabaja was genuinely shocked at this complaint, as all matters relating to the Bundu Society were secret and discussion of them in public by the men, particularly in the presence of a stranger, was taboo. The young men realized that they had overreached themselves and withdrew the complaint.

My task was to record all the complaints and do what I could to pacify the aggrieved taxpayers. They certainly had the impression that the local tax they paid, which this year had been 30 shillings, was all 'chopped' or consumed by the chief and her cronies. I explained that her salary and other administrative expenses had to be met from the tax, but that there were also some benefits for the general public good. I was able to instance the motor road, which was now open as far as Galu, as well as a school that was functioning in the chiefdom. Whether my emollient words made any impression is difficult to say. I advised the members of the tax assessment committee that in future they must not make any levies of food on their tours of the villages, but should just accept hospitality to the extent of cooked meals provided while they were there. I advised Madame Mabaja that she must cease demanding forced labour for working on her farms, though she was entitled to expect each section of the chiefdom to contribute some labour towards building her house. A temporary settlement was reached on these lines at a meeting attended by over 2000 people, at the end of which the young men appeared to be satisfied and went home.

This was the most tiring trek I ever undertook. On one day in particular I walked more than 20 miles, held three meetings in different section towns and sat up till almost midnight in the rest house writing a long report. At a time of stress every effort was needed from all officers to maintain a precarious peace. I was away from Bo, cut off from official sources of news for over a week, and was perturbed by rumours that reached me of disturbances in neighbouring chiefdoms. I was uncomfortably aware that riots and rumours of riots close by might easily spark off trouble in Bagbwe chiefdom. I had only two policemen with me and there was little chance of being able to get reinforcements if I needed them, as police strength in the protectorate was already stretched to the limit.

In the event there was no trouble and the young men dispersed, seemingly satisfied at having been able to give vent to their grievances. It is possible that my visit was timely in that it afforded the young men a safety valve at a time when there might otherwise have been an explosion. If this surmise is correct, then I can take some retrospective pride in having performed in the course of this trek one of the classic tasks of British colonial administrators in providing an opportunity for grievances against traditional rulers to be aired and rectified, and ensuring that good government and common sense prevailed.

At the end of my visit I decided to climb Mano-Pendorbu, a hill two miles from Galu of extraordinary appearance, set down like an outsize boulder in the middle of the surrounding plain, thinly covered with wiry savannah grasses, a local miniature version of Ayers Rock. It rose to a height of about 2000 feet above sea level and on two sides rose sheer from the plain. It had a commanding view of the northern part of Bo District and on a clear day the reflection of sunlight on corrugated-iron roofs in Bo, over 20 miles away, could be seen.

Bobo Samai, the paramount chief's son, accompanied me and, as there was no path up the hill, I also engaged a number of men to clear a way through the bush. The village headman of Mano-Pendorbu and some of his people met us.

I greeted him and told him that I wished to climb the hill that bore the name of his village. He did not object, but told me that spirits inhabited the hill and that if I propitiated them some sacrifice would have to be made — the locals were ever inventive in finding reasons for demanding money. I gave the headman five shillings, which would enable him to sacrifice a chicken if he were so minded, and began the climb.

To the local people it was incomprehensible that one should want to climb a hill simply to have a view or for no special reason other than for exercise. However, the ways of Europeans were often inscrutable. It was a hard climb, and for the first few hundred feet we toiled up an almost sheer tree-covered slope. The men went ahead of me clearing the undergrowth with their machetes, which made the going a little easier. When we emerged above the tree line we were on grassy slopes whose gradients became steadily easier until we finally reached the plateau on top. This was the dry season and the grass was tough, thick and wiry; as we walked we sank into it a little. I was a little afraid of snakes, which regularly hide in long grass, but we did not see any.

We went to the southern end of the plateau, from which we had an extensive view of the surrounding country. The plain immediately below us was mostly grassland, good for grazing, and we could see one cattle enclosure or *warri* near the village at the foot of the hill. Further afield, for a distance of several miles, we could see bumpy hills and valleys, covered with low bush and palm trees. Bo was pointed out to me, but I confess that I did not see anything recognizable. Seen thus, the green landscape and vegetation of West Africa look exciting, to the untrained eye a virgin land untouched by man. The practised observer notices the absence of high forest, which in a well-watered country of luxuriant growth indicates over-farming and erosion, and is able to pick out patches that have been cleared for farming during the current season.

But the grosser manifestations of man's presence, huge

cities, broad roads, electricity pylons and large industrial buildings were and no doubt still are missing from most of Africa, and it is their absence, the feeling that nature still has to be tamed here, that can evoke in the spirit of one born in a developed country something of the thrill that early explorers felt, their main reward for the sweat, disease and danger that were their travelling companions. The knowledge that very few white men had ever set eyes on most of the landscape, and those few belonging to the select band of administrators, no mere tourists or big game hunters, lent an additional cachet to the experience of trekking on foot. I am drawn to make comparisons with the jungles of the East, where the scenery may be more awe-inspiring but where one's exhilaration must be tempered by the perhaps unconscious realization that one is looking upon the homeland of ancient civilizations, whose history is well chronicled, whose fortresses and temples remain.

The African bush lacks a known temporal dimension. Its history is unwritten and can be presumed to comprise mainly small-scale primitive wars. One may sketch in this dimension according to one's imagination, or one may assume that since the history is unknown, as the interior of tropical Africa was itself unknown until the final quarter of the nineteenth century, then it can be deemed not to exist. This lack of any atmosphere of a known past and the absence of any surviving artefacts from earlier periods enable one to ignore the aspect of time and to perceive Africa as visibly new and raw.

I felt that the climb had been worth the effort and that it was a welcome and relaxing end to a visit that had had its harassing moments. That afternoon I returned to Bo to report on the results of my trek. I found, as I had expected, that the reports I had heard in Bagbwe had been exaggerated. There had been no violence anywhere in the district, though there had been several mass meetings at which either the DC or my fellow ADC had been present and had pursued a course of energetic conciliation similar to that which I had undertaken in Bagbwe. By February 1956 the riots had spent themselves in the Northern Province and government was left with the task of clearing up the mess and appointing a commission of inquiry to investigate these disastrous events.

8

First Home Leave

I arranged to go on leave in March 1956 after a tour of 19 months. I packed my personal belongings that were to be left behind and put them into a government store in Bo. Much as I had enjoyed my first tour, it was a relief to be taking leave, and on my last night in Bo I was in high spirits and treated some friends to a bottle of champagne at the club. The following morning I set off for Freetown in the provincial commissioner's lorry, that well-tried Bedford that had first met me at Bo station on arrival and had since carried me on countless journeys. We had travelled perhaps a third of the way when we had a breakdown, the inevitable petrol blockage. It seemed that even my departure on leave was to be in the best African tradition. The trouble seemed to be more serious than usual and the driver and his lorry boy were tinkering with the engine for a long time.

I was lounging in the shade by the roadside waiting for the repairs to be completed when a familiar vehicle came up behind us and stopped. It was my friend George Crichton, divisional forest officer from Bo, who was on trek. He was in no hurry to reach his stop for that night, so he brought out two camp chairs from his truck and we sat near the vehicles in these, sucking oranges and chatting. The roads in Sierra Leone carried few vehicles and travelling was often a most friendly affair; people travelling in opposite directions could stop their cars alongside each other and talk without any fear of holding up the traffic. Encounters such as these did much to brighten otherwise lonely and tedious journeys.

In Freetown I stayed again at the notorious transit camp for two days, which gave me time to collect my leave papers and sailing ticket, sign the visitors' book at Government House — a routine piece of colonial protocol — and make other necessary preparations for leaving. On the Saturday morning, 19 months after my first arrival in Freetown, I embarked on the *Apapa*, older sister ship of the *Aureol*, bound for Liverpool. Mr MacDonald, the retiring colonial secretary, was a fellow passenger. Most of the secretariat staff was on the quayside and the governor also came down to say goodbye. Three police buglers were on the quay and as the ship moved out into the river they sounded the 'Hausa Farewell', the bugle call of the West African Frontier Force, which was always played on such occasions.

The colony hills fell behind us as the ship gathered speed. Coupled with the pleasurable anticipation of leave was a sense of satisfaction at having concluded my first tour and being no longer a raw and inexperienced cadet. The exercise of responsibility had given me a degree of confidence I had never known before and I felt that I would be more than equal to whatever task my next tour of duty might have in store for me.

The chief steward in the dining room assigned me to a table with three officers from Gold Coast, the colony that became Ghana on independence in 1957. One was an education officer, one a superintendent of police and the third an auditor. With independence imminent they were planning their career moves and there was much talk among them of possible transfers to other territories, of the compensation they expected to receive for loss of career prospects and of the possibility of taking up employment in very different fields. Although independence for Sierra Leone was still a distant prospect I became uncomfortably aware of the shadow hanging over my own future, but at this stage was not very worried.

A biting March morning greeted us in Liverpool. The docks, landing stage and Liver Building and the gaunt cranes of the Birkenhead shipyards across the Mersey against a backcloth of grey sky in the early dawn made a cheerless setting for any wanderer's return. The ferryboats plying to and from the pier head, carrying the early commuters between Liverpool and Birkenhead gave us our first reminder of the workaday world we had all forsaken. Dockers in cloth caps and overcoats and countless officials of the shipping line, port authority, immigration, post office, British Council, RSPCA and other bodies took possession of the ship as soon as it was tied up. We were caught up in a bewildering, rushing world and the ship's officers and stewards who had ruled over our lives for nine leisurely days faded into insignificance. The ship itself, whose bulwarks had briefly marked the confines of the world for us all, was now diminished in stature, stripped of the aura of romance of the high seas, and had become a mere banausic appendage of the land.

We had our last breakfast on the ship and disembarked soon after 9.00 a.m. I took a taxi to Exchange station where a porter opened the door and took my luggage. I told him that I wanted to go to Blackburn and he took me along to the enquiry office and found out for me the time of the next train. The train was at the platform, but would not be leaving for half an hour. The porter told me that if I would care to get myself a cup of coffee in the refreshment room he would find me a seat on the train, put my luggage on board and look after it for me until I was ready. I have rarely experienced comparable politeness and attentiveness anywhere in the world on my travels. It was a wonderful reintroduction to England for a temporarily returned exile. I took pleasure in my cup of coffee and in reading that morning's *Manchester Guardian* — still its title at the time — which I bought from the bookstall. The *Guardian* was for long my favourite newspaper, though sadly not for many years now, and I regularly savoured its lively prose. My train was due to leave and I boarded it in a contented frame of mind having generously tipped my amiable porter.

Leave is an interlude to which every exile looks forward, the more so if he normally lives in countries where amenities are few. It is a chance to spend time with family and friends and to savour with intensified appreciation the material pleasures of civilization which people who live all their lives in developed countries take for granted. Travelling on good roads or in fast trains, going to cinemas, theatres and concerts, downing pints of bitter in a pub, all these everyday experiences had been denied to me for the past 19 months. I now had four months with nothing else to do except enjoy myself within the limits of my salary. I had ordered a car, a new Standard Vanguard, while I was still in Sierra Leone. This had meant taking a loan from government of over £700, not far off the equivalent of a year's salary for me at the time. I was, however, determined not to put up with another 18 months of the kind of inconvenience I had had to endure in Bo without a car.

I collected the car from the Standard factory in Coventry a few weeks after my arrival and drove it cautiously back to my home in Lancashire at a steady 30 miles an hour — in those days the manufacturers strongly recommended a running in period of some hundreds of miles at prescribed low maximum speeds. I was very proud of it and excited at being a car owner for the first time in my life. I loved the gleam of the polished paintwork and the smell of the new upholstery.

Already, although I had been away from the United Kingdom for a comparatively short time, I felt out of touch. Friends who had been my contemporaries at Cambridge were now established in professional or commercial careers and though still friendly now regarded me as a colonial curiosity. The personalities of television, which at this time was in its first phase of rapid development, were unknown to me and my ignorance was taken as a mark of eccentricity, almost as a social gaffe. At the house of some friends whom I was visiting there was talk about Sabrina, the lady who was making a fortune by exhibiting her remarkable body. My plaintive question, 'Who is Sabrina?' was greeted with a mixture of incredulity and amusement. Such charmingly naïve ignorance of the modern world evidently put me into the category of High Court judges who were supposed to ask witnesses questions such as 'Who are the Beatles?'

I felt most at home in the company of a friend who was on leave from Nigeria and of a colleague from Sierra Leone whom I met in London. All three of us had been on the same Devonshire Course. We had all just completed our first tours and were full of the enthusiasm of newly fledged cadets. Talk of paramount chiefs, of riots, trekking and other subjects dear to the heart of every administrative officer evoked polite interest of other acquaintances up to a point, beyond which they became bored and tried to bring the conversation back to sensible topics such as the price of property in London. I cannot be critical of my friends and acquaintances. A conversation becomes a monologue or may simply dry up if there is not a sufficient common ground between the participants, and my experience in West Africa was usually remote from that of my listeners.

One close friend, a chartered accountant in London, asked me, 'What do you eat out there? Lots of *bonga* I suppose?' 'No', I replied, '*bonga* is very popular with the Africans but I have never known Europeans eat it.' He had intended to be whimsical in inventing what sounded like a vaguely African word. He was astonished to learn that there was such a food as *bonga*, this being the name given in Sierra Leone to smoked, dried fish, the local version of kippers.

Leave came to an end and I enjoyed one last weekend in London, finishing with a visit to The Prospect of Whitby at Wapping, overlooking the Thames, where one had to fight one's way to the bar for a drink through a crowd of people on a slumming expedition from the West End to this then fashionable venue set in the most unlikely surroundings of docks and slums.

Next morning I took the airport bus from Brompton Road to Heathrow, where the terminal was still a collection of wartime prefabricated huts on the Bath Road. By 9.00 a.m. we were airborne and heading for Tangier, our first night stop. The plane was a Viking owned by Hunting Clan Airways, a name long since disappeared. It was small, cramped, uncomfortable and slow, most unsuitable for long distance flights such as this. The actual flying was a penance, made bearable, however, by the charming ministrations of a ravishingly beautiful blonde stewardess, though at the time they were still called air hostesses.

At this time air travel was something new and exciting for most people, myself included, despite the discomfort of having to travel in a small and unpressurized aircraft, bumping along at 5000 feet over Spain in the midday heat. It had the attraction of being still a leisurely form of transport and providing a far more personal service than that to which we are all accustomed nowadays. On our first day we landed at Biarritz for lunch and arrived in Tangier at 4.00 p.m. Cars took the passengers to our hotels in the city and on the way we had a brief glimpse of the unfamiliar and slightly exotic world of North Africa in the cosmopolitan setting of Tangier. Beggars, pimps, importunate guides and bootblacks pestered tourists wherever they walked. Rags and poverty were to be seen in striking juxtaposition with Cadillacs and wealth. After dinner at the hotel I set off to explore the kasbah in the company of some of the other passengers, escorted by an English-speaking guide, without whose assistance we would soon have lost ourselves in the narrow and tortuous alleys. Here and there brightly lit establishments indicated the existence of a sordid nightlife.

Our party went into one bar that was also a brothel. It was run by a tough and beefy *señora* who had in her charge several young but rather haggard looking Spanish women. Some of the men disappeared upstairs with one or other of the women, having first paid the appropriate fee. The rest of us sat in the bar drinking beer bought at exorbitant prices and talking to the other women, though conversation was limited by our lack of Spanish, and what English the women knew consisted in large measure of obscenities picked up from merchant seamen. The *señora* was keen to stage an 'exhibition'. I am not sure what this would have involved, but to judge from tales I have heard of similar shows in other Arab cities, it would not have been suitable for a maiden aunt. We did not take advantage of the offer as we felt that the evening was already costing us enough. One middle-aged Australian engineer who was on his way to Nigeria insisted that it was his party and that he must pay for the drinks, but we did not wish to abuse his hospitality. All the time, our guide, an Arab in gown and fez, sat at a table by himself, his face impassive and his eyes tired. As a good Muslim the pleasures of alcohol and fornication were denied to him and he simply sat and drank Coca-Cola. I would have liked to know his private views on the decadent Europeans whose vices afforded him a livelihood.

At 4.00 a.m. I was tired and bored and there were no signs of the party coming to an end. A Scotsman and I decided that we would like to go back to the hotel. The guide took us out of the maze of alleys to a street where there was a taxi rank, accepted his baksheesh and went back to look after our friends. It was almost 5.00 a.m. by the time we reached the hotel and as we were to be called at 5.30 there was no time for sleep. I lay down partly dressed for half an hour.

After an early breakfast, with cups of black coffee to revive those of us who had been out all night, we drove out to the airport and took off for the next stage of our journey. For most of the day all we could see beneath us was the endless Sahara. We had a refuelling stop at Casablanca and the second one after lunch at Villa Cisneros, a dismal outpost in the Spanish Sahara since renamed Ad Dakhla, with the Atlantic Ocean on one side and the desert on the other. There were no proper airport buildings and just a sand runway. There was no trace of vegetation anywhere and the only sign of civilization was a group of whitewashed, barrack-like buildings. It was a forlorn and desolate place.

Our second night stop was Bathurst (renamed Banjul after independence), capital of the Gambia, still a colony, which I had already visited twice on outward and homeward voyages on Elder Dempster's ships. The airport was at Yundum, 20 miles from the town and the former site of the Gambia poultry scheme, one of the Colonial Development Corporation's failures in the early postwar years. It was an ambitious project for undertaking poultry farming on a large scale, but unfortunately there was an outbreak of Newcastle disease among the chickens and the scheme had to be abandoned after huge sums of money had been spent on it. Vast areas of cleared bush and derelict buildings and machinery remained to remind us of a failure that had cost the British taxpayer dearly.

As we sat in the bar of the recently built Atlantic Hotel before dinner, there were soon plenty of signs, notwithstanding the relative luxury of our surroundings, that we were back on 'the Coast'. The atmosphere had that warm and soupy feeling I shall always associate with West Africa, and I was sweating freely. Nowadays one would expect air-conditioning in such a hotel, but at that time it was a very rare feature of buildings in hot climates. Next to the bar was a billiard room and several men were playing snooker, dressed in the daytime uniform of West Coast Europeans, sports shirts, shorts and woollen stockings. In the bar men sat in little groups at tables, drinking bottled lager and boring each other with tedious tales. It was Bo Club again, with more elegant trimmings. Bathurst had none of the diversions of Tangier and we all went early to bed.

From Bathurst to Freetown was only two hours' flying time. The second night stop would have been unnecessary, but the plane had to go on to Accra, where it ended its journey. We disembarked at Lungi airport and after lunch in the restaurant there were taken by bus some 12 miles to a jetty on the north bank of the Sierra Leone River. Familiar sights came crowding in on me, reminding me that leave was at an end — a bumpy laterite road, thick bush and palm trees on both sides, small villages of mud huts, women dressed in *lappa*s and head ties carrying loads on their heads and babies on their backs. It was an overcast and cheerless day in the middle of the rains, and the hills of the colony peninsula, seen across the harbour, looked forbidding, with thunderclouds nestling against their summits, threatening Freetown.

An hour's journey by launch took us to Government Jetty, just below the secretariat building. This had been the hub of Sierra Leone's commerce with the outside world before Freetown acquired its Deepwater Quay in the early 1950s. Ships used to anchor a few hundred yards off the jetty and passengers and cargo were carried to and fro in lighters. It was still used by a few ships, and the railway continued to land all its coal there. A car was waiting for me and took me to Hill Station, where I had arranged to stay with a friend.

9

Bonthe I

I was posted to Bonthe, 80 miles from Bo and one of the four districts of the South-Western Province. I was pleased to be told that I was to act as district commissioner on my own for a few months until the regular DC returned from leave. After a few days in Freetown I caught the train to Bo, where I had to collect the loads I had left in store there. I felt myself to be a very different person from the apprehensive young cadet who had made the same journey two years earlier. I was delighted at the prospect of having my own district, even though it was to be for only a short time. It gave me much confidence to feel that at the age of 25, after two years in the service, I was entrusted with so much responsibility.

At Bo the provincial commissioner's lorry was waiting for me at the station as it had waited so many times before. I stayed at the house of a friend and Devonshire Course contemporary, John Cook, who had succeeded me as assistant district commissioner in Bo. After two nights there I set off for Bonthe in the lorry. I travelled as far as Mattru Jong, 54 miles away, where I had to transfer from the lorry to a launch the DC had sent to meet me. The town of Bonthe, the district headquarters, was a port on a large island, Sherbro Island, where the estuaries of several of Sierra Leone's major rivers met before entering the sea. The Atlantic Ocean washed the southern shore of the island. Most of the district was low lying and swampy and rivers and creeks were the main arteries of communication. The chiefdoms immediately neighbouring Bo District had a few miles of motor road, but there were no roads to the south of Mattru, which marked the upper limit of navigation on the Jong River.

Sierra Leone had many broad rivers, but rock bars and rapids limited their value to trade and communication. Mattru, for example, was only 30 miles from the sea, but launches drawing three or four feet of water often scraped the river bed when going there or coming from there during the dry season.

My loads were put on the launch at Mattru's wharf and we moved off down the river. My servants and the launch crew occupied the stern, aft of the engine casing, while I had the foredeck to myself and was able to relax in a deckchair and watch the banks slip by. For the first few miles the vegetation was the same as that which covered most of the protectorate, thick bush and low trees, many with their branches partly immersed in the water. Further downstream mangrove swamps became predominant. These are the characteristic vegetation of the coastal regions of West Africa, unhealthy, unattractive, reeking and forbidding. Mangrove trees grow close together in salt water, forming an impenetrable mass. They grow to a great height and propagate themselves by sending down shoots, which take root in the bed of the river. The trees arch over with the weight of the new shoots pulling them down, and advance into the water over the years like a grotesque series of croquet hoops.

Mangrove swamps are one of nature's ways of reclaiming land and counteracting the effects of erosion caused by the heavy rains inland. Much of the rich topsoil is washed out to sea by the rivers, but a great deal of it is caught up in the interstices of mangrove roots. Eventually a shelf of mud is formed, which is left to dry when the river is low. The mangrove cannot, however, thrive in mud, which tends to choke it and continues to send out shoots further into the river. The process is self-perpetuating. In some parts of West Africa large areas of mangrove were cleared, a backbreaking task but one that brings rich rewards. The fertile alluvial mud left behind is ideal for certain varieties of rice and produces good crops many years in succession, sometimes twice in one year.

The river broadened out and was joined by tributaries and creeks as we came nearer to Bonthe. There were a few small villages on the banks and from time to time we saw fishermen in their primitive dugout canoes, which are just the hollowed out trunks of trees. Seen from midstream, the increasingly distant banks resolved themselves into a thin, dark green line. The launch reached Bonthe three hours after leaving Mattru.

Bonthe was a small township, one square mile in area, and had formerly been an important port, second only to Freetown. With the silting up of the estuary and the diversion of traffic to the roads, however, it had been in decline for some years. It had become important through trade in produce, brought down in canoes and launches from the other parts of the district. In addition to the usual palm kernels and groundnuts, Bonthe was still at this time noted for its piassava. This fibre, which is used for making stiff brushes, is won from the stalks of the raffia palm fronds that grow in abundance in riverine swamps throughout the district. The stalks are shredded, dried in the sun, graded according to quality and bundled for shipment. The best quality is 'Prime Sherbro', taking its name from the island, the river and the tribe that mostly peoples the district. Even in 1956, when I was there, at least one cargo ship a month still came to load piassava. Ships had to anchor or tie up to a buoy five miles down river from Bonthe, and the cargo was taken out to them by launches and lighters. Years ago ships had been able to anchor off Bonthe or York Island, two miles away, but this was now no longer possible.

The town bore some signs of its former prosperity. The four main European trading companies operating in Sierra Leone all had branches there, but most of their warehouse space was no longer used. One of the two French companies had a huge derelict house in its compound, which had once accommodated over a dozen European assistants — a 'chummery' in former Anglo-Indian parlance. Business was now on such a small scale that one Frenchman was able to run the branch with a small number of African clerks and shop assistants. There were also Syrian and Lebanese merchants in Bonthe, some of whom shipped fibre, but their community was in decline. Any Levantines who had spare capital used it to set up shops in the diamond areas, where fortunes could be quickly made.

I have sometimes thought of Bonthe as the Venice of Sierra Leone. It was on an island with no motor traffic and served only by boats. Like Venice it had known better days and was now to be compared with the dowager who had both feet in the water. The architectural and artistic splendours of Venice, the gondolas and the tourists had, however, no equivalent. Bonthe was a town of old buildings, many of them with rusting corrugated-iron roofs. It was a typical West Coast trading station, whose seedy and decayed air evoked the shades of palm oil ruffians of the nineteenth century, the merchant adventurers who had established the first regular contacts between West Africa and Europe. It was still part of the colony of Sierra Leone, both *de jure* and *de facto* and a large proportion of its population was of Creole stock. In consequence, it was well provided with churches, missions and schools run by a variety of Christian denominations.

The DC was busy when I arrived and his wife came to the public jetty to meet me. I had lunch with both of them while loads were taken to the house that I was to occupy and my servants began to unpack. I had just over a week in which to take over and we made a start the following morning. The district had 11 chiefdoms, four fewer than Bo. Nearly all my trekking would have to be by launch, which meant that I must expect to be away from my station much more than I had been in Bo. The launches could seldom travel at higher speeds than nine knots, even with a favourable tide, so except for the two chiefdoms on Sherbro Island near at hand I would have to spend at least one night away from Bonthe every time I went anywhere. The DC's launch fleet consisted of four vessels, at least one of which could be expected to be under repair at any one time. The DC had to maintain regular mail services and provide transport for any government officials visiting the district and for the local medical officer on occasional trips. All these commitments put a heavy strain on the tiny fleet, and scheduled regular trips often had to be cancelled because no launch was available.

The launches were under the immediate care of Gbana Fai, the chief coxswain, an amiable Sherbro with great strength of personality. There were 20 crew members, plus a fitter, storekeeper, shipwright and two assistants. Supervision of the maintenance of the fleet was always an unfair assignment for a DC, who invariably knew nothing about marine engines or the construction and repair of hulls. He simply had to trust that the fitter and shipwright had done their jobs properly. Administrative officers had to be versatile and turn their hand to many different tasks in which they had little or no expertise, but this was a demand too far.

Bonthe had been unaffected by the anti-chief riots which had swept through the Northern Province and parts of South-Western Province. This was explained partly by remoteness from the area in which the disturbances originated and partly by the less powerful hold that Sherbro paramount chiefs had over their people by comparison with those of the Mende or Timne. The main occupation of the coastal Sherbro was fishing, farming being secondary. This meant that there was less dependence on the land than else-where; hence there was less scope for the chiefs, who were the principal arbiters in land matters, to control the liveli-hoods of young men and exact tribute from them. Further-more, a man might be away fishing for several days at a time, and it was difficult to get him to attend the native court or otherwise answer the chief's summons.

The DC was the senior government officer and first citizen of Bonthe. There were also a medical officer who ran the hospital and an agricultural officer, police and other depart-ments being represented by more junior officers. The other Europeans were branch managers of the trading firms and the manager of the local branch of Barclays Bank, an Irish Roman Catholic father and a mother superior who managed a girls' school. It was a small but cosmopolitan community that included several Frenchmen, two Greeks and one Scots-man and, of course, the inevitable Lebanese and Syrian traders.

Bonthe had acquired an unsavoury reputation as a govern-ment station and legend had it that administrative officers were sent there as a punishment, though I never believed that. It was, however, an isolated station, linked with the rest of the world only by water. It formed part of the coast and was low lying, was hot and damp and did not cool off at night as did places inland. Mosquitoes and sandflies abounded; as protection against the latter when sleeping a net of extra-fine mesh was needed, as the holes of an ordin-ary mosquito net were big enough for them to crawl through. Other disadvantages were the difficulty of getting food and other supplies. Fresh meat was never obtainable. The local butcher had a feud with Bonthe town's grandly named local authority, the Urban District Council, regarding the fees to be paid for use of the slaughterhouse, and for a long time, including my few months in the district, refused to kill any cows. Although fishing was the main economic activity of the district, fresh fish was a rarity. Most of the fishermen preferred to have their fish smoked and dried and sent to the diamond areas where it brought a good price as *bonga*. My office was on the waterfront and at high tide the water was just a few feet from the office door. From time to time, one enterprising fisherman would tie up his canoe alongside the office and the clerks and I would rush out to buy his catch of very welcome fresh fish.

I enjoyed my few months in the district, but a much longer stay would have been trying. Soon after I arrived, a European manager for one of the trading companies was taken to hospital suffering from *delirium tremens* and had to be sent back to the United Kingdom. The previous year a medical officer had gone berserk; he had attacked his night watchman with a cutlass and had to be locked up for the night by the police. An earlier medical officer had committed suicide. I would certainly not have enjoyed even my few months there if I had had to spend the whole time within the narrow confines of the town, seeing the same collection of dismal buildings and the same faces every day, with no possibility of escape. I had to spend at least half of every month on trek and therefore found my short spells in Bonthe town all the more tolerable.

My territorial responsibility at the age of 25 was for some 3000 square miles of bush, swamp, river and creek. In principle it included also a three-mile belt of the Atlantic Ocean, as about a third of Sierra Leone's coastline was in Bonthe District. I was responsible for the law, order and good government of a district that comprised 11 chiefdoms plus those parts of the district, notably Bonthe town, which were part of the colony of Sierra Leone and not within any chiefdom. I had to look after four launches and somehow keep the mail services going. I was also harbour master of Bonthe, though this post was a sinecure. There was never any occasion for me to go out to any of the ships which sometimes tied up in the estuary, and regulation of launches, tugs and lighters in the harbour did not present any problems. The responsibilities were considerable, poorly rewarded even in 1956 by a salary of £922, with no acting pay for taking charge of a district. Becoming a district commissioner was not a promotion but simply the assumption of a new title on reaching a certain point in the long incremental scale. From the point of view of pay and promotion the administrative service was not exciting.

My first task was to conduct elections to the district council. Hitherto these councils had consisted of all the paramount chiefs of the district plus certain nominated members. Under legislation that came into effect in 1956 each chiefdom was entitled to elect one member in addition to the chief, and additional members in the ratio of one per thousand taxpayers over the first thousand. Every taxpayer, that is every adult male over the age of 21, was entitled to vote.

Holding ballot box elections in African conditions presented all kinds of problems that did not occur in more advanced countries, problems that arose mainly from poor communications and the illiteracy of the electorate. The first problem to overcome was a total lack of understanding and general indifference. Much time had to be spent touring in order to hold public meetings at which the significance of elections and the procedure involved were explained, sometimes with the aid of practical demonstrations. The average peasant or fisherman in Sierra Leone had only a very vague idea of what the district councils were or what they were supposed to do, which was not surprising since they provided few tangible services. Election of district council members was generally regarded as a new way of appointing a superior kind of subchief and members once elected were not averse to being regarded in this way.

Having at least made a token effort to overcome ignorance and apathy, the administrative officer was next faced with the formidable task of organizing the holding of elections. Voters' lists were prepared from the tax rolls in each chiefdom and the usual motions of making the lists available for inspection and giving opportunities for claims and objections were gone through. Nominations of candidates were called for on the appropriate day and each candidate whose nomination paper was accepted had a symbol allotted to him. These symbols were drawings of easily recognizable objects and were fixed to the outside of each candidate's ballot box for identification; they included a palm tree, a cow, a house and a canoe.

Polling stations had to be arranged with a view to limiting as far as possible the distance the voters would have to walk, but even so many voters might have to walk as far as 20 miles in each direction to vote. Each station had to be provided with two officials to mark off names on the lists and issue ballot papers. Government and district council clerks, junior officials and schoolteachers were conscripted into this work. In addition, groups of stations had to be supervised on polling day by assistant returning officers, a capacity in which senior government officers, missionaries and others were employed. The district commissioner was the returning officer for all the wards within his district.

In Bonthe District the elections had to be spread over three polling days in three consecutive weeks, partly because of a shortage of suitable polling station staff and partly because of the peculiarly difficult communications. All the ballot boxes had to be brought at the end of the day to wherever the assistant returning officer was staying, and during the day this officer had to visit the polling stations for which he was responsible to ensure that all was in order. There were simply not enough launches to meet these needs for all wards on one day.

My first trek in the district was to Dema chiefdom, at the western end of Sherbro Island. It was a little over 20 miles from Bonthe and accessible by bush path, but the journey by launch was easier and pleasanter. It was a delightful spot at the western mouth of the Sherbro River, popular with many people from the governor downwards, who went there for the fishing. Close at hand were the Turtle Islands, part of the chiefdom, and all inhabited by fishermen and their families.

The rest house stood on an open patch of ground looking towards the Turtle Islands and across the wide estuary. It was little more than a minute's walk from the Atlantic Ocean, where I went one evening for a swim. This was, however, disappointing. A heavy surf pounds the Atlantic coast of Sierra Leone, which makes bathing difficult and dangerous. The beach is of coarse sand and steeply sloping. I soon found that swimming was impossible and all I could do was sit on the sand and let the surf break over me.

The soil in this part of the island was sandy and little would grow other than palm trees and cassava, a root crop of very low food value. The people had to live mainly on fish, which was fortunately plentiful. The chiefdom was notorious for the Tun Tun Society, whose aim was to ensure good fishing for its members and which was alleged on occasions to make human sacrifices to this end. The evidence for this was uncertain and confusing, but there had at various times been mysterious deaths and disappearances, which had come to the notice of the DC. It was widely believed that the members of the society not only used parts of the bodies of victims for ritual purposes, but also that they ate whatever was left. Considering the monotony of their diet, this would not be surprising. Information about the activities of the society was hard to come by, as it was proscribed and had to function by stealth. During my stay in the district three men were convicted by the Supreme Court and imprisoned for being in possession of instruments that linked them to the society.

I have long held the theory, unproven by anything more

than casual observations such as those of the Tun Tun Society, that although cannibalism in Africa and elsewhere has often been explained by anthropologists in terms of ritual sacrifice, another and possibly primary motive is dietary. The people of Bonthe District were generally fortunate in being able to get protein from fish, but in the inland parts of the country there was little meat to be had other than from scraggy chickens and very occasionally from underfed cattle. Many local people probably had to subsist on a vegetarian diet for much of the time and it would be understandable, if deplorable, if they sometimes turned their thoughts hungrily towards the idea of supplementing this with protein in the form of the flesh of children or adolescents.

Since the purpose of my visit to Dema was to receive nominations for the elections, I spent one full day there. It was a chiefdom all DCs loved to visit on account of its idyllic setting and the feeling of utter remoteness it afforded. I was able to understand something of the joy men could derive from administering lonely islands in the middle of the Pacific. On a later visit I was able to obtain a closer insight into the life of the people of Dema. I was canvassing the idea of setting up a fishermen's cooperative society, with a view to helping the fishermen extricate themselves from debt and borrow capital to buy better fishing nets and other tackle than they were able to make themselves.

I have already mentioned the considerable trade in *bonga* between Bonthe District and the diamond areas. The Sherbro people caught and dried the fish but trade was entirely in the hands of Foulah and Mende traders — the latter almost exclusively women, who formed 'friendships', the local euphemism for casual sexual liaisons, with the fishermen. Payment of interest on loans of money or for the women's services to the fishermen was made in fish, so that it was unusual for any man ever to receive cash in return for the fruits of his labour.

I called a meeting of the fishermen on one of the islands to discuss the formation of a credit society. The islands formed part of what on Admiralty charts was known as the Turtle Bank and even at high tide the water around them was very shallow. My launch anchored about 100 yards out and I had to wade ashore. Here a cheerful gathering met me. None of them had gone out fishing that day so that they could be present at the meeting, and while waiting for me to arrive they had been drinking palm wine. By the time I arrived they were all merry and pleased to see me. They listened politely while I put forward my ideas and the feeling appeared to be that a credit society would be a worthwhile scheme to pursue. I doubted at the time, however, that their appreciative remarks indicated anything more than the normal courtesy towards strangers that is part of the African way of life. One of the Foulah traders at another meeting had already expressed it as his frank opinion that so long as the Mende women continued to participate in the fish trade and had something even more attractive than hard cash to offer, no society would have much hope of success. He was almost certainly right.

The island was small, no more than a few acres in area, and a few huts were the only settlement. There were plenty of signs of the inhabitants' main occupation — nets being repaired or pegged out to dry and canoes drawn up on the beach. Near the huts were the *banda*s, where fish were dried and smoked. The fish were first dried in the sun on rough trestle tables made of sticks tied together and then put inside the *banda*s, long low buildings made from local materials. Here were more trestle tables with smouldering fires under them, which smoked the dried fish. This was a simple and effective way of preserving fish and *bonga* could be kept unrefrigerated for two or three weeks, even in that climate.

After the meeting was over the fishermen took great delight in showing me this process and gave me some fresh fish as a present before I left. Later I submitted a report saying that I thought the idea of a credit society was worth trying, given competent management — a most important proviso. The scope for increasing the fish trade was considerable and a properly organized society would be able to exploit this. One much needed improvement was in transport. None of the traders at Dema owned launches and those from Bonthe called infrequently. A prosperous credit society would have been able to buy a launch for itself in order to ply regularly carrying fish between the islands The final decision on whether a society should be started rested with the registrar of cooperative societies in Freetown, to whom my report went. What his decision was I never knew, as it had not been taken before I left the district. Whatever it was, the necessary investigations had afforded me one of the friendliest and most pleasant visits I had ever paid to any chiefdom.

On returning from my first visit to Dema I encountered one of the minor problems that a waterborne administrator has to face. High tide on the day I wished to go back to Bonthe was at about 3.00 a.m. and, as the channel that launches had to use to reach the middle of the estuary was very shallow, it was not possible to move off at low tide. I had to get up soon after 3.00 a.m. to see that my camp bed and remaining loads were packed and carried out to the launch anchored offshore, all by the light of my pressure lamp. We were able to leave by 4.30 a.m., by which time the water level had already dropped, and we bumped the keel several times on the bottom before we got out into the river.

Soon after my first visit to Dema I supervised polling in Nongoba Bullom chiefdom, 30 miles east of Bonthe, up the Sewa River, which I was now beginning to regard as an old acquaintance from my days in Bo District. For the last 60 miles before it joins the Sherbro, the Sewa runs parallel to the Atlantic coastline and is separated from the ocean by a long narrow strip of sandy terrain, Turner's Peninsula, which in places is little more than 100 yards wide. The banks were open swamp and grassland and there were no mangrove trees. In places the coconut palms and rich green grass coming down to the water's edge created a scene of idyllic beauty such as one rarely meets in West Africa.

Along this river the agricultural department had started an ambitious scheme for rice production with the aid of mechanical ploughing. The department allocated land to farmers from all over the district and not only from the riverine chiefdoms. Ploughing in preparation for sowing rice seed was carried out by tractors supplied by the department. These were kept at a station set up on the river and looked after by a European mechanical superintendent. He and his young wife were occupying possibly the loneliest and most remote of all stations in Sierra Leone, but both loved it.

In the course of polling day in this chiefdom I became aware of some more of the difficulties to be faced in introducing so complex a procedure in a backward country. I soon realized that it was no use following the normal practice in the United Kingdom whereby the voter gives his name to the official in charge of the station, who checks his lists, ticks off the name and hands the voter a ballot paper. Often a voter in Sierra Leone would have one name on the list but would give a different one when he came to vote. This was not because of deliberate duplicity but simply because it was a local custom to use more than one name. A man would often genuinely forget that he had been using another name a few months previously. Furthermore, the names on the lists were not arranged in alphabetical order; to do so would have been a formidable undertaking beyond the capacity of the staff that prepared them. They were grouped together by towns and villages, so that it might take half an hour or more to trace the name of a man from one of the larger towns with 100 or more taxpayers.

Fortunately, there was an easy solution to this problem. Villagers invariably travelled together to vote; voting was regarded as a communal rather than an individual matter. The officer in charge of a polling station could therefore take each village as a whole and call out the names of the voters in the order in which they appeared on the list. The individuals came up when called, took their ballot papers and voted. This was always a satisfactory and quick method.

An occurrence at one of the polling stations showed how careful one needed to be that instructions were not misunderstood. All the polling station officials had been lectured in detail about their duties before the elections. Among other things they had been told that each candidate was entitled to have an agent present at the polling station throughout the day to ensure that no one voted twice and that there were no attempts to impersonate voters. I arrived at one of the stations and found a crowd of people waiting there and the presiding officer and his assistant were both sitting idle. It was early in the afternoon and I asked why they had not begun to issue ballot papers. The presiding officer told me that he was waiting for the candidates' agents to arrive; I told him that although the candidates were entitled to have agents present, the failure of agents to appear would not invalidate the proceedings and they should have started at 9.00 a.m. whether the agents were there or not. I made sure that voting got under way as rapidly as possible before I left.

I was thankful when the elections were over and the results had been declared. I found the duties of a returning officer tedious and troublesome and was not without doubts about the value of the exercise.

10

Bonthe II

Trekking by launch was unquestionably far pleasanter than by any other form of transport. The speed was leisurely and there was time to savour the passing scene; the launches were big enough to ride comfortably on the water without any rocking or pitching. There were none of the dust, mud, potholes and corrugations of the roads, none of the vagaries and exasperating delays of the railway, none of the sweat and aching muscles caused by walking. Frequently I took the contents of my 'in' tray with me on journeys and drafted replies to letters for the clerks to type while sitting in my deckchair. At other times I was content to relax with a bottle of beer or a book. I love sea travel and found river travel equally to my taste.

I had to spend more than half my time touring the district, but at weekends in Bonthe it was a pleasure to accompany the rest of the small European community on the regular trip they made to the eastern mouth of the Sherbro River. For this we normally travelled in one of the trading companies' launches, faster and more comfortable than any of the government vessels. We took bathing trunks, food and drink, plus a pack or two of cards, and left after breakfast on Sunday. It took us just over an hour to reach the mouth of the river, where we landed at a spot known as 'Sheba', a corruption of 'sea bar' and a reference to the sandbanks marking the mouth of the river where it met the Atlantic.

At Sheba we waded ashore and spent the idle hours of daylight on the beach eating, drinking, playing cards, swimming or sleeping. It was an unreal and hedonistic day off in surroundings suggestive of a small Pacific island. Everything was there, the silvery sand, the swaying coconut palms, the endless ocean — but no coral reef and no dusky meridional belles in sarongs and with frangipani flowers in their hair. A few such maidens or a selection of their fairer sisters wearing brief bikinis or less would have made the day perfect for the predominantly bachelor party. Towards evening we would pack up and return to Bonthe. On the launch, so long as daylight lasted, some of the more enthusiastic bridge players would continue the rubber they had started at Sheba.

As well as Dema there were some other attractive spots at which to stay in the district. Just across the river from Bonthe was Bendu on the mainland, half an hour away by launch and the headquarters of a small chiefdom. Here there was a recently completed rest house sited on high ground, perhaps 20 feet above the beach, with a view over the river towards the waterfront at Bonthe, whose lights could be seen from there at night. Bonthe District Council had plans to build a road to link Bendu and other towns in the area with Mattru, and a garage had been optimistically included in the plan of the rest house. At one time long ago there had been plans to build an extension of the railway to Bendu from Bo, but nothing ever came of that. I doubt whether it ever became possible to reach Bendu by road, as construction over such swampy and low-lying ground would have been a difficult undertaking and one major river crossing would have needed a bridge or more likely a ferry, but at least the garage provided a roomy and waterproof home for the rest house-keeper.

On one occasion while I was having breakfast on the veranda, I saw two young women walking along the beach just below me, carrying a large fishing net between them. The Sherbro women regularly fished in shallow water by the shore, two holding a net and dragging it through the water. These two women were evidently just about to start fishing, for they were both naked except for their head ties. They were perhaps 17 years old and I found their brown nubile bodies in brilliant sunshine on a sandy beach a most delectable and stimulating accompaniment to my breakfast. They had forgotten or not realized that I was staying at the rest house. When they saw me they giggled and paused for a moment to take off their head ties, short pieces of cotton cloth wound round their heads in turban fashion, and made from them an extempore and exiguous covering for their loins, leaving the rest of their bodies naked. Having done this they gave me a friendly wave, which I acknowledged, giggled again and waded into the water to start their fishing. Sad to relate, whenever after this I stayed at that rest house the women did their fishing in the evening, just after sunset.

Another spot on the mainland to the north of Bonthe was Gbangbama, which had to be reached by road. It was set in undulating country and behind the town was an imposing hill over 1500 feet high. It had 30 years before been a district headquarters, and on one of the lower peaks were the former district commissioner's house, office and prison. The house had been used as a rest house since the station was closed and was reached by a steep pathway leading up the hillside. Steps had been cut to make the climb easier and later a motorable road, also very steep, was added. The house was built to the common T-shaped pattern, with dining room, veranda, two bedrooms and kitchen and servants' quarters separate. It was built on a grand scale such as would have befitted a house for a provincial commissioner or some other senior official. The rooms and veranda had an enormous floor area and a very high ceiling. The walls were of laterite stone and the roof of corrugated iron, whereas other government quarters built at the same time were usually of mud block with a thatched roof. When it was built it was still normal practice for government to call for forced labour to put up and maintain public buildings in the protectorate, and it was clear that a great deal of such labour must have gone into the building of this house.

The ground had been levelled to make a lawn in front of the veranda and at the edge of the lawn the ground fell steeply away. The view from the veranda was magnificent. Nearby could be seen some small villages in clearings in the middle of the dense bush and forest, but not Gbangbama itself, which was tucked away out of sight at the foot of the hill. Beyond there stretched a seemingly endless plain, merging with the mangrove swamps and rivers in the dim distance. The hill was clearly visible from Bonthe, and was the only high ground in an otherwise mostly flat district, but Bonthe itself was too far away to be made out from the top of the hill.

The house was at this time occupied by a geological prospecting party sent out by a British company interested in the rutile deposits occurring in this part of the district. Rutile and ilmenite are the ores from which titanium is extracted. The chief merit of this metal is that it has a higher melting point than any other and at this time it was seen as the answer to the serious problem of metal fatigue in jet aircraft travelling at high speeds. Winning the metal from the ore is an expensive and difficult process, and large-scale investment in mining the ore would be justified only if a large and continuing demand for titanium could be assured. At this time the company had high hopes of a steady demand arising from the production of military jet aircraft. Writing now in 2001 I am aware that the company did begin mining many years later, but I doubt whether it has been able to continue its operations in the chaotic and dangerous conditions of the interior of Sierra Leone.

In 1956, however, prospecting was being carried out with great vigour and enthusiasm. In a large area around Gbangbama, lines were cut through the bush and drilling was

undertaken at fixed intervals along these lines. Samples of
earth were tested and an accurate picture of the location,
magnitude and quality of the deposits was created. It was
exciting work and the Europeans in charge of the drilling
teams, the chemists and others went about their tasks with
tremendous energy in very trying conditions, not troubling
to count the hours. A new and very good road had only
recently reached a point near Gbangbama and this linked
them with the rest of the country. In the areas where they
were prospecting the company had to build whatever roads,
bridges and other infrastructure it needed. The drilling and
road construction kept a labour force of several hundred
men employed and brought much prosperity to the chiefdom.

The rest house was used as a mess and living quarters for
the European staff; those who could not be fitted into it
were lodged in prefabricated huts put up around it. The
building had been well decorated and furnished and a small
generator supplied electricity. It was not politically desirable
that I should appear to identify myself too closely with the
company, and after my first visit I always asked the
paramount chief to provide me with a house in the town.
On my first visit I stayed in the rest house as a guest of the
company and enjoyed a degree of comfort and good living
that was untypical of trekking. I discovered that this had
made me a little suspect with the chief and local people and
on later visits I accepted the company's hospitality only to
the extent of one or two meals in the evening.

The manager in charge of this operation was fond of
animals and kept among others a baby chimpanzee, a mon-
goose and two boa constrictors, Gert and Charlie. On one
occasion he insisted on introducing me to these two. They
were kept in cages just outside the main building whenever
there were visitors but at other times were allowed to glide
freely around the place. My host hauled Charlie out of his
cage and held him out for me to stroke. He was five feet

long, fat and not at all friendly in appearance, but he was somnolent after a good meal. I stroked his skin hesitantly and was surprised to discover for the first time that the skin of a snake is not clammy and unpleasant to the touch as is often supposed, but dry and firm.

After I had been in Bonthe for two months my car arrived in Freetown and I had to collect it. I arranged to travel in a small coastal vessel belonging to one of the French trading companies, which frequently went to Freetown carrying piassava fibre and bringing back cloth and other consumer goods. The distance was about 100 miles and the journey took 12 hours. The boat had to reach Freetown during working hours and left Bonthe at 4.00 a.m. I went aboard the previous night and slept in my camp bed, which was put up in the small cabin. I was disturbed after a few hours' sleep by the clatter of feet on the iron deck as the crew came aboard and made ready to leave. I heard the ring of the engine room telegraph, soon followed by the throbbing of the diesel engines as they started up and quickened their rhythm in answer to fresh instructions from the wheelhouse.

By daylight, soon after 7.00 a.m., Sherbro Island and the Turtle Islands were well astern and we were heading towards Shenge, a fishing village on the mainland on Yawri Bay. Like Dema this was a popular resort with administrative officers and others who were fond of fishing and was just over 50 miles from the district headquarters of Moyamba by road. We passed close to Shenge and the boat stopped for a few minutes while the crew bought fresh fish from canoes that came alongside. After Shenge we spent several hours crossing the mouth of the bay and were in the open sea, though never out of sight of land. Sussex, a small village on the southern tip of the colony peninsula, was the opposite headland of the bay from Shenge, looking out to the Banana Islands a few miles offshore. From Sussex onwards I was able to enjoy a first-class view of the peninsula's palm-shaded beaches and the tall, forested hills behind them. It was a beautiful unspoiled coastline and could hold its own with any of the scenic attractions the West Indies offered.

We passed Lumley Beach, Freetown's popular bathing spot, rounded Aberdeen Point with its lighthouse and chugged up the estuary of the Sierra Leone River. I disembarked at the trading company's private wharf where a car was waiting to take me up to Hill Station.

After my subsequent return to Bonthe came the highlight of my time there, an official visit by the new governor, Sir Maurice Dorman. This was his first visit to the district and I was naturally anxious that everything should go off properly. For several weeks beforehand I was busy planning a suitable programme and making arrangements.

Sir Maurice arrived at Mattru by road from Bo, accompanied by Martin Page, the provincial commissioner. I met him at the offices of Bonthe District Council on the edge of Mattru and introduced him to the president of the council, the secretary and other officials. He was shown round the offices, introduced to the clerical and other staff and had informal discussions with the president on some of the problems facing the council and some of the projects for which the council was seeking government assistance. The governor made it clear that while he was happy to discuss matters of this kind he was not prepared to make any promises unless he was certain that they could be fulfilled.

What became apparent on first acquaintance with Sir Maurice in these circumstances was his keen interest in people and his retentive memory for faces and names — valuable assets for any governor. Equally apparent was his desire to see things for himself. The president of the council mentioned the need for a ferry across the Jong River at Mattru, giving the town a ready link with Gbangbama on the other side of the river. On learning that the proposed site for the crossing was only a mile away, the governor's immediate reaction was that we should go and look at it, which we did. Afterwards we drove into the town of Mattru, where a large gathering awaited us. All the members of the tribal authority were in the *barri* and a large crowd was clustered round the outside. On both sides of the pathway leading into the *barri* the local schoolchildren and boy scouts were lined up and, as the governor got out of his car, they came to attention and sang 'God save the Queen'.

In the *barri* the governor was introduced to the paramount chief and section chiefs, after which the usual address of welcome was delivered, to which the governor replied. The business was brief, formal and friendly. When it was concluded, the governor and his party consisting of Lady Dorman, Martin Page and myself, plus the governor's aide-de-camp, military orderly and interpreter, walked through the town down to the wharf. Schoolchildren lined both sides of the road and a crowd of several hundred people had collected at the wharf. An American missionary who ran a secondary school in Mattru was waiting with his camera and the governor obligingly paused to allow him to take pictures.

We boarded the governor's launch *Cara*, which had come up from Freetown two days previously. Most of His Excellency's trek loads had already been taken down the river on one of my launches, the remainder being loaded on board *Cara*. There was much cheering and enthusiastic waving as the launch moved off, and Governor and Lady Dorman stood for some time on the foredeck waving back to the crowd. The governor was genuinely pleased at such a friendly reception, for he had not long before completed a tour of the Northern Province, where the grievances that had caused the riots of the previous dry season were still uppermost in the minds of the people and they were not yet well disposed towards any representative of government.

We were now able to relax for two and a half hours. *Cara* was a beautiful and luxurious launch in which it was a pleasure to travel. I do not know what her dimensions were, but she was certainly much bigger than any of my launches and was very well fitted out. She had a spacious cabin with bunks and table, plus bathroom and toilet. Astern of that was the wheelhouse, then the engine room, whose two powerful engines kept the boat moving at a steady 12 knots. Further aft again was the galley, complete with refrigerator, then a cabin for crew and servants in the stern. The governor and his party sat on the open foredeck under a canvas sun awning and here, high above the water, we sat and drank welcome bottles of cold beer and ate a sandwich lunch. From time to time we passed villages on the banks and the villagers came running down to the water's edge to wave to us.

Our first call was at York Island, an appendage of Bonthe. Here were a small settlement and a store belonging to Paterson Zochonis & Company (known locally as PZ), an Anglo–Greek trading firm. The island's only jetty belonged to PZ and it was customary for the governor to ask permission to land when he visited the island. I asked on his behalf and the Greek manager, who was standing waiting at the end of the jetty, readily granted it. I introduced the manager to the governor and we walked through the store compound where all the company's labourers, 40 to 50 of them, were lined up as though on parade; in an attempt to give them a smart and uniform appearance, the manager had issued yellow singlets to all of them with SHELL BP in large green letters on the front. It was an incongruous but effective touch. After a short walk round the town, a smaller replica of Bonthe, we again boarded *Cara* for the last part of our journey.

I had given 3.15 p.m. as the expected time of arrival at Bonthe in the programme of the visit I had circulated. We were a little ahead of time and I had to ask the coxswain to go at half speed for a while so that we would not arrive too early. I felt very pleased with myself when we reached the public jetty at exactly 3.15. Such precise timekeeping is rarely achieved in Africa.

At the jetty all the town's leading citizens lined up to be presented to the governor — the chairman of the Urban District Council, medical and agricultural officers and representatives of the churches and trading companies. Schoolchildren and townspeople lined both sides of the road from the jetty to the district commissioner's house, where the governor was staying. There was no cheering, the predominantly Creole citizens of Bonthe being sedate and more reserved than the less inhibited ones from the protectorate who had seen us off so enthusiastically from Mattru, but many people exchanged polite greetings with the governor.

The governor's programme comprised mainly visits to chiefdoms plus the customary cocktail and dinner parties. On the Saturday night Martin Page and I accompanied Sir Maurice and Lady Dorman to a dance that was being given in the town hall, a building of much more modest proportions than its name might suggest. Dances of this kind were invariably referred to in Sierra Leone as 'ball dances' to distinguish them from dances of the traditional African kind. We danced to gramophone records of calypsos and 'highlife', the latter a dance originating in Ghana, having similar rhythms to some of the dances of the West Indies. The record that proved to be the hit of the evening and was played at least a dozen times was 'The Zombie Jamboree', a calypso on the macabre theme of corpses or 'zombies' dancing by night in a cemetery. It began with the lines 'Zombie jamboree took place/in Long Island cemetery' and there was an oft-repeated chorus:

> 'Back to Back,
> Belly to belly
> I don't gove a damn,
> 'Cos I dun dead a'ready!'

The Dormans left at midnight but the dance continued. Martin Page and I stayed until the end, long after the rest of the European community had gone home. At 4.00 a.m. I walked home wearily and thankfully to bed. Unfortunately, I was not able to stay in bed as was my wont on Sunday mornings, for I had to accompany the governor to church. An unpleasant incident, which marred the day, was a row with my cook, Musa, which ended in my sacking him. This held me up a little and I had to cycle furiously through the town in order to meet the governor at 9.00 a.m. I was a minute or two late, but Lady Dorman very kindly excused me, as she knew that I had had very little sleep.

I felt the need of a rest after the church service and, in company with the governor's ADC, Donald Mackay, one of my Devonshire Course contemporaries, and the agricultural officer, I went off to Sheba in one of my launches for a swim. We took beer and a picnic lunch with us. I was feeling the strain, but the visit was not yet over. That evening, I again accompanied the governor to church and the following morning we had to leave early on the morning tide to go up the Sewa River. The agricultural officer came with us because the main interest of the day's programme was to see the mechanical cultivation of rice.

We called at Gbap, headquarters of Nongoba Bullom chiefdom, where the usual address of welcome was made to the governor. The address made reference to the fact that the farmers engaged in rice cultivation had had a bad year and asked that in consideration of this government should agree to write off the ploughing fees still owing. This is the kind of exaggerated pessimism one expects from farmers the world over, and the agricultural officer and I agreed that although yields that year might have been a little lower than usual there was no justification for the allegation the farmers made that all their rice had been spoiled. In any event they must be prepared to take the good years with the bad and it was unreasonable to expect government to meet all the losses in a relatively bad year while the farmers kept all the profits in a good one. The governor agreed with us and gave a firm reply to the effect that government could not possibly agree to the write-off that was requested. Notwithstanding this reply, however, collecting ploughing fees continued to be difficult and it was necessary to take legal action to recover some of the money due.

Further up the river, at the small village of Messima, the agricultural officer and I said goodbye to the governor and disembarked. *Cara* went on to Gbundapi in Pujehun District, which the governor was visiting. At Messima, Turner's Peninsula was little more than 200 yards wide and in less than a minute we were standing on the Atlantic shore. Here we spent the night in a small rest house overlooking the ocean. This was the only time I ever visited Messima and I was able to capture there something of that peace of mind induced by the nearness of the ocean, idyllic surroundings and remoteness from civilization I had experienced at Dema. I was able to bask in the satisfaction of knowing that the governor's visit had gone off without any serious hitch so that I could resume my normal duties with a feeling of virtuous satisfaction. The next morning the two of us, with servants, were again able to use *Cara*, which called to collect us, and enjoy its comforts for the return journey to Bonthe. The governor would be continuing his travels from Gbundapi by road and no longer needed his launch.

In November the schools closed for the Christmas holidays, which were in the middle of the dry season, the longest break of the year. Several schools marked the occasion with performances, which I was expected to attend. They consisted of long programmes of recitations, sketches in English or Mende, songs and dances. The school halls were always packed and, while the audience might become restive during a dramatic representation of *Cinderella* or an extract from

Julius Caesar, they enjoyed the dancing and humorous sketches given in their own language. I was in a quandary when I received invitations for two events on the same night. If I had had more warning I would have asked the head teachers to change their dates to avoid a clash; there was so seldom entertainment of even a rudimentary kind in Bonthe that it was a great pity to have competing performances. However, it was too late to change anything, so I decided to divide the evening between the two, going first to the Minnie Mull Girls' High School, run by an American nonconformist mission and after the interval to the concert being given by the Roman Catholic Boys' School. Both the head teachers thought this was a good idea and the Irish father, after accepting my suggestion, added 'And if you care to come up to the house afterwards there'll be a drop of whisky for you and that's something you won't get from the Americans!' — all the American missions being notoriously teetotal.

I was working in my office one afternoon, pausing from time to time to contemplate the river at high tide lapping gently against the sea wall a few feet from the office window, when a message reached me from the manager of one of the French trading companies. 'Heard the news?' It read, 'The British and French have bombed Cairo and paratroops have landed in the Canal Zone.' He had heard this on his radio. I was aware that Nasser had nationalized the Suez Canal, but this news made me uneasy. I went to see my French friend to get more details. I found him in exuberant mood, delighted at this bold return to what he evidently perceived as the traditions of the *entente cordiale* and Anglo–French hegemony. I was unable to share his enthusiasm.

The Lebanese and Syrian traders in Bonthe were very worried because of their countries' close ties with Egypt and did not know where they stood. They were not at all anxious to be identified with Nasser and wanted to be left alone to carry on their peaceful trade. Their sentiments were wholly practical and one of them who had lived a long time in Sierra Leone brought to my office a hasty application for naturalization as a British subject. The British members of the European community treated the affair with some degree of levity and one or two of them frivolously offered their services as special constables in case I wished to arrest the Syrians! I had no powers to make such arbitrary arrests and would not have wished to exercise them if I had. The Suez crisis passed off without any repercussions for Sierra Leone, but it brought added prosperity on account of the great increase in the numbers of ships calling at Freetown for oil and other supplies, which were obliged to go round the Cape of Good Hope while the Suez Canal was closed.

Two other events stay in mind from my time in Bonthe, one tragic and the other frivolous. Late one afternoon I was on one of my launches going down the Jong River back to Bonthe after one of my many visits to Mattru when we came upon a launch that had very recently sunk and was just visible on its side where it had capsized. It had obviously been very crowded and the survivors were stranded on the bank to which they had managed to wade. A number of people had drowned in the accident and their bodies were trapped inside the launch. It was already getting dark so we picked up the survivors and took them with us on my launch.

Word about the sinking had already reached Bonthe and I arrived in darkness to find the local African police inspector ready on the quayside with some of his men, waiting to use my launch to go back up the river to try to bring out the corpses. I judged that this would be a perilous mission, involving diving under the water without the benefit of searchlights or any other form of lighting, and I suggested to him that he should instead leave at first light in the morning, a suggestion he accepted. I cannot now recall the exact numbers of those who had died, I think about 20. Late the following day the bodies were brought back and the medical officer had to carry out postmortem examinations. I saw some of the corpses being carried out of the hospital for burial and can still recall their pervasive and sickly sweet smell. This was not long before I left the district and I was unable to pursue the necessary coroner's inquest or any other investigations, but I served a notice under an ordinance relating to river traffic, requiring the owner to cause warning lights to be placed on the wreck.

The frivolous incident was a football match. One of the trading company managers accepted a challenge on behalf of the small European community from a team made up of more senior local schoolboys, without any consultation with any of us. We had no more than a few hours' notice that we were expected to turn out and face these young and athletic men without having had any opportunity to train or indeed to object to the fixture. I have never had any interest in or aptitude for football and was a most unwilling participant, but honour had to be obeyed. The result from our point of view was a disaster. None of us was particularly fit and if it had not been for the Irish father, who had some hitherto undiscovered talent as a goalkeeper, the score against our team would have been even more humiliating than it was. The match attracted a lot of attention from the people of Bonthe, who stood on the touchline and vigorously cheered the schoolboys. It was all good humoured, but not a glorious day for our team.

Early in January 1957 a telegram arrived summoning me to transfer to Kambia District in the Northern Province as soon as possible. I had already handed over the district to the regular district commissioner, Mike Westcott, who had returned from leave, and arranged to leave a day or two later. It was a long journey, starting off by launch to Mattru, then going diagonally across the country by road from southeast to northwest. I spent a night in Bo on the way as the guest of my friend and contemporary John Cook. This

was the last time I saw him as he died in mysterious circumstances a few months later. The next day I drove to Kambia,
a distance of 180 miles including a ferry crossing, which
made it a particularly long journey in Sierra Leone terms,
and arrived at 7.30 p.m. when it was already dark.

11

Kambia I

Kambia District was small, comprising only seven chiefdoms, and in the normal way did not have an assistant district commissioner. It had, however, been a major trouble spot in the Northern Province's riots of the previous year and normal administration had not yet been restored. The district was still unsettled and there was more work than one man could adequately manage.

It was generally considered isolated, 120 miles from Freetown along a road interrupted by the Mange Ferry, which had to be used to cross the wide and turbulent Great Scarcies River. In the rainy season the ferry was often out of action for weeks on end and at the best of times afforded a slow and laborious crossing. For long the DC had been the only senior government officer stationed there, now joined by myself as assistant and later by a permanent deputy superintendent of police. Before the riots an African inspector had commanded the police detachment in the district. There was no medical officer and the MO visited us occasionally from Port Loko, 40 miles away on the road to Freetown and on the other side of the ferry.

The district was a long, narrow strip of country straddling the banks of the Great Scarcies River and never more than 30 miles wide, running from northeast to southwest. The lower reaches of the river, below Kambia, were the richest of the rice growing areas in the country and one of the richest in West Africa. Rice was grown in the alluvial riverine swamps from which the mangrove trees had been cleared long ago. A rice research station had been set up at Rokupr, ten miles downstream from Kambia, and it carried out research into the breeding of rice for the benefit of Nigeria, Gambia and Ghana as well as Sierra Leone. Around Kambia in the northern part of the district there was undulating upland country, bush and grassland, much of it barren, and the poverty of this area contrasted strongly with the relative prosperity of the rice farmers down the river.

The western boundary of the district was also part of Sierra Leone's long international boundary with what was still at this time *French* Guinea, one of the eight territories of the former Afrique occidentale française. The river was the obvious boundary, but a large chunk of territory on the west bank of the river was within Sierra Leone, and the river became the boundary further upstream, northeast of Kambia. In the 1890s, when international frontiers came to be demarcated, the British exchanged the îles de Loos, on which Guinea's seaport and capital of Conakry now stands, for this piece of land. It was a curious bargain, but typical of the horse-trading in fragments of Africa that took place at that time.

The district, which marked the western extremity of Timne country and covered over half of Northern Province, contained a mixture of tribes. Two of the chiefdoms were Susu, a tribe domiciled mainly in Guinea, and one was mixed Timne and Susu. There was also one Limba chiefdom and there were pockets of Bulloms, a race of fishermen living on the coast at the mouth of the Great Scarcies.

At first I had to live in a rest house, as there was no other accommodation for me. The government reservation was on a plateau on top of a hill outside the town of Kambia. The district commissioner had a fine, modern, two-storeyed house, built a few years previously to replace an old one that had collapsed. There were two rest houses and another permanent house intended for a medical officer, which I subsequently occupied. Some 200 yards away was the usual group of administrative buildings — the DC's office, court *barri* and district lockup. The laterite road that led down from the DC's house to the office was lined on both sides with a carefully tended hedgerow and an avenue of flam- boyants. These trees, known in India as gulmohrs, put forth a vivid red blossom for a few weeks a year during the dry season, and a whole line of them created at that time a beautiful display. Like many other stations, Kambia had had much loving care from successive district commissioners, many of whom took a keen interest in landscape gardening and in making their stations attractive oases of beauty in the middle of the unruly African bush.

Kambia was my first truly 'bush' station. Bonthe was small, but had a number of Europeans, and I was never lonely there. At Kambia, however, for much of the time the DC, Mike Sandercock, and I had the station to ourselves, and when one of us went on trek the other was very much alone. There was no electricity and I soon became accustomed to dining every evening by the light of hissing pressure lamps.

One consolation I had was that all the chiefdoms were accessible by road and the roads were good by Sierra Leone standards, as little traffic used them; this meant that I could now use my car regularly, whereas in Bonthe it had had to be kept in Mattru and was only rarely usable, as most of my travelling was by launch. Here also the district commissioner had a launch, which was frequently used for treks down the river. Kambia originally owed its importance as a trading centre to its being the head of navigation on the Great Scarcies, just as Mattru was on the Jong River, though in the dry season it was accessible only at high tide.

Rokupr, some miles downstream, could be reached at any stage of the tide throughout the year, and had outstripped Kambia in its importance for trade. Most of its trade was in the hands of a Swiss company, owned by the Galfettis, a family of Swiss–Italian brothers that had been established in Sierra Leone for more than 30 years. They were good businessmen with an intimate knowledge of the country and its people. All of them could speak Susu and Timne fluently, as well as English and its Creole offshoot, Italian, French and German. They performed a valuable service to the small European community by bringing up from Freetown tinned goods, fresh vegetables and other products not normally available in the protectorate.

The Cox Commission had long since published its report into the disturbances in the Northern Province generally, but inquiries into allegations of misrule and oppression by individual paramount chiefs were still continuing to determine whether removal from office or some lesser punishment was merited. When I arrived in Kambia, Sir Harold Willan, a former chief justice from Malaya, was in the middle of investigating the conduct of the paramount chief of Mambolo chiefdom, having completed several other inquiries. Meanwhile, normal administration was at a standstill in all but one chiefdom in the district. No taxes had been collected for two years and the chiefdoms were being supported by government loans, which were unlikely ever to be repaid. The district council, dependent on chiefdom taxes for its revenues, was in a similar plight.

There had been no major disturbances since the end of the riots the previous year, but the chiefdoms were divided into bitterly opposed factions and occasional clashes could not be avoided. The police had been strengthened and a number of posts set up in Samu chiefdom on the west bank of the river, where the troubles had been particularly virulent. A most unpleasant incident here, which had no parallel in anything that happened elsewhere, was the murder of three policemen towards the end of the riots. They were taken prisoner by the rioters, tied to stakes driven into the river bed at low tide and left there to drown as the tide rose. Theirs must have been a horrible death. The leader of those responsible had been identified, but he had escaped into French Guinea and his whereabouts were not known.

At the time of my arrival in Kambia, the government's work was confined to maintaining an uneasy peace and dealing with complaints. No major settlement was possible until the commissioners investigating the conduct of individual paramount chiefs in the district had finished their inquiries and the government had decided what action to take on their recommendations. I found it difficult to understand why there had been so much urgency about my transfer from Bonthe. On my first day in the office the DC suggested that I could usefully occupy myself by writing the annual report for the district for 1956. This was a chore few administrative officers liked, for it meant a great deal of research into files, compiling statistics and much writing. For me it had some value as it gave me the opportunity to find out what had been happening in the district during a crucial year. I worked at the report by fits and starts over the next few weeks in intervals between more pressing duties.

After I had been in Kambia for a few weeks Mike Sandercock asked me to visit Forecariah, the nearest district headquarters in French Guinea, in order to make contact with the *commandant du cercle*, our opposite number there. The commandant had written some time before inviting Mike to visit, but he had been unable to take advantage of the invitation and in any event preferred to send me because I could speak French.

I left one morning, accompanied by an office messenger in uniform to make it clear that I had some official status. I first had to cross the ferry at Kambia and the frontier was eight miles further on the other side of the river, marked by a large sign on the side of the road, put up by our Public Works Department. On our side was the legend, 'FRENCH

GUINEA — KEEP TO THE RIGHT' and on the other, 'SIERRA LEONE — TENEZ A GAUCHE'. The road was so narrow that it was not possible to drive anywhere but in the middle, but the warning was necessary. Even so, accidents occasionally happened when a vehicle near the frontier moved over to the wrong side of the road and had a head-on collision with another vehicle coming in the opposite direction.

There was a customs post and road barrier at Pamelap, the first town in Guinea, but after I had explained who I was and said that I was going to see the commandant, I was allowed to go through without hindrance. Some miles further on, there was yet another post, at Mellikuri, but here again I was not held up. With no passport and no papers for the car I must have been guilty of several offences at once, but no one seemed to mind as I was on an official visit. After Mellikuri the road was excellent. It was unsurfaced laterite, the same as the roads in Sierra Leone, but wide, well aligned and obviously maintained by a mechanical grader, unlike our roads, which were maintained entirely by labourers with hand tools. I was able to travel at a good speed without slowing down or stopping when a vehicle came in the opposite direction, as one normally had to do in Sierra Leone.

There was a perceptible change in the landscape and vegetation soon after one entered Guinea. There was little dense bush and much open grassland, and on both sides of the road were many acres of well-kept banana plantations. Bananas were an important cash crop in Guinea and some of the bigger plantations were owned by Europeans, many of whom had been in the country for two generations and looked on it as their home. Other plantations were owned by Lebanese and Africans. It was a well-organized and prosperous industry. An unsuccessful attempt to start similar plantations in Sierra Leone had foundered some years before.

The main obstacle to development of this kind was the system of land tenure in the protectorate, which vested all land in the tribal authorities in trust for the people of their respective chiefdoms. No individual freehold title was recognized by law and the best form of tenure trading companies and other non-Africans could obtain was a not very secure lease of 50 years at the most. The intentions behind the law were good, as it was designed to protect the rights of African farmers and make it impossible for them to sell their land; in theory at least it prevented the growth of a class of landless peasants. It was, however, a major impediment to agricultural progress as no company or individual would contemplate investment in land with such a limited tenure. Consequently, agriculture was left to the ordinary farmers with their traditional and wasteful methods.

Forecariah was 30 miles from Kambia, very like any other small West African town, with its corrugated-iron roofs and nondescript houses and stores, but one touch, which made it refreshingly different, was a small bistro, with tables on a veranda outside, run by a Frenchman. The approach to the commandant's office was along a broad straight avenue, lined on both sides with tall trees, reminiscent of a small French town. The office was a long, single-storeyed building with a crowd of petitioners and uniformed guards on the veranda. It might well have been a district office in Sierra Leone but for the tricolour fluttering on top of the flagstaff.

I introduced myself to the commandant, a middle-aged Martinican who had been in the French overseas civil service for 20 years. Before the war he had been in Indo-China, a posting once much sought after by French administrators. He had recently been transferred from Fort Lamy in Niger, not far from Maiduguri in Northern Nigeria. He introduced me to his adjoint or assistant, an army captain in uniform, seconded to the administration. This was mainly a courtesy visit, but I took the opportunity to discuss security problems with him, particularly the situation in Samu. This chiefdom had been divided into two when the British and French settled their frontier in the nineteenth century, and there was a canton of the same name in Guinea. The people on both sides of the border were Susu and closely related to each other.

I accepted an invitation to lunch and was escorted across to the commandant's residence, an imposing building set in the middle of a well-kept garden. Madame Jalton, the commandant's wife, was away, and his 18-year-old daughter Colette, a charming and attractive young woman, acted as hostess. I had expected to be offered a Dubonnet or similar aperitif before lunch, but to my surprise my host suggested whisky. Notwithstanding the reputation of the French as wine drinkers, in my experience they are very fond of whisky. I had brought a bottle with me as a present, as it was difficult to obtain and expensive in Guinea. I always adhered to the colonial tradition of not drinking whisky until after sundown and I therefore asked instead for beer. After an excellent lunch, the commandant suggested that I might like to see something of Forecariah and its immediate surroundings and said that his daughter would be pleased to act as my guide while he went back to the office.

There was little to see in the town so we went to a banana plantation kept by a Frenchman. We walked around it and looked at the hundreds of banana trees planted in neat, orderly rows, with drainage channels between them, and looked also at a field of pineapples. As an indication of the painstaking care taken of these valuable crops, every individual plant had to be kept covered with a handful of grass to protect it from the fierce rays of the sun, which would otherwise cause it to dry up and wither — and the one field I saw had thousands of plants in it. I was told something of the speed and organization that were needed when bananas were being shipped. When it was known that the banana boat was expected in Conakry, cutting would begin immediately and the stems would be packed into lorries and sent off as soon as they were cut. It was necessary to load them onto the ship and into the refrigerated holds within 36 hours of cutting; otherwise they would rot. At that time of course refrigerated road vehicles were unknown, at least in West Africa.

From this and subsequent meetings with Monsieur Jalton I realized that the French colonial administrators had status and privileges denied to us. British colonial governments always had some residual misgivings about delegating too much authority to district commissioners as their local representatives, though in most colonies this was the only practical form of administration. The French on the other hand never had such qualms, having had from the days of Napoleon all-powerful prefects in the departments of metropolitan France. Administrators in a French territory had a much higher status than the specialist officers of the agriculture, forestry, public works and other departments; they were employed and paid from Paris and had a more generous leave allowance than the rest. They exercised direct control over the police and other organs of government operating within their circles. Such customary chiefs as were retained by the French were treated as minor functionaries and could be removed by the commandant at will.

There were no native courts other than one for the circle, over which the commandant, assisted if need be by assessors, presided. His position can best be compared with that of the district collector in British India, who as a member of the Indian civil service enjoyed many privileges that were denied to departmental officials, and had wide powers within his district. By comparison, the British administrative officer had a very lowly status. He was on the same salary scale as departmental officers, had poorer chances of promotion than most of these and had no special perquisites or privileges. Furthermore, such powers as he was entitled to exercise were circumscribed and looked upon with ever increasing suspicion by the rising class of African politicians.

The French empire in Africa was a very different creation from our own haphazard collection of territories, acquired in a fit of absent-mindedness. The French appear to have a taken a pride in ruling over a huge area of the continent and to have regarded themselves as the modern successors of the Romans. The sheer extent of their former African colonies was impressive, stretching from the Mediterranean to the Congo and from Dakar on the Atlantic to the borders of the Sudan. The territories of French West Africa and of French Equatorial Africa were administered as unities from Dakar and Brazzaville respectively, sending deputies to the legislature in Paris and forming parts of that homogeneous entity, *la France d'outre-mer*.

French influence was much more pervasive in Africa than ever British influence was in our colonies. Frenchmen were to be found living in out-of-the-way places, doing humble jobs, running garages, driving buses and working as waiters in hotels. Settlers in small numbers were permitted and do not appear to have created any racial problem such as used to bedevil those British territories, Kenya in particular, where European settlers were allowed.

In British West African colonial territories settlement was not allowed, rights to the land being reserved for the natives, namely the indigenous peoples of the Protectorate, as explained earlier. The French took their colonies much more seriously than we took ours; they not only invested substantially in them but also even contributed from metropolitan funds to the costs of administration. British policy on the other hand, to the extent that there could be said to be any policy at all, was to require each colony, no matter how small and poor, to manage as a self-sufficient unit. The French could therefore say with some justice that we were not making any sacrifice in giving our colonies independence, as we had never invested in them. They on the other hand were virtually compelled to follow our example by making their colonies independent or face the opprobrium of the rest of the world and in so doing to throw away a great heritage and abandon a civilizing mission — perfidious Albion again.

In 1957 Guinea, in common with the other French territories in Africa, was still a closely controlled colony with no elected legislature and no ministers to whom any share of the responsibilities of government had been transferred. In 1958 revolutionary changes took place following the coming to power of General de Gaulle and the September referendum. In this Guinea said 'no' to the proposed constitution of the Fifth Republic and was given immediate independence. Such dramatic events could hardly have been foreseen 18 months earlier.

* * *

The social life of Kambia was severely limited but friendly. Mike Sandercock and I inevitably saw a great deal of each other both in the office and off duty and it was fortunate that we got on well together. When I had been there five months he was joined by his wife Helen and one of his two sons, who was not yet at the age when it was necessary for him to be left behind in England for his education. We were regular visitors to the Rice Research Station at Rokupr, ten miles or so away by road and staffed by a number of young expatriate scientists, all of whom had their wives with them. It was here that for the first and last time in my life I attempted to play golf. The station covered a large area and a rough-and-ready nine-hole course had been laid out on the undulating parkland created by clearing the bush. It was provided with a respectable number of hazards such as ravines and clumps of tall trees between tee and green. There were six or seven of us who played regularly, including some of the wives, and we shared the two available sets of clubs between us. I was never a great games player and did not discover any hidden talent for golf. I would be ashamed to admit the number of strokes per hold I took and I often lost count of my score.

In addition to golf we played tennis and also spent many happy evenings playing poker, pontoon and other unintellectual card games. There was some shooting to be had for those keen enough to own shotguns. Guinea fowl, pigeon, small deer, fretambo and other small game could be shot in the upland area around Kambia and the Great Scarcies offered wild duck. (This part of Africa has no big game. Leopards and wild boar are occasionally killed and from time to time marauding elephants may be hunted, but the vegetation is usually too dense for large mammals.) The river was a fruitful fishing ground, and sometimes when travelling by launch I tried trailing a baited hook and line from the stern. All that happened, however, was that the line broke as a result of the tension caused by the speed of the launch.

In February the commissioners' reports into the conduct of the paramount chiefs of four of our chiefdoms were published, along with the government's decisions on their recommendations. One chief was deposed, another was permitted to resign his office and a third was indefinitely suspended. The chief in Samu, Yumkella by name and with a worse reputation for extortion and maladministration than any other, was for inexplicable reasons exonerated by the commissioner, but the government at least recognized that this astonishing verdict was unlikely to be popular with large sections of the people in his chiefdom. He accordingly retained his office but was required for the time being to refrain from exercising his functions as chief until a chiefdom court could begin to operate and the tribal authority could be reorganized. Samu continued to be a trouble spot and police posts had to continue being maintained in all main towns of the chiefdom.

Regent chiefs, who would hold office pending the election

of paramount chiefs, were elected in the three chiefdoms other than Samu. Logically, our next step should have been to set about restoring normal chiefdom administration, which would be a long and laborious business. We were, however, faced with a more pressing task, which could not be post-poned, the holding of Sierra Leone's first general election under the recently introduced revised constitution. Hitherto, the Legislative Council had had elected members from the colony, and protectorate representatives had been nomin-ated by the district councils. The chief secretary, chief com-missioner for the protectorate, attorney general, financial secretary and other senior officials were also members. Now the council was to be renamed the House of Representatives, in which there would be no officials; all the members of the house for the colony and protectorate were to be elected by popular franchise, except for 12 paramount chiefs who would continue to be nominated by the district councils and two members nominated by the governor to represent com-mercial interests. Each district of the protectorate was to have two single-member constituencies. The franchise was substantially the same as that for the district council elections that had been held in 1956.

The two Kambia constituencies were known as Kambia west and east, consisting respectively of the riverine and upland chiefdoms. Voters' lists presented a problem, as there had been no tax assessments for the past two years and the available lists were likely to be far from accurate. However, there was no time for the major task of revision and we had to hope for the best. In Samu the tax rolls had been des-troyed in the course of the riots and early in the year a special team of government clerks and others had been sent round the chiefdom to prepare a list. This was a long and expensive operation, but the result was the most accurate and up-to-date voters' list in the district.

A particular day was appointed for the nomination of candidates and the regulations provided that no nominations could be accepted after 4.00 p.m. One would-be candidate for Kambia West turned up at the district office just before 4.00 p.m. and was unable to get her nomination paper or have her deposit paid into the sub-treasury. She was a Creole lady from Freetown and was most indignant when I told her that she was too late. For half an hour the office was the scene of an angry tirade by this lady and her supporters, but there was nothing we could do except advise her to wait until next time and try to be more prompt in filing her nomination paper. She returned to Freetown and later protested to the governor, but he was unable to help her.

The general election presented again most of the problems I had already experienced when running the district council elections in Bonthe. Shortage of suitable polling station staff and police made it necessary to have two polling days, one in each constituency, with a gap of two days between them. Lectures had to be given to the clerks and others who were to run the stations to make sure that they were familiar with their duties. Our clerks spent long hours typing out copies of voters' lists and other essential documents. Ballot boxes had to be prepared and stocks of numbered ballot papers and other stationery carefully checked to see that nothing was missing that would be needed on the two days. All the staff involved had to work under pressure at a pace to which they were not accustomed and I had to stand over them, goading them on to maintain their efforts. This slave driving of staff unused to long hours and concentrated effort was the most exhausting part of the preparations.

Planning the two polling days and the subsequent counting of votes was like drawing up orders for a minor military operation. I worked out the polling stations for each constituency and sent out notices all over the district announcing where they were to be and which sections of the chiefdoms in which they were located were to vote there. As far as possible I made sure that no one would have too far to walk to vote. As the time drew nearer I allocated the staff to the stations, one presiding officer and one polling assistant to each. These officials had to go to their stations either the previous day or two days before polling day, so as to arrange the hire of a house or other suitable building and prepare their stations for inspection by the assistant returning officers.

I had been promised one government lorry, which would be sent up from Freetown, and was authorized to hire others as necessary. I drew up an elaborate transport schedule whereby each lorry would take the staff for specified stations, wait at a given place and bring back the staff and ballot boxes when polling was over. The launch was used for some of the stations on the river and some staff had to walk to the more remote stations. I had several conferences with the local police superintendent and with the senior government officers, mainly from the Rice Research Station, who were to act as assistant returning officers and take responsibility for a number of polling stations each.

For each station a parcel of necessary materials had to be made up, comprising voters' lists for the villages using that station, ballot boxes, an adequate number of ballot papers, copies of instructions, sealing wax, rubber stamps, pencils and other articles. It was important that nothing should be missing from these parcels and I personally checked every one before handing it over to the presiding officer. The lorries filled up one by one with the people assigned to them; I called the roll and sped them on their way. The next day I inspected the polling stations I was personally supervising to make sure that all was in order and called on the assistant returning officers looking after other stations to see whether they had encountered any difficulties.

Polling days went as well as could be expected. The district's roads were probably busier than they had ever been before, with assistant returning officers, police, candidates and their agents rushing from place to place. One of the Kambia West candidates was a Freetown contractor and had brought several of his lorries to take his supporters to the poll. There were one or two arguments between agents who wanted to inspect the ballot boxes after voting had started and presiding officers who rightly refused to allow them.

At a station down river from Rokupr the presiding officer found that some pages of his voters' lists were missing and had to face an angry mob of villagers who belonged to the anti-chief faction and suspected that some trick was being played to prevent them from exercising their votes. I received word of this from the assistant returning officer responsible and rushed to Rokupr as soon as I could find a spare copy of the list. At Rokupr wharf I met the presiding officer, a schoolteacher, getting off a launch with the rest of the staff of the station. He had become scared of the mob and was unwilling to return. I had no time to argue and handed him the list I had brought and ordered him to return to his station immediately.

Counting could not take place in Kambia West until the following evening, as one of the stations was in a remote village up one of the creeks, not accessible by road, and the ballot boxes were not brought back from there until the afternoon of the next day. We eventually started the count in the district *barri* at 7.00 p.m. by the light of pressure lamps, with a large crowd watching. The counting ended and the result was announced just before 11.00 p.m.

This of course was only the first round, ending on a Saturday night. I was obliged to call in the flagging office staff for a few hours on Sunday morning to prepare parcels of materials for the Kambia East elections. They came a little unwillingly, some of them complaining that the work was killing them. I tried to console and encourage them by telling them that this was part of the price of democracy. On Monday the same routine of handing out parcels and dispatching lorries was followed and polling took place on Tuesday. In this constituency all the stations could be reached by road, and we were able to count and declare a result the same evening.

The following day Mike Sandercock closed the office at 10.00 a.m. to give the office staff and ourselves a much needed rest. All that now remained to be done was to parcel up all the ballot papers and other documents and send them off to the election officer in Freetown. I also had to write a report on the election.

Psephologists have written many learned articles and books on running British-style elections in underdeveloped countries. An outstanding feature of doing so is the huge cost, a serious matter in a country with only meagre resources. The cost was probably comparable with that of a Western country because of the large territorial area a thinly populated rural constituency covers, necessitating numerous polling stations and much travelling. In the district council elections the cost was borne by government, for some of the councils would have been bankrupted if they had had to foot the bill. Elective democracy is an expensive luxury.

I was in charge of all the preparations for the general election and had control of the funds allocated for meeting election expenses in the district. Allowances for the extra work involved had to be paid on a generous scale to the staff and lorries had to be hired at great cost. I found myself obliged to spend public money with a gay abandon that normally would have brought down on my head the wrath of the audit department and the accountant general in a very short time. Expenditure of public money was tightly controlled by a host of regulations, which officers responsible for spending ignored at their peril. Few were able to obtain all the funds they needed to do their jobs properly and the most parsimonious management was necessary at all times. When it came to financing elections, however, the normal canons of caution were relaxed and we had no difficulty getting whatever money we needed.

Another striking feature of the conduct of these elections was the strain they put on the machinery of government, never too robust at the best of times. In the weeks before polling, almost all our time was taken up with preparatory work, to the neglect of other tasks of routine administration, and for five days the work of other government departments was disrupted because their staffs were engaged on polling duties. The police too had their manpower strained to the limit by providing staff for duty at the many polling stations while trying at the same time to keep a minimum number of men on essential regular duties.

Polling was generally low in the protectorate and in few districts did more than 50 per cent of the voters on the lists register their votes. Of those who did, probably very few realized the true meaning of a secret ballot. The traditional African method of election or of dealing with any contentious matter is to gather together to hang heads (this is an expression translated literally from the Mende *'wu hitie'*) and after heated discussion reach a unanimous decision. This practice was adapted to modern times by having meetings before polling day of all the voters of a village who would agree, were it not already a foregone conclusion, on the candidate for whom they would vote; later they would walk to the polling station in a body to register their ostensibly secret votes.

I found my car indispensable for the management of the elections and logged more than 1000 miles during May 1957, a high mileage for a district in which the furthest motorable point from headquarters was only 47 miles. Already the car was beginning to suffer from travelling on bad roads. The door catches had become faulty and I was unable to close the rear doors properly. The suspension left much to be desired and during my stay in the district I broke two rear springs. The car bounced excessively on particularly bad patches of road and the sump frequently hit the ground.

I knew nothing about cars before I came to own one, but in these surroundings I had perforce to learn to carry out my own maintenance. I became adept at using the grease gun, changing the engine oil, adjusting valve rocker settings and plug gaps, topping up the battery, cleaning the terminals and other odd jobs. It was dirty work, usually reserved for Sunday mornings while it was still cool, and at the end I would be covered with oil, grease, mud and sweat. I have never been a practical minded man and the completion of a thorough servicing gave me a degree of satisfaction out of all proportion to my modest achievements.

Now that the general election was over it was time for us to resume our normal work and catch up on arrears. In particular, it was important to make a start on the collection of local tax, already delayed a year because of the riots. Although this was in theory and by law a function of the tribal authority in which the district commissioner played very little part, in practice very close supervision was still needed. We decided to begin in Tonko Limba chiefdom, which had been less affected by the disturbances than any other in the district. The Limba were known as palm wine tappers and carried on this trade all over the country. They were less inclined to active political intrigue than some of the other tribes.

The beginning of my trek was a minor disaster, illustrative of the many hazards a European working in out-of-the-way corners has to face. I was staying in a rest house that belonged to the Public Works Department, used from time to time by engineers inspecting roads and bridges. It was partly furnished, not usual for a rest house away from a government station. This was almost the end of May and the rains, which usually arrived in early April, had not yet broken. The countryside was parched and burned. On the first afternoon of my trek, however, not long after my servants had unpacked and set up my camp bed, there was a cloudburst and torrents of rain began to fall. The rest house had a thatched roof, which gave me no protection, and it was not long before the rooms were half an inch deep in water. I soon realized that I would have to evacuate the place, but my lorry had long since gone back to Kambia, over 20 miles away, and I could not get all my loads, plus interpreter, messenger and servants into my car.

I had not come prepared for rain so in going out to get into the car I simply had to get wet. I started off down the road, hoping to find a lorry I could hire. To add to my problems, one of the fuses had blown and the windscreen wipers were not working. I had to get out of the car at the paramount chief's town to tell the chief that I was leaving the rest house, and again to ask a lorry driver if he would agree to collect my loads. By the time I had arranged for a lorry and arrived back at the rest house I was thoroughly soaked and miserable. The only dry place was the kitchen in a small outhouse behind the main building. It also had a thatched roof, but as it regularly had a fire lit, this had dried out the thatch and prevented it from rotting. My cook had kept a fire going and I was grateful for its warmth.

I loaded as many of my personal belongings as possible into the car and set off for Kambia with my two servants, leaving the other members of my party to wait for the lorry and return in it with the remaining loads. I continued my business in Tonko Limba by travelling out to the chiefdom each day by car. This was not the most satisfactory way of dealing with chiefdom affairs, as it limited contacts to working hours and prevented an administrative officer from keeping his ear to the ground to the extent considered desirable, but at least I had a good roof over my head every night.

12

Kambia II

S upervision of tax collection was a tedious but essential chore, and during the next two months we were able to get in most of the tax for all the chiefdoms except the much-troubled Samu. For some time we had become aware of a mounting number of disputes over the ownership of land and at one time I had at least 30 on my list. The lack of properly functioning native courts made it necessary for us to deal with these ourselves, though until tax collection was completed it was not possible to make a start. Soon after I took up my duties in Kambia I had dealt with two upland bush disputes involving small areas of land. Most of the disputes were about the much more fertile and valuable alluvial rice swamps on the lower reaches of the Great Scarcies and they usually had a political complexion in that the parties represented pro-chief and anti-chief factions.

Unsettled land disputes were always a threat to the peace, and I began to deal with these as soon as I was free from other work, even though it was by now the height of the rainy season and not a good time of the year for walking around swamp farms. I had to stay in small villages reached by launch, on foot or a combination of both. There were no rest houses in the villages and I would send a messenger ahead of me to make sure that a suitable house was vacated for my use. Rest houses were invariably located on the edge of towns or villages to provide a little privacy, a luxury I had to forgo on these visits. I came to appreciate more than ever how much a DC needed to have a disciplined body of men under his control to provide such assistance in the manner of the former Court Messenger Force, for administrative officers often had to dispense justice under difficult conditions. Preparation of suitable accommodation, maintenance of order among crowds gathered for the hearing of a dispute and supervision of the cutting of a boundary were all tasks that needed the help of people who had some understanding of the substance of such disputes and of the steps needed to bring about peaceful settlements.

For keeping order I was able to call on the police, though the constables were not always happy about soiling their shiny boots in the mud of the swamps. The other tasks were beyond the normal competence of the police, but fortunately we had at the district office two messengers who had been members of the Court Messenger Force up to the time of its disbandment and who were familiar with the routine of land disputes. When the first complaint was made by one of the parties that the other party was unlawfully farming or otherwise making use of his land, I would send one of the messengers to investigate briefly and 'flag' the land in dispute. This involved sticking a pole into the ground in a conspicuous spot with a large piece of white cloth tied to the top of it, a conventional indication that no one was allowed to carry out any farming operation until the case had been settled. I also took one messenger with me for the actual hearing of the dispute.

I would begin by hearing evidence from both sides. It was always difficult on this basis alone to decide who had the just claim. In many cases the quarrel would be between competing sets of cousins with differing political allegiances who were closely related to each other and lived in neighbouring villages. Sometimes evidence would come to light that a subchief had intervened by awarding the land to a relative or supporter, regardless of the strength of any claim. One bogus claim was historically interesting in that the status of slavery was material to it. Slavery had not been finally abolished in Sierra Leone until 1926, and one of the complaints made in the course of the 1956 disturbances was that the chiefs were trying again to make slaves of their people. In this case it was alleged that an ancestor who had died many years before had left the land to his slave to look after for him; it was also alleged that he had written down instructions for the eventual disposal of the land and that the slave had deliberately destroyed the document and kept the land, which the descendants were now claiming.

The issue of written documents was irrelevant, for customary African law did not recognize any form of testamentary disposition of land or any other property. The story of the slave holding the land as a trustee was most improbable and the claim of the descendants of the original 'testator' was fictitious. I had no difficulty in disposing of the case and awarding the land to the other party. In this, as in so many other cases, the losing side did not mind losing so long as the winning side agreed to swear on African medicines that they had a right to the land; no one ever refused to swear. When swearing was agreed I would ask each side to deposit £5 or some other suitable sum towards the cost of obtaining the medicine, and would then arrange for someone to be sent to the home of one of the well-known medicine men in the protectorate. Its keeper would eventually bring the medicine and both parties would assemble on the land for the ceremony, with myself as witness.

The medicine would usually be a basin full of all kinds of ritual objects such as a leopard's teeth and bottles of mixtures of herbs with supposed magical properties. First the keeper would speak to the medicine and explain the nature of the case for which it had been brought. The leader of the winning side would then take a handful of piassava stalks or a large feather with which he would repeatedly tap the medicine and repeat an oath such as, 'if it is not true that this land belonged to my father and now belongs to me and the members of my family, may this medicine kill me.' This was sometimes followed by the sacrifice of a chicken, which would have its head severed over the medicine and its blood would be allowed to drip into the basin. The final part of the ceremony would consist of the oath-taker swallowing a vile mixture of unleavened dough and some nameless liquid as an earnest of his being bound by the oath. Then would often ensue an argument over the period for which the medicine should be deemed effective. It was important to agree on this, for if the oath-taker died within the effective period the losing party could then claim the land as theirs. Usually a period of not longer than six months was fixed.

The reader may have certain preconceived notions of the electric atmosphere of ceremonies of this kind, derived from television films and plays, or descriptions in novels. Fancy conjures up an awesome gathering around a fire at dead of night, presided over by an all-powerful and malevolent sorcerer in elaborate garb and headdress, muttering arcane incantations and holding his audience in a spell of terrified fascination. The drums begin to beat in a steadily quickening rhythm and the listeners stand up and begin to gyrate around the fire, a circle of half-naked black bodies streaming with sweat, dancing an unholy conga. The pace begins to become hotter and the dancers work themselves into a frenzy.

But the reality as I experienced it was lacking in outward drama. The ceremonies tended to become disorderly and I would deliberately interfere as little as possible, preferring to let the parties to the dispute and the medicine keeper settle their own procedural wrangles. I had, after all, performed my own function of adjudicating on the dispute and my presence at the ceremony was necessary only to be a witness and to make sure that it took place without the parties coming to blows. The proceedings were little more dignified than an everyday squabble in the marketplace and would not have been thought remarkable by any casual, unin-structed observer. Their power was to be sought, not in any physical manifestation of ecstasy or terror, but rather in the minds of the participants, imbued as they had been all their lives with a fear of the supernatural, and innocent of any sophisticated notions about the logical causes of natural events.

I could have refused to countenance this piece of ritual, as I had used the district commissioner's statutory authority to hear the dispute and my order had the force of law, but it was conducive to peace and good order to accept it. One or two enlightened people to whom I have described this pro-cedure have expressed astonishment that we availed our-selves of so primitive a way of reinforcing legally binding decisions and appear to give official blessing to sanctions based on superstition. There is some force in such criticism, but much could be said in defence of the use of swearing on medicines in cases of this kind. First, their use is consonant with customary law, which we were required to follow in adjudicating on cases between natives. Second, it was acceptable to both parties. Third, it was effective; Africans generally feared an oath on strong medicine far more than any bailiff or policeman. Finally, we were trying to keep the peace in difficult circumstances and with inadequate resources in a country where communications were poor. Any effi-cacious means of seeing that an order made at the end of a land case would be respected without the need to send police to enforce it was welcome, ethical and other objections notwithstanding.

In most of these cases there was no need to divide the land because the decision was normally that it belonged to one or other party, subject to the swearing having taken place. For record purposes, it was necessary for me to make a detailed sketch plan of the land. This involved pacing the boundary from corner to corner and checking the direction of the boundary line with the aid of a prismatic compass. Proper surveys were never made in land disputes because it was impossible to finding qualified surveyors, whose services would in any event have been prohibitively expensive for ordinary African peasants, and a rough-and-ready survey of this kind was adequate for the purpose of recording and defining the boundary. Usually trees would be planted or piles of stones placed on corners, and these would be referred to in the description and sketch plan that eventually found their way into the formal record known as the District Decree Book after the provincial commissioner had confirmed the decision of the DC or ADC, as required by the Protectorate Ordinance, the source of the powers under which we acted.

Walking around swamps in the course of adjudicating on these disputes was tiring, as at almost every step one sank into the mud a foot or more. I was well protected by a pair of gumboots and admired the hardiness of the Susu, who at this time of the year were busy transplanting their seedlings from upland nurseries into their swamps. It was common to see groups of men and women on cold and miserable days, hard at work on their farms, almost naked beneath a heavy downpour and up to their knees in thick, oozy mud. I sometimes reflected that if I or any other European had tried to emulate them we would have been dead in a few days.

There were some interesting trends in the development of African land tenure on the banks of the Great Scarcies. Its alluvial swamps were probably the most valuable agricultural land in Sierra Leone, and it was not surprising that wealthy men should try to acquire a dominant interest in them. Traditionally, customary law did not recognize any form of individual ownership and land was held on a communal, village or family basis. A widespread practice had, however, grown up of pledging land as security for a loan of money, and the pledgee usually took possession of the land

and cultivated it. Few farmers were ever able to repay loans obtained in this way and the pledge became a *de facto* alienation, which defeated the rights of the pledgor's heirs. Pledgees held large areas of swamp along the Great Scarcies. It was but one step from pledge to outright sale, and I frequently heard statements that one party had sold a particular swamp to another. Such a sale was impossible according to *Native Law and Custom of Sierra Leone*, the standard work of reference written by a long retired provincial commissioner called Fenton, but practice was developing ahead of traditional customary law and it seemed to me that in time individual title would have to be recognized.

The peculiarities of land tenure inevitably had a political significance. Many of the farmers in Kambia District, whether holding by pledge or by hereditary and customary title, were wealthy men, able to afford the luxury of an independent outlook. Some of them were not natives of the chiefdom in which their land was situated and visited the land only at the times of planting and harvesting. It was from these farmers that much opposition to the chiefs came.

My interest in customary land law grew as I dealt with more of these cases. It seemed to me doubtful that the traditional native courts in the troubled areas would ever again be able to sit effectively in judgment on land disputes, as they had a bad record and there was no prospect of any quick improvement in their standing in the eyes of the local populace. A basic problem was that it was almost impossible to find impartial court members, since most members of the tribal authority from whom they were chosen would be either interested parties or related to such parties. At the same time it was too much to ask that administrative officers should have the task of adjudicating on all land cases; this would have meant an appreciable increase in their numbers, which would have been politically unacceptable.

I made bold to suggest, in a memorandum to the provincial commissioner, that it was time to give serious thought to the best way of dealing with land litigation and that the first necessary step was to take it away from the jurisdiction of the native courts. Since there were 12 paramount chiefs in the new House of Representatives, all of them supporters of the government party, I realized that this revolutionary suggestion had little hope of finding favour. I went on to propose that a land causes tribunal be established for dealing with these cases, which would continue to be decided in accordance with African law and custom. Administrative officers would need to exercise the powers of the tribunal in their own districts, but I envisaged that ultimately a tribunal presided over by trained adjudicators would be able to handle all land disputes.

I limited my proposal to making recommendations only on procedure, apart from saying that the tribunals should apply African law and custom. I said also, however, that some reform was needed to bring land law into line with modern conditions, create some form of recorded individual title and make land more readily saleable. I did not presume to make any recommendations for substantive reform, which would need to be preceded by prolonged study by experts. In retrospect, this was a bold and impertinent proposal to be produced by a young administrative officer with only four years' experience, and if my proposals had been taken seriously and pursued they might well have resulted in some form of recorded title, but most probably would have resulted also in a takeover of much land in the protectorate by wealthier people and the creation of a large class of landless peasantry. I have no idea whether any kind of land law reform has been undertaken by the government of Sierra Leone as an independent nation in the past 40 years, but I suspect that the general chaos and anarchy, which have plagued the country for so long, cannot have been conducive to any kind of reform that may have been attempted.

13

Of Crocodiles

The value of the traditional office of coroner, an ancient British institution, was once questioned by Sir Alan Herbert in one of the fictitious and amusing cases in his satirical series *Uncommon Law: A Selection of Misleading Cases*. I am inclined to agree with him that there is nothing a coroner can do about cases of violent or suspicious death that cannot be done just as effectively and to better purpose by an efficient police CID. It is up to the police to start investigations into deaths in the first place, and they have to produce witnesses and other evidence from which the coroner, with or without a jury, is required to ascertain the cause of death. If the coroner reaches the conclusion that there may have been foul play, then he must adjourn the inquest and ask the police to pursue their investigations with a view to making an arrest and bringing a prosecution for murder or manslaughter. Since the police already have a good idea of the cause of death and are able to judge for themselves at the appropriate stage in their investigations whether there is enough evidence to present to the Crown Prosecution Service for the latter to decide whether there is enough evidence to support a prosecution, this seems to be a pointless proceeding.

In Sierra Leone, which followed the British model in this as in so many other institutions, it was made doubly pointless by the fact that if and when a decision was made to launch a prosecution, the accused person would have first to be brought before the same official who had started the inquest sitting as coroner, but sitting this time as magistrate at a preliminary investigation and taking the same evidence in the form of depositions, in order to decide whether or not there was a *prima facie* case to commit the accused person to the Supreme Court for trial.

At least half the inquests arose out of road accidents and most of them were boring. When sitting as coroner I sometimes called to mind the words of a High Court judge who complained that he spent most of his time in court listening to cases between two insurance companies about head-on collisions between stationary vehicles. Once or twice, however, there were more colourful cases, and I particularly recall one death I investigated in Kambia District that had an aura of mystery about it. The corpse of a young woman was brought to Kambia with one leg missing and pieces of flesh torn from it. The body was sent for a postmortem examination. The death had taken place near Mambolo, a chiefdom headquarters on the Great Scarcies River, 35 miles southwest of Kambia. I had already made plans to visit Mambolo and decided to hold the inquest while there. The first witnesses told a straightforward story of how they had gone down to a creek to bathe one evening in company with the deceased woman.

While they were there a crocodile attacked the woman, bit off one leg and caused her to drown in deeper water. This was not an unusual event, as there were plenty of crocodiles in the river, and they could sometimes be seen on the banks lazing in the sun. The last witness had a more startling tale to tell. She said that she was a member of the Crocodile Society, and that while they were all bathing she had got into the skin of a crocodile and attacked the woman, whom she had killed as a sacrifice for the society. I questioned her at length, but she stuck to her story. She appeared to be demented and it was obvious that no matter what we might think of her fantastic story she was a prey to some nameless fear. As she had publicly confessed to murder, I had to order her immediate confinement in the African administration lock-up. I adjourned the proceedings and raced back to Kambia in my car in order to bring the deputy superintendent of police. He also questioned the woman and the other witnesses and was told the same story I had already heard.

The woman was formally charged with murder so that she could be kept in custody. It seemed certain, however, that she would never be convicted, for the only evidence was her own confession and in her mentally deranged state this was of doubtful value. The police later found out that a devil had accused her of belonging to the Crocodile Society. There were many kinds of 'devils' in Sierra Leone, usually associated with a secret society. This was an itinerant one, dressed in black from head to foot, with no part of his body visible and with strings of hammer heads and other metal charms hung about him. He had recently visited Mambolo and with his ironmongery jangling had gone around the town accusing various individuals of belonging to the Crocodile Society.

Such devils and medicine men were often charlatans playing on the superstitions of simple villagers. Their technique was to accuse people of harbouring evil medicine in their houses, or of belonging to secret societies such as this one, named after baboons, leopards and other predatory animals. Such accusations were believed and would have the effect of cutting off the persons thus named from their families, who would drive them away out of fear. The medicine man or an accomplice would then undertake the task of exorcising the malign influence, for which the unfortunate victim and his or her family would have to pay a large fee. Money was not always the motive, however, and I suspect that, in this particular case, enemies of the woman's family might have persuaded the devil to make the accusations as a revenge for some wrong. She was later released when it was decided that no case could be made against her and I do not know what happened to her. It is possible that with such a weight of fear on her mind she simply died.

From the medical evidence of the postmortem examination alone it seemed certain that a crocodile had killed the young woman. However, Africans seldom accepted such obvious explanations and were wont to attribute any death or lesser misfortune to evil spirits or the machinations of enemies — hence the widespread belief in crocodile and other societies, depending on what large animals inimical to man were prevalent in a particular place. Such beliefs were not always without foundation. In one chiefdom in Bonthe District, for example, several killings were committed by members of a baboon society, two of whom were convicted of murder and hanged shortly after I went to Bonthe. It was impossible to draw a clear dividing line between truth and superstitious belief in matters of this kind.

I had one encounter with a crocodile that was unquestionably the real thing. This was on another occasion when I was staying at Mambolo. The rest house there was on the riverside a few yards back from the edge of the water. One evening after supper when it had gone dark I was sitting on the veranda in a deckchair reading a book by the light of a pressure lamp. A slight noise caused me to look up and I was horrified to see a long, fully grown crocodile a few feet away from me by the side of the veranda, which was only a few inches above the level of the surrounding ground. Fortunately its tail was nearer to me than its head; it was motionless and did not appear to have noticed me. I shot into the rest house as quickly and silently as I could, closing the door behind me, and did not go back to the veranda until I was sure that the beast had gone away. I had no shotgun or other weapon, and I doubt in any case whether it would have been wise to try shooting the crocodile when it was near enough to retaliate with its dreadful jaws. Acquaintances to whom I later related this incident were amused by it and suggested in jest that the crocodile was no more substantial than the more conventional pink elephant. In fact I had had no alcohol that day, but I treated myself to a strong whisky after the event, to steady my nerves.

Another coroner's inquest that stands out in my recollection also arose out of a death in the Great Scarcies. In this case, all the witnesses told me that they had been fishing in the shallow waters near the bank and that the deceased had been one of their party. They saw him get out of his depth, struggle and eventually disappear beneath the water. Their evidence was suspect at several points. All said that the man did not cry for help at any time; none of them appeared to have made any effort to try to save him and they could not agree among themselves on how many times he had come up to the surface before going under for the last time. Most significant of all, their evidence showing that the man had died by drowning was at variance with that of the medical officer, whose examination of the corpse showed that there was no water in the lungs. There was, on the other hand, a bruise on the back of his head, which might have been caused by a blow with a blunt instrument.

Medical officers were not normally called in person to give evidence at inquests; this was to avoid their having to waste a lot of time in court that would be better spent looking after their patients. The Coroners' Ordinance permitted them to give evidence by a signed statement in writing. On this occasion, however, I concluded that the medical evidence was more telling than usual and that I ought to go into it in detail. I asked the medical officer to see me on one of his routine visits to Kambia. He explained to me that the man had probably been unconscious before he entered the water. He might have revived with the stimulus of air, but under the water this was lacking, and he had therefore died as a result of suffocation and the traumatic shock from the blow to the head. Again I had to refer the case to the police for further investigation, but without result.

Mysterious deaths were a common occurrence. I have previously alluded to the death of my close friend and contemporary John Cook. In 1957 he had been transferred to Kono District and, on returning from a walking trek, he had to cross a river by canoe. However, as so often happened in Africa, when he reached the river bank the canoe that should have been waiting for him was missing. According to the evidence of his servants and other camp followers, he undressed and dived into the river to get a canoe from the other side. This I find hard to credit, for it was dark at the time and such an irrational and foolhardy act was out of keeping with John's level-headed temperament. He died in the water, but not from drowning. It was surmised that he had died of shock, perhaps as a result of having touched, or imagined that he had touched, a crocodile. As in so many cases the evidence of witnesses was contradictory and unreliable. It was doubtful whether any of them spoke the truth and possibly they felt compelled to tell a roughly consistent story of drowning through fear of the consequences that would ensue if they told the truth.

* * *

No account of Kambia District would be complete without mention of a notable episode in its history, the Haidara rebellion of 1930. I was able to read the contemporary record of this in a carefully preserved file in the district office, which would certainly deserve a place in Sierra Leone's official archives, though I doubt very much whether it has survived. Islam was a strong influence in the district as in other parts of Northern Province, by contrast with the general paganism and superficial smattering of Christianity of the other two provinces. Haidara was a fanatical mullah from French Guinea who gathered around him a large crowd of adherents in Bubuya, the headquarters of Tonko Limba chiefdom. His preaching became seditious, as he openly claimed that he would have all the Europeans in the district killed, including the district commissioner, and he boasted that the government was powerless against him. He advised his followers not to pay any more taxes. He boasted also that bullets could not harm him but would pass straight through his body.

The DC soon realized that Haidara was a dangerous man and he asked for a deportation order to be sent up from Freetown so that he could have Haidara removed from the country. The colonial secretary sent the order and the DC went to Bubuya with a posse of court messengers to serve it. Haidara was openly defiant and refused to leave. The DC evidently did not consider that the forces he had with him were strong enough to arrest the man and deal with the possibly violent reactions of his hostile followers, so he returned to Kambia. He sent a telegram to Freetown saying that the situation was out of hand and asking for military assistance. The following day, in response to this request, a platoon of soldiers of the West African Frontier Force under a Lieutenant Holmes left Freetown by launch, this being at the time the only way of reaching Kambia.

Although Kambia was not linked to the rest of the country by road until 1942, in 1930 work had already started on the Kambia to Kamakwie road, running in a northeasterly direction parallel with the frontier with French Guinea. Progress was obviously slow, as in 1957 when I went to the district it was still 30 miles short of Kamakwie, a town in neighbouring Bombali District, northwest of that district's headquarters town of Makeni. In 1930, some 20 miles of it had been built, starting from Kambia and going just beyond Bubuya. There was one motor vehicle in the district, a Chevrolet lorry that belonged to the Public Works Department, and a European inspector of works who was supervising the construction of the road had a motorcycle. An advance party of troops and court messengers commanded by Lieutenant Holmes and a sergeant left on the lorry as soon as they arrived at Kambia. The lorry set them down near Bubuya and went back to Kambia for the DC and more court messengers. There is no explanation of why the DC did not go with the lorry on its first trip.

The court messengers, acting as guides, advised Lieutenant Holmes to take a bush path that led off the road to Bubuya, but the officer suspected an ambush and was reluctant to leave the road. Some of Haidara's followers were known to be armed. What he possibly did not realize, though the court messengers must have been aware of it, was that Haidara had threatened to kill any European who crossed a certain bridge on the motor road. Lieutenant Holmes advanced up the road in front of his party and was the first to cross the bridge. Some men appeared from the bush on the side of the road and opened fire with shotguns, killing the young officer outright. The sergeant took command, rallied his men and returned fire. Haidara and several of his followers were killed. The rest fled and in next to no time the rebellion was at an end and all the remaining rebels had disappeared.

The DC arrived soon after the shooting was over. As soon as he learned what had happened he asked the European inspector of works to return to Kambia on his motorcycle and send a telegram to Freetown containing a report of the day's events. He posted troops and court messengers at Bubuya and returned to Kambia on the lorry, taking with him the body of Lieutenant Holmes, who was buried with full military honours near the district office that evening. His grave, surmounted with a concrete cross and gravestone on which appear his name and a brief account of how he met his death, was still to be seen at Kambia when I was there.

The provincial commissioner arrived the next day and took charge. It was obviously felt that the government's prestige had suffered a setback as a result of these events, and not only in Kambia District. Accordingly, a route march of West African Frontier Force units was arranged to show the flag in parts of the Northern Province that had become disaffected and to make it clear that the government was reasserting its authority.

The older Swiss partners running the trading company at Rokupr remembered this incident. At the time there was no motor road between Kambia and Rokupr, but with local people coming and going all day along the bush paths, news spread quickly. The names of the partners had been on the list of Europeans Haidara had intended to have murdered. They knew of his proclaimed intentions and on the day the troops arrived — they called at Rokupr on their way to Kambia further up the river — they were aware of a mounting tension in the town and among the people who came to their store. They were defenceless and realized that there was no hope for them if the local population turned against them. However, in the afternoon came the news that Haidara was dead and the rising was at an end. Everyone was friendly again and they were able to relax.

From the DC's official report in the file it was impossible to tell what his personal feelings had been. He must have been a worried man, feeling at least partly responsible for the deaths of a young army officer and of Haidara and several of his followers, which might well have been avoided by a more adroit and firm handling of the rising before it got out of hand. However, it is unfair to pass judgement on another man's conduct when that man has no chance to explain his actions and one cannot fully appreciate all the factors that influenced him at the critical time.

There was no comparable dramatic incident in 1957, though the events of 1955/6 had been far more tragic and catastrophic than those of the 1930 rebellion. We had our quota of shouting and demonstrations in the divided chief-doms, and without careful handling there might easily have been fresh riots. Attempts to elect regent chiefs and appoint African court members often reactivated rivalries that had come to a head during the riots, but it was essential to try to get some form of chiefdom administration functioning.

Late one night we received a report of a clash between pro- and anti-chief factions in a town on the other side of the Great Scarcies. The DC went off with the police and I was given the task of contacting police headquarters in Freetown to ask for reinforcements, for we were afraid that this might be a major outbreak. Kambia had a direct radiotelephone link with Freetown as well as a police radio transmitter. It appeared, however, that all stations on the police network closed down at night, so that was no use. This discovery astonished me. The police network was obviously useless at a time of emergency, so I wondered why it existed at all. I went to the post office in Kambia and woke up the postmaster. He started the generator that supplied the power for the telephone link, there being no public electricity supply in Kambia, and began trying to contact the Freetown exchange, which, he assured me, maintained a 24-hour watch. For an hour he tried in vain to get a response, but in the end we gave up. In spite of all the riots there had been in the Northern Province not so long before, in an emergency outside office hours we were on our own and very vulnerable.

Fortunately, the disturbance was less serious than we had at first thought and the local police were able to cope. However, this lack of a means to communicate with Freetown or anywhere else gave us food for thought. The Mange Ferry, the crossing of the Great Scarcies, closed every night at 7.00 p.m. and the ferrymen slept on the far side of the river, making it impossible to go from Kambia to

Freetown at night. With this and the total shutdown of radio or telephone contact, we were completely cut off from the rest of Sierra Leone at night, and the only way of contacting the capital would have been to drive to Conakry, the capital of French Guinea, 90 miles away and much more easily reached, from where there was a submarine cable to Freetown. This was a deplorable state of affairs.

* * *

My experience in Kambia of trying to resolve situations that were sometimes verging on anarchy and of dealing with countless land disputes led me to reflect at length on the state of the protectorate and in particular on the role of administrative officers. The Cox Commission's report had diagnosed many ills in the body politic of Sierra Leone and had made recommendations aimed at curing those ills. Nowhere in the report was there any adverse comment on the part played by district commissioners in coping with the riots and their aftermath. Reading between the lines it was clear that the commission had come to the conclusion that the provincial administration was the one institution in the country in which ordinary people continued to have faith and that, given the central government's unequivocal support, it was still capable of pulling the country out of its dire straits, despite the provincial administration's prestige having been lowered by political measures such as the abolition of the Court Messenger Force. The commission may not have considered the provincial administration's actions to have been beyond reproach at all times, but if it did have any but the mildest criticisms it was careful to withhold them.

The last few years had seen a basic change in the pattern of government in the protectorate. The original theory under-lying the administration of the protectorate was that of indirect rule, made sacrosanct by Lugard in Nigeria. In typically British fashion this doctrine developed to justify a purely pragmatic policy. When Lugard took charge of Northern Nigeria he soon realized that he had neither men nor other resources to exercise complete control over the territory, and accordingly he adopted the obvious and sensible course of allowing the Muslim emirs to carry on with the internal government of their emirates, subject to the overriding jurisdiction of British administrators. This system was copied in other territories and indirect rule became a hallowed principle.

The emirs were powerful rulers of large numbers of people and had developed a sophisticated form of government; in some ways they could be compared with the nabobs who continued to rule their own states in India in the days of the raj, subject to limitations in foreign affairs. They appointed their own ministers, treasurers and judges and maintained their own police forces. It was a far cry from them to the paramount chiefs of the sometimes tiny chiefdoms of Sierra Leone, but nevertheless the same principle was applied there. There was no interference with African law and custom, though certain criminal offences such as murder were taken out of the jurisdiction of the native courts, which were empowered only to hear civil disputes between natives. Disappointed litigants had a right of appeal to the district commissioner, who could also if he thought fit transfer a case from the native court to the magistrate's court, which meant of course that he could dispose of the case himself, sitting as a magistrate.

The district commissioner had powers under the protectorate ordinance to investigate land and other disputes and make any order he thought fit; this was the provision I used to adjudicate on land disputes. Paramount chiefs were elected by the members of the tribal authority under the supervision of an administrative officer, usually the provincial commissioner. After the election the commissioner would present to the successful candidate his staff of office, a polished stick with a brass knob at the top bearing an embossed crown, the traditional symbol of a paramount chief officially recognized by the government. Once elected, a chief held office for life and could be removed only after an inquiry into his behaviour had found that his conduct had been subversive of good government, and the decision to depose him must be taken by the governor-in-council. The office of chief was therefore very secure.

Apart from this ultimate sanction, the provincial administration had at its disposal no legal sanction of any significance against chiefs who misbehaved; if district commissioners had always stuck to the letter of the law the colonial government's control over the protectorate would have collapsed at an early stage. But the *de facto* power and influence of the provincial administration were far in excess of anything laid down in the statute books, and many district commissioners of the older school freely admitted that they ran their districts largely by bluff. Chiefs did as they were told and if they stepped out of line there were ways of dealing with them. It was once the practice of district commissioners to suspend a recalcitrant chief and debar him from exercising authority by taking away his staff. The law made no provision for such suspension but nobody questioned the practice.

As an illustration of the kind of power that could be exercised in lesser matters, it was not unusual for a district commissioner to forbid the holding of dances in politically troubled chiefdoms. Dances were invariably accompanied by singing, and many songs had political import, praising one faction and abusing the other, sometimes in obscene language. They were often sung in deliberate provocation and led to fights. Such bans had no legal basis, but were always effective and continued to be respected even in my time in Sierra Leone.

An allegedly true story is told of one provincial commissioner who had to deal with a particularly wicked paramount chief. The commissioner was trying to persuade the chief to resign to avoid the otherwise troublesome need for an inquiry into his conduct, but the old man was obdurate and refused to be browbeaten. Finally, the commissioner gave up and his parting words at the end of the interview were, 'Very well, if you won't resign, then you will be destroyed!' Within a fortnight the chief died of a mysterious and sudden illness. For the rest of his service the commissioner never again had any difficulty persuading paramount chiefs to do his bidding; the commands of a man possessed of such devastating super-natural powers could not with impunity be ignored.

With such a degree of control over his paramount chiefs and with an active and loyal body of court messengers to ensure that his orders were carried out, it is hardly sur-prising that the district commissioner found it unnecessary to ask the government for extra legislative powers to enable him to administer his district. Unfortunately, after the abo-lition of the Court Messenger Force the chiefs became less compliant and the legal powers, the need for which now became so apparent, were not available; and there was no prospect of obtaining them because the provincial adminis-tration was anathema to the politicians.

When this stage was reached, indirect rule became for the first time a disastrous reality instead of the polite fiction it had hitherto been. The chiefs were well protected and virtually irremovable. They were in a stronger position than they had ever known and no sanctions could be applied against them. In the days before British rule a Timne chief who incurred the extreme displeasure of his people could be removed from office by the expedient of cutting off his head. Now a chief whose hold on his chiefdom was uncertain could claim police protection against any attempt to oust him, and if he was guilty of misgoverning could be removed from office only by a most elaborate procedure.

As the results of the inquiries into the misdeeds of indi-vidual paramount chiefs in Kambia District showed, the politicians in government who now had the final say on whether or not a chief should be removed, were most reluctant to take such a decision, even in the face of overwhelmingly damning evidence. The case of Paramount Chief Yumkella in Samu chiefdom was the most glaring example of this. His conduct in oppressing his people had been far worse than that of any other chief and without question he should have been removed from office, but the ministers who had to take the decision were unwilling to do anything so drastic. As a consequence, he retained his office but was forbidden to exercise his functions as a chief — an edict that in retrospect probably had no proper legal basis but was nevertheless obeyed. The anti-chief faction was dissatisfied and the obvious potential for further serious disturbances meant that police posts had to be set up in all the main towns in the chiefdom. It was a decision that gave us the worst of all possible worlds.

I would never dispute that at this time chiefs had and would continue to have an important role in Sierra Leone. However, it was wrong that they should be regarded as almost sovereign monarchs and I felt that the government should take powers to exercise stricter control over them. It was also my opinion that they should hold office for a fixed term of not more than ten years and not for life and that the district commissioner should have the power to suspend any chief for good cause pending an inquiry.

There was insufficient recognition of the need for strong government at the centre, exercising undisputed authority throughout the country. The misplaced emphasis on local government, the dominant Colonial Office policy of the post-war years, obscured this need. Local government is a valuable institution in developed countries, where sufficient funds will be forthcoming in the form of council tax or whatever, to make local councils viable units and where there are large numbers of educated people from whom councillors and officials can be drawn. Local authorities can and do perform a wide range of functions, good communications make close supervision of their working possible, and a well-developed civic sense ensures that they work efficiently and that a high level of integrity on the part of councillors and officials can be assumed. In the United Kingdom nowadays there is much criticism of and cynicism about local government, and central government does not always seem to appreciate its merits, but I would still hold to this brief assessment of its virtues.

African conditions in the 1950s were very different. Councillors were often illiterate and seldom well educated and the motive for seeking office tended to be personal aggrandisement and illicit gain rather than a desire to serve the community. The provision of even the most basic range of public services required a staff of educated and competent people who were hard to find. Creating such local units of administration merely added to the burden of the costs to be borne from taxation without giving the taxpayers any worthwhile extra services. Decentralization of power encouraged fissiparous tendencies that were never far below the surface and could easily damage whatever national unity had been built up over the years.

I am thinking mainly of the much cherished but sadly disappointing district councils, but the same criticisms could be made of the older native administrations, the lower rung of local government. In a typical district there would be one district council and possibly a dozen native administrations, the main source of revenue for all of them being the local tax at 25 shillings a head for perhaps 10,000 taxpayers. Most of this money went in salaries and other administrative expenses and there were seldom more than the most rudimentary services available. Most services had perforce to continue to be provided by central government — roads, the railway, telephones, electricity in those districts that had a supply, hospitals and schools. The hold the paramount chiefs, who had a strong vested interest in the continuance of both district councils and African administrations, were able to exercise in national politics meant that there was little chance of any reform of this wasteful and inefficient system.

Colonial Office apologists and their advisers in the academic world used to defend the introduction of elected local councils into African territories with the argument that it was the only system of local government of which we in the United Kingdom had any experience and this therefore had to be the model we followed. This argument seemed to presuppose that there was a mysterious perfection about British institutions that made them readily adaptable in any part of the world. But local government in this country has never stood still and has been continuously evolving for decades, so there was an obvious fallacy in taking as a model for Sierra Leone the stage of development that local government in the United Kingdom happened to have reached in the 1950s.

The basic assumption that we know only one form of elected local government is false; the survival of the office of Lord Lieutenant, the sovereign's representative in each county, now confined to ceremonial functions, is a reminder of an earlier system. For much of our history, unpaid justices of the peace who had administrative as well as judicial functions carried on local government in the name of the sovereign. During the Second World War, the government appointed regional commissioners throughout the country who, in the event of an invasion, were to assume dictatorial powers, overriding all other authorities, in the regions for which they were responsible; they were required if necessary to continue organized resistance to the enemy even though central government had broken down.

Finally, and most relevant, in the Indian Empire and in African and other colonial territories we had for long had vast experience in local government through officials appointed by and responsible to a central administration.

For reasons that are not immediately apparent in retrospect, it was decided that local administration of this kind was incompatible with political independence, and that it should be regarded as a temporary and interim form of government. Its officers were expected loyally to administer themselves out of existence by building what were fondly hoped to be the foundations of democratic government at local level. It was common to talk of the provincial administration as the scaffolding of a new building in the course of construction, which could be removed when the building was complete — in my view a seriously misleading metaphor. It would have been much more realistic to regard the provincial administration as the foundations of the building, which could be dug out once the walls and roof were up.

Unfortunately, most administrative officers were white expatriates and independence, the sloughing off of alien rule, came to be equated with getting rid of district commissioners. In nearly all territories formerly under British rule, the provincial administration has proved to be an essential organ of government since independence. It seemed to me at the time that the sensible course of action must be not to abolish the provincial administration, the avowed aim of the African ministers, but to Africanize it.

At the time of writing Sierra Leone is already independent. In the former protectorate resident ministers have taken the place of provincial commissioners and district commissioners remain. I am sure that the government will find it necessary to retain control from the centre through the agency of local officials.

14

Home Again

I was due to go on leave again at the beginning of February 1958, but as I did not care to face the tail end of an English winter I obtained permission to extend my tour of duty by three months. I would in any case have had to stay longer than the usual 18 months because I was a witness in a criminal case that did not come up in the Supreme Court until the beginning of April. In June 1957 I had carried out a routine check on the accounts of one of the African administrations in Kambia District. The cash-book showed a balance of £200, but the clerk was able to produce only £7 in cash and a number of payment vouchers, which, he said, he had not yet had time to enter in the cash-book. My suspicions were aroused by the fact that all the vouchers bore that day's date, and one of them purported to cover a payment of £160, no small amount at that time. The voucher stated that it was a payment to one Alkali Kamara for digging wells in various villages at £10 each. There was a space for the payee to sign on having received the money, and all that appeared in the space was a cross, evidently made by the clerk himself. Many payees were illiterate and the custom was that they would acknowledge payment by thumbprint, which would be witnessed by the signature of a literate person other than the clerk making the payment. There was no signature of any witness on this voucher.

I questioned the clerk at length, for part of the time in the presence of the paramount chief who was unaware of the tribal authority having approved any project for digging wells. No one else had ever heard of Alkali Kamara, but the clerk was adamant that he was speaking the truth. I asked the police to investigate and eventually the clerk was charged with embezzlement and falsification of accounts. The evidence against him was clear, but he pleaded not guilty to the charges, made no statement in his own defence and called no witnesses. He was convicted and sent to gaol for three years.

Peculation of this kind was all too common among native administration clerks. In most chiefdoms there was no supervision of their work other than occasional inspections of their accounts by a visiting administrative officer. Most paramount chiefs were illiterate and it was a great temptation for the clerks to steal some of the money for which they were responsible. Few of them were clever enough to conceal their frauds effectively. If they tried to cover up their traces at all, it was usually by some naïve device such as this, which gave useful evidence to the prosecution and made possible the additional charge of falsification of accounts. If the clerk in this case had not forged the voucher for £160 but had simply offered no explanation for the missing money, it would have been difficult if not impossible to obtain a conviction. The courts generally took the view that a mere shortage of cash without any other evidence, was insufficient proof of embezzlement — there were, after all, other possible explanations for the shortage.

※ ※ ※

No ticket for my homeward journey had been bought for me, for I could not be certain how soon the case would be over and I could leave the country. As soon as the judge had passed sentence I telephoned the secretariat in Freetown and asked for a ticket on the first available flight. I left Kambia at a few days' notice. Before I left I was very touched to receive a present from the staff of the district office. They gave me a pair of locally made leather slippers, with no backs to the heels and extravagantly pointed toes, a style much favoured by the Mandingoes of Guinea, and an African gown. I took these presents as a great compliment to me.

I returned home by the same service that had brought me back to Sierra Leone at the beginning of my second tour in 1956. In the meantime, however, the airline had bought Viscount turboprops to replace the piston-engined Vikings and was able to offer a faster and more comfortable journey. Instead of two night stops we now had only one, at Las Palmas in the Canary Islands.

Feeling at last in a holiday mood after a 21-month tour of continuous duty, I settled into my seat for takeoff and soon afterwards was having my last glimpse of Kambia District for some time as the plane flew over the mouth of the Great Scarcies River, heading for our first stop at Bathurst, Gambia, a place with which I now felt familiar. A few minutes later another passenger of about my own age came up to me and asked whether I remembered him. He was Leslie Stones, a near contemporary of mine at school and at the same Cambridge college. He was employed by a British bank in Nigeria and, like me, was on his way home on leave. This was an occasion to celebrate, which we did as soon as the air hostesses started serving drinks. Leslie's travelling companion, a district officer from Western Nigeria, joined us and a small party was soon under way.

We landed at the airport of Gran Canaria in the late afternoon and then travelled 20 miles by coach across the island to Las Palmas where we were to stay the night. Nowadays many thousands of Britons take holidays in the Canary Islands every year, particularly in Tenerife, but 1958 was before the age of mass tourism and the islands were still considered to be a fairly exotic destination known only to a select band of travellers, including those of us who from time to time had to travel between West Africa and the United Kingdom by ship or plane, for they provided a convenient stop *en route*. They are not far from the coast of Africa, but their landscape, atmosphere and inhabitants are — or at that time were — wholly European. We went on a winding road through vineyards and ploughed fields, past villages of whitewashed peasants' houses and barren hills marked by deep vertical gullies, a sign of serious erosion. The development of the tourist industry has transformed the islands, but at that time they could be described as poor but picturesque.

At Las Palmas we were accommodated in a town centre hotel. My hopes of a delicious Spanish meal were dashed when I sat down to dinner and read the menu: soup, roast beef with Yorkshire pudding and vegetables. Clearly the airline did not wish to risk upsetting its passengers by offering unfamiliar fare. The British were always conservative in their eating habits, especially when travelling, and this does not seem to have changed so much when one considers the vast numbers of restaurants in so many popular holiday resorts in Spain and elsewhere that offer fish and chips and similar homely dishes. English food prepared by continental cooks is perhaps the gourmet's nadir.

After dinner Leslie Stones and I, along with one or two other passengers, decided to see something of the town and one of the hostesses accepted our invitation to accompany us. We hired a taxi and explained as best we could to the driver that we wanted to go somewhere to dance. In spite of our poor Spanish he understood us and drove to a café in a side street near the harbour. Here a small band played and there was a dance floor. We gathered around a table and for two or three hours drank tots of *fundador*, a mild vinous brandy, talked and danced from time to time. Such evenings made us aware of some of the deficiencies of life in West

Africa. I allowed myself the luxury of feeling tired at the end of a long tour of duty. In the taxi on the way back to the hotel there were not enough seats to go around because the driver was giving a lift to a friend of his, so it was my pleasant duty to have the air hostess sit on my lap. After a while she sweetly asked me to stop muzzling her. I was beginning to make good other deficiencies.

Next day, on the last leg of our journey, we landed at Lisbon to refuel. From the air the red brick houses and green fields took on unbelievably rich hues. I do not suppose that the colours were any different from those of the suburbs surrounding Heathrow, but the clear air and sunshine gave them a lustre and picture book quality never seen in our climate. We sat on the terrace outside the airport restaurant. Behind us we could see the city not far away, and on the concrete dual carriageway outside the airport a procession of cars and green double decked buses finally convinced us, if it were necessary, that West Africa with its wild and unkempt scenery and untidy clusters of corrugated-iron roofs was a long way away.

Trouble with the pressurizing equipment made a further stop at Bordeaux necessary and it was almost dark by the time we reached London. Here we were ushered into plush waiting rooms and sat in comfortable armchairs while elegant airport hostesses with cultured accents murmured a series of messages and announcements into microphones. Soon we had cleared immigration and customs and were on the coach to London. This was long before the opening of the M4 and the Great West Road was a mass of lights of thousands of vehicles. For one who had just spent the better part of two years in remote places where the passing of a motor vehicle was an event, this abrupt transition to the maelstrom of London's traffic was overpowering, and by the time we reached the air terminal in Brompton Road I was exhausted.

The district officer from Nigeria had invited me to join

him at the Naval Club in Hill Street, Mayfair for supper and so, after saying goodbye to Leslie Stones and the other passengers, we went off there in a taxi. We savoured with relish our first draught bitters for a long time.

Having completed a long tour I was entitled to a long leave of five months, much of which I spent in London. I took a short trip to Brussels for the International Exhibition, which took place there in 1958, and went on from there to Paris. I had visited Paris on numerous previous occasions in my undergraduate days, but on this occasion I found it a disappointment, so after two days I returned to London. It was an expensive city for a poorly paid colonial civil servant and in any case I was on my own there, another kind of loneliness after long periods alone in the bush.

My future was becoming a problem. Ghana had become independent in 1957 and the pace of letting other African territories off the colonial leash was quickening. Conversation among the small communities of European government officials in Sierra Leone ran more and more on the theme, 'Where do we go from here?' Some younger men had already resigned and taken up other careers and the older ones strongly encouraged men of my generation to follow their example. I was set to some serious thinking on meeting a former acquaintance from Cambridge in Oxford Street. He had gone to Kenya as a cadet at the same time as I went to Sierra Leone. He told me that he had left the service because he felt that within a few years there would no longer be a career for him and was now working as a trainee manager at one of the stores on Oxford Street. He admitted that he had had problems in being accepted for a suitable post in Britain, but having now succeeded he was very happy.

This was shattering. Whatever the pace of political advancement in the territories on the west coast, one always had the general impression that the East African colonies were the last bastions of empire and would need expatriate administrators for many years to come. I had been contemplating the possibility of applying for a transfer to East Africa, preferably Uganda or Tanganyika. The realization that career prospects for expatriate officers there were no brighter than in West Africa came as a shock.

Perhaps I ought to have taken the courageous step of resigning before I left Sierra Leone to give myself the impetus to find another job. However, at the time I did not feel prepared to do that and I contented myself with applying to one or two of the bigger companies to see what if anything they had to offer. I had two preliminary but fruitless interviews and eventually resigned myself to going back to Sierra Leone for a third tour. I was in no way discontented with my work, apart from feeling that a little less interference from politicians would have been welcome, and could gladly have gone on being an administrative officer for the rest of my working life. However, as this was obviously not going to be possible, I had to try seriously to find other work before I became too old to be readily employable in industry. Pusillanimously I postponed the irrevocable decision and breathed again.

Tearing myself away from Britain after five months was painful, but if my leave had not come to an end I would soon have been in financial difficulties. I had no regrets about my extravagance, as I had enjoyed myself, but it could not have gone on much longer. I wanted to go back to Sierra Leone by sea and was annoyed when I received instructions from the Crown Agents that I had to go back by air because the Sierra Leone government had asked that I return as quickly as possible at the end of my leave. I flew by Air France and, while changing planes at Orly, was able to read in the evening papers the results of the referendum on the proposed constitution of the Fifth Republic. Today was Tuesday, the voting on the referendum had taken place on Sunday and I was staggered to read that Guinea, the only colonial territory to vote '*non*', was being given immediate independence as from Thursday! General de Gaulle had had a very unfriendly reception when he visited Conakry, Guinea's capital and, not being a man to trifle with, had cut off the recalcitrant colony without even the proverbial shilling. The generous subventions from Paris, which bolstered the revenues of all French colonies, were being stopped forthwith. Such a lightning decision contrasted starkly with the stately progress over many years of British territories from crown colony government via internal autonomy to full independence.

Armed guards patrolling the tarmac in front of the main airport buildings were a sign of some of France's other colonial troubles. Algerian terrorists had attempted to sabotage aircraft and, among other precautions, passengers' baggage was being searched.

From Paris I flew in a Super-Constellation non-stop through the night to Dakar, the capital of Senegal. A wonderful champagne dinner, cooked in the galley on board, was served soon after takeoff, but I found it poor compensation for the nine days at sea, of which I had been cheated. At Dakar we had breakfast in the airport restaurant, and the black faces, Europeans in shorts and hot sticky air even at that early hour made me feel once more back in my proper environment. At Conakry I changed from the Super-Constellation to a DC3, which operated the local service from there to Freetown and Monrovia, Liberia. This was something of a come down. The elegant upholstery and carpets of the Super-Constellation were exchanged for a floor covered with battered linoleum, old leather seats and a generally dilapidated interior, with the luggage stacked near the door. In place of chic hostesses in smart uniforms, murmuring bilingual announcements in dulcet tones over the public address system, the DC3 had a male steward dressed in shirt and shorts, who contented himself with announcing laconically to the passengers just as the engines were being started up, '*Une demie heure de vol jusqu'à Freetown*' and thereafter performed no apparent function.

And so it was back to Lungi airport; the ride in the bus with a crowd of Africans, mostly junior civil servants chatting volubly in Creole; the trip across the estuary of the Sierra Leone river in the launch; a sky overcast with rain clouds; the familiar outline of the hills behind Freetown. Then Government Jetty and no sign of the car I had asked to be waiting for me. The non-appearance of expected vehicles was one of the regular hazards of Africa, and I gave an exasperated sigh at not being spared for even 24 hours.

I was able to get a lift to the secretariat building and my car was waiting for me there. I learned that I had been posted to Kabala in Northern Province. Knowing that this would be a station where it would be difficult to get supplies, I bought a bumper load of groceries and other essentials in Freetown before I left. A lorry took my loads, which had been stored in Freetown during my leave, and two days later I followed by car. It was 200 miles to Kabala, all but the first 47 on laterite roads and therefore a slow journey. I stopped at Makeni after 120 miles and spent the night there with friends. Next day I continued my journey, breaking new ground and entering Koinadugu District for the first time.

The northern part of Sierra Leone forms the foothills of the main West Africa massif, with the Fouta Jallon highland of Guinea at the western end. The hills begin in the northern part of Bo District, but it is only north of Makeni, the headquarters of Northern Province, that the higher ranges begin to appear. Many of them are covered with thick bush and forest, but there are also scrub and grassland, which allow the traveller along the road to Kabala to see something of the magnificent scenery. The road climbs steadily through difficult terrain and there are hills on all sides, usually very steep and sometimes offering a sheer cliff face. Where the rock shows it is a rich purple colour. From time to time the road crossed streams that were in spate, and the rushing water breaking over rocks was reminiscent of mountain streams in Scotland or North Wales. It was noticeable that the villages were at much longer intervals than in other parts of the country and I gained an impression of spacious emptiness. I met only two vehicles on this 80-mile journey; one was the government lorry that had taken my loads and was now returning empty to Freetown.

I reached Kabala in the early afternoon and went to the DC's house. It stood on top of a steep wooded hill, 1300 feet above sea level and 600 feet above the surrounding country. The top of the hill had been cleared and levelled when the house was built, giving it a site and outlook of unparalleled magnificence. The house overlooked a broad valley in which could be seen the town of Kabala and the road leading out of the town northward to the rest of the district. The vegetation in the valley was mostly grassland, good grazing for the cattle that abounded in the district. On the opposite side of the valley was Alibataia Hill, a long ridge rising at its highest point to 2400 feet, dominating the surrounding area. It formed a superb backcloth for the small and otherwise featureless town in the valley beneath it.

The house was 35 years old, built of mud block before there was a motor road linking the district with the rest of the country. Its dimensions were ample, though less generous than those of the house at Gbangbama in Bonthe District. The compound of the house had been laid out and maintained with loving care by previous DCs and was superior to anything I had seen elsewhere in Sierra Leone. There were lawns on three sides of the house and on one side they had been made at two levels because of the steep slope of the ground, with a retaining wall to support the higher one. Bougainvillaea, poinsettia, hibiscus and other flowering shrubs were planted all round the house and tall hedgerows screened off the kitchen, outhouses and an unsightly but necessary 10,000-gallon water tank at the back of the house.

The steep road leading down to the office past the two-level lawns was lined with flamboyants and elsewhere in the compound were a few alamanders and frangipani. From the edges of the lawns one could look down an almost sheer hillside, thickly clustered with tall trees, which one would hardly have thought capable of taking root on so sheer a slope. They were so close together that they shut out the sun and there was little vegetation on the ground beneath them. I have never before or since lived in such beautiful surroundings, and from the first had no difficulty understanding why so many administrative officers had loved Kabala.

Koinadugu (the district was named after a town some miles from Kabala that had been the original district head-quarters) had produced more than its share of odd characters, mainly because of its isolation. Even in 1958 when I arrived there, the only senior government officer there apart from myself was an African medical officer, and the only other Europeans in the district were the agricultural officer and his wife, 15 miles away at Musaia. There were also a few American missionaries running schools and churches scattered around the district, some in very out-of-the-way villages. For many years the district commissioner had run the district entirely alone and often saw no other European from the beginning to the end of his tour of duty.

It was only in 1930 that the road from Makeni first entered the district. It might have been built earlier but for the resistance put up by Mr Harnetty, a reactionary officer who was the DC for several years in the 1920s. He felt that a motor road would bring contaminating corrupting influences and would spoil the simple innocence of the people. In those days the district commissioner's wish was law and no road was built until he had left the district. It is also alleged that he would not permit the building of square or rectan-

218

gular houses. The traditional African dwelling is a round hut and Mr Harnetty was unwilling to see this disappear in favour of decadent modern styles of dwelling, even though both designs used the same mud and wattle for the walls and palm thatch for the roof. I have no doubt that in his attempt to freeze the people he governed in their customary and unsophisticated lifestyle he was sincere and well intentioned but perhaps also a little misguided and over zealous.

My cook, Johnnie Gorvie, a Sherbro whom I had engaged in Bonthe after sacking Musa during the governor's visit there, had worked for Mr Harnetty in the late 1920s and was coming back to Kabala after almost 30 years. All the people he had known before were now dead. There was, however, one station labourer who had looked after the compound of the house since Mr Harnetty's day and he showed me an old bridle path zigzagging down the side of the hill down which Mr Harnetty used to ride his horse. My cook was able to confirm another story about this legendary figure, namely that he was fond of cricket and used to have his servants bowl to him so that he could keep in practice.

Another district commissioner had been an amateur poet who had succeeded in having a volume of verse published. He built a stone bench 50 yards from the house on the edge of the hill, looking across to Alibataia. The bench was still there in my day and may still be there now. In the evenings he would sit there seeking inspiration from the view as he composed his poems. I often sat there myself before sunset, but confined myself to admiring the view.

In the days before the road reached the district, one officer went on leave, walking first by stages to Makeni, from where he could take the train to Freetown. Here he called on the provincial commissioner, who subsequently wrote in a confidential report that he did not think it would be advisable to send this officer back to Kabala after his leave, as the long months of solitude had obviously had an effect on him. The officer concerned discovered this report some years later when he was promoted to provincial commissioner and was astonished that his predecessor had had the impression that he had become a little unbalanced mentally. To the best of his own recollection he had felt normal when he saw the commissioner, but evidently the latter thought he was behaving strangely.

One of the consolations of going slightly mad is that the sufferer is not usually aware of his own condition, and the lack of awareness acts as a kind of anaesthetic against trying conditions that might otherwise become unbearable. Hence the formerly well-known West African adage, 'You have to be a bit mad to put up with this place, or you'd go completely round the bend!' The isolation expatriate officers had to endure for long periods in the years before communications began to improve must in many cases have caused mental strain and accounted for the eccentricities attributed to so many of them. The problem was still there in my day, though perhaps in a less chronic form than in earlier times.

On trek and sometimes also on station, especially in Kabala, I was alone for long periods apart from my servants, clerks and other members of my official entourage. I read many books and had newspapers sent out from the United Kingdom. I had the *Manchester Guardian Weekly* by airmail, which kept me in touch with the wider world. I also received the *Observer* by sea mail, which meant that it was some weeks old when it arrived, but I devoured it greedily. Inevitably I began to talk to myself, a habit I still have. It is more than a little understandable that bachelor officers and for that matter married officers who had to leave their wives and children in the United Kingdom once the children were of school age, frequently had African mistresses for the comforts of company as well as sex.

* * *

Within a few days of my arrival I took over the district and my predecessor went off on leave. I was in charge of the largest district in the country, 4700 square miles, almost a fifth of the country's total area. The population of about 80,000 was made up of several different tribes. Limba and Koranko predominated, but there were also pockets of Yalunka and Mandingo. The Foulah, ubiquitous cattle owners all over West Africa, were well represented and many of them were wealthy. Some were itinerant, crossing regularly between Sierra Leone and Guinea with their herds, but others had been settled in the district for years. Their economic and social importance was recognized by the appointment of a Foulah headman for the whole district. He was paid by contributions from all the native administrations of the district and was answerable to the DC for the good behaviour of his people. He regularly attended sessions of native courts when cases involving Foulahs, especially complaints of cattle damage from farmers, were being heard.

The Foulah are a virile race of tall people of Hamitic stock and are mostly Muslim. Their dominant position in Koinadugu District was to be explained by the healthy climate, good for cattle as well as for human beings, and by the abundant good grazing land. Their relations with the indigenous people of the district were usually good, though some of the less responsible herdsmen took too little trouble to look after their cattle, with the result that some of them strayed and damaged growing crops. The practice of fencing farms to keep out cattle was beginning to be adopted, and some of the farmers bought rolls of wire netting for the purpose. Most farms, however, were unprotected and there were frequent complaints of damage.

Most of the district was 500 feet or more above sea level and temperatures were markedly lower than nearer the coast. At night I often found that I needed two blankets on my bed, whereas in Kambia and Bonthe I had had no blankets and sometimes had even lain on top of the sheets. On New Year's Eve 1958 I was glad to sit near a wood fire in the agricultural officer's house at Musaia. In December and January came the harmattan, the cold wind bringing dust from the Sahara, and every morning I could look out and see the town of Kabala and the lower slopes of Alibataia covered in wreaths of ground mist formed by condensation of moisture round the dust particles. The climate and scenery drew many tourists of the hardier kind to the district and the rest houses were regularly in demand.

In the few months of my tenure I met several young national service officers from the Sierra Leone Regiment, part of the West African Frontier Force, taking local leave from Freetown to visit the district. Two officers who had just been demobilized from Nigeria arrived one night by car, having travelled all the way from Lagos on their way to London — no mean journey by road. Two travellers from Bo passed through on their way to Timbuktu, more than 1000 miles away on the edge of the Sahara, and called again to tell me about their adventures on the way back. Lecturers from Fourah Bay College in Freetown and others came up to spend part of their vacations there.

Perhaps the main feature of the district, which endeared it to administrative officers, was its freedom from political troubles. The riots in Northern Province two years before had upset Bombali District to the south, but Koinadugu was unaffected. The paramount chiefs were less sophisticated or rapacious than their fellows elsewhere and the district had poor communications, was undeveloped and relatively cut off from the rest of the country. Equally important was the absence of any pressure on the land in the sparsely populated chiefdoms, so there were no disputes for the chiefs to meddle in and thus stir up that ever-potent source of discontent. Perhaps, most important of all, there were no diamond deposits. The district was no longer as trouble free as formerly, though by comparison with others it was a blissful haven.

Another of the joys of Kabala was the cost of living, probably the lowest in the protectorate. Meat was one shilling and ninepence a pound, compared with three shillings and sixpence in Bo and even higher prices elsewhere. It was furthermore of much better quality, coming from cattle that were still fat, not having been herded on the hoof over long distances before being slaughtered. In addition, fresh vegetables grown in the district were available in much greater quantities than elsewhere.

Guinea, the newly independent republic, previously a French colony, had a long common boundary with Sierra Leone, of which much was also the northern boundary of Koinadugu District. Dabola, the nearest administrative headquarters, home of Guinea's first president, Sekou Touré, was 60 miles away and could be reached by road, though I never attempted the journey. One or two of my visitors who called on me in Kabala told me of some of the confusion in Guinea at the time and particularly of disconsolate Frenchmen suddenly having to give up their life work at a few days' notice. Rumours began to reach me of large-scale persecution of the Foulahs in Guinea and were to the effect that the Yalunka, Mandingo and other non-pastoral tribes were taking advantage of the turmoil of independence to confiscate cattle belonging to the Foulahs, exacting in this way vengeance for real or supposed wrongs in the past in a manner that would never have been tolerated by the French. Many of the Foulahs were said to be fleeing across the frontier to seek asylum in British territory. Mention of this very plausible rumour in one of my routine intelligence reports caused a stir in Freetown, but it proved to be without foundation. The police originally confirmed it when I asked them to send a Special Branch investigator to the frontier area, but the Foulah headman for the district knew nothing about it and proved to be a more reliable source of information.

An excited messenger bringing a letter from the paramount chief of Sinkunia chiefdom interrupted one of my evening walks round the spacious bungalow compound. He reported that a marauding elephant had attacked one of the villages in the chiefdom and asked for help to hunt it down. Fortunately, the village in question was on the motor road north of Kabala, so access would not be a problem. I was aware that for hunting an elephant a special large bore rifle was needed and no such weapon was available. The police had their Lee Enfield .303 rifles, which were unlikely to be effective because the bullets would probably bounce off the elephant's hide. However, we had to do something.

I went down to the police lines and told the inspector in charge to muster as many men as possible and to issue fire-arms and ammunition. As an afterthought I asked him to take an extra rifle for my own use. Within a few minutes the normally sleepy police station was filled with a mêlée of bustling, chattering constables in various stages of dress and undress. The police sergeant major, a former court messenger, was in his element as he handed out weapons from the armoury and cursed at the more dilatory men struggling into their boots. Some were delighted at the prospect of the expedition, but others were not at all happy about hunting something so much bigger than themselves.

The chief clerk from the district office, who lived close by, fired by the general excitement, asked me whether he could come along as a spectator, and I readily agreed to take him. The police started off in a Land Rover and I followed close behind in my car, with the chief clerk as passenger. We had 20 miles to drive and it was dark as soon as we left Kabala. This seemed an unfitting way to go chasing elephants, unarmed, at night and sitting in a comfortable car, but then Africa is seldom what one expects. After a few miles my chief clerk, at first cheerful and garrulous, began to show signs of nervousness.

'S ... suppose we come upon the elephant on the road?'

'Oh well, I would put the car into reverse and shoot back towards Kabala as quickly as possible.'

This attempt at levity failed to reassure him and a further idea of mine, that we might try driving between the elephant's legs, brought him no cheer either. The thought of the car's headlights suddenly shining on a rampaging pachyderm worried him more and more and he began to cackle hysterically. At last he could stand no more and he begged me to set him down at the next village, where he would wait for me to come back. This I thankfully did.

Alas for our disappointment when we reached the village. The villagers, huddled in frightened groups outside their houses, told us that the elephant had disappeared into the bush. Trampled crops and a rough path stamped out by huge feet through the vegetation showed us where it had been, but our efforts to track it were in vain. After wandering through the bush for an hour or more by the dim light of hurricane lamps and torches, I decided to give up the search. It would in any case have been dangerous to shoot at anything in the darkness, as we could easily have hit each other. Sad but relieved at this anticlimax we returned to Kabala, leaving two armed constables at the village overnight as guards. On my way I picked up a chastened and shamefaced chief clerk. The police resumed the search for the elephant the next day, but with no success.

15

Positively the Last Outpost

I knew when I went to Kabala that I was not going to be there for long and that I would be transferred elsewhere when the permanent DC newly assigned to the district returned from leave. At first I was told that I would be returning to Kambia as acting DC, a prospect that appealed to me greatly. After the successive transfers I had had in my comparatively short service I liked the idea of returning to take charge of a district with which I was already familiar. However, posting plans were changed and I was next told that I would be going to Magburaka, the headquarters of Tonkolili District, south of Makeni, as assistant district commissioner. This was disappointing; I had had my heart set on Kambia and on being once again in charge of my own district, not an unreasonable expectation after four-and-a-half years of service.

A posting to Magburaka would mean going to an unfamiliar district as assistant to a man who, though I liked him personally, was only two years my senior. Early in January there came a further and final change. There had been fresh outbreaks of violence in Kono District in the South-Eastern Province, the centre of the country's diamond mining areas. The police had been making a record number of arrests, the gaol was overflowing and the magistrate who visited there for a fortnight each month was unable to cope with the volume of cases. Since I had a law degree, though I was not at

226

the time professionally qualified, and had some experience of sitting as a magistrate, I was sent to Kono in that capacity.

Kono had a long boundary with Koinadugu District and in a straight line the headquarters towns were perhaps 100 miles apart. There was, however, no road linking them and the boundary ran through some of the most mountainous country in Sierra Leone, between Bintimani and Sankanbiriwa, the two highest ranges in the land, both rising to 6000 feet. The area was also undeveloped and thinly populated.

It was typical of the communications in Sierra Leone that although these two districts were next to each other, I nevertheless had to take a long detour of more than 300 miles to drive from Kabala to Sefadu, the headquarters of Kono District, passing through Makeni, Magburaka, Bo and Kenema. I stayed one night in Bo and a second night in Kenema as the guest of Hugh Beattie, the commissioner for South-Eastern Province of which Kono District was a part. I had never before travelled beyond Kenema and was breaking new ground. The DC in Kono was my old friend Jack Wann, who had been my first DC in Bo four-and-a-half years earlier. I was his guest for my first night in Sefadu, after which I moved into one of the rest houses. The several emergencies in Kono in recent years had necessitated increasing the staff of what had hitherto been a placid district, and the building of permanent houses for newly posted officers was lagging behind. The rest house was small and far from luxurious, but there was nothing else available.

The government station of Sefadu was over a mile outside Koidu, the main town of the district. Koidu had merged into Tankoro, a town in a neighbouring chiefdom, and a stream marked the boundary between them. Koidu–Tankoro had a population of 30,000, most of them people who had come in search of illicit wealth from diamonds in the past few years. The town was an outstanding illustration of Professor Kenneth Galbraith's one-time theme of private affluence and public squalor. Diamond dealers and Syrian and Lebanese traders had made vast fortunes and the signs were huge houses built with permanent materials, often with their own generators, large and expensive cars and an opulent display of imported consumer goods of all kinds.

On the other hand, the town had few roads and even some of the bigger houses were accessible only on foot. What roads existed were in a terrible state, churned up by heavy traffic, unsurfaced and full of potholes. There was no public water or electricity supply. A post office had just been opened and offered a radiotelephone link with the rest of the country. There was no telephone exchange and anyone who wished to make a call had to do so from the single instrument at the post office, which as often as not was out of order. Kono was the main source of Sierra Leone's wealth and of the government's revenue, but disgracefully little money had been spent there on providing amenities.

For the next six months I worked almost exclusively as a magistrate. The conditions under which I had to do so could serve as a good example of the shoestring basis on which our African colonies were administered. I had no proper courtroom. The *barri* at district headquarters was almost permanently in use by the visiting magistrate and I had to occupy a borrowed native administration *barri*, normally used as a market, which was cleared of its usual occupants. It was a few yards from a busy laterite road and the noise and clouds of dust thrown up by passing vehicles often held up the proceedings. I had no court furniture other than two tables and half a dozen chairs borrowed from a nearby police station. Witnesses, policemen, prisoners and warders had to sit on the floor or stand by the *barri* wall. A convention was soon established whereby prisoners stood on my right and witnesses under examination on my left; there was neither dock nor witness box.

For law books I had my own set of the *Laws of Sierra*

Leone. With much difficulty I had managed to obtain copies of the supplementary volumes added in recent years, which the Government Printer never produced in adequate numbers. I wrote to the master and registrar of the Supreme Court, asking him to send me reasonably up-to-date practitioners' reference books on criminal law and evidence. He sent me an obsolete edition of Archbold's *Criminal Pleading, Practice and Procedure* and I had to make do with that. I had a constant struggle to keep myself supplied with stationery. I sometimes sat for seven hours a day or more, writing all the time and using foolscap paper at a tremendous rate. Repeated letters and telegrams to Freetown requesting further supplies were ignored and eventually in exasperation I sent my court clerk to Freetown with instructions to bring back as much stationery as he could get. He managed to bring me enough to last a week. Had it not been for the constant scrounging of stationery from the DC's office I would have been forced to suspend all cases for want of paper on which to keep the court record. The story about an administrative officer who in similar circumstances began to keep the court record on torn up cement bags is probably apocryphal.

A further embarrassing difficulty was the need to appear each day dressed in a suit. Our normal working dress of open-necked shirt and shorts would not do for court, and I had only one suit, made of linen and not a very good fit. I had long ago realized that the tropical outfitters in London who had sold it to me in 1954 had not gone out of their way to give me good value for money, but it was only now, when I was wearing it every day, that its most serious shortcomings became apparent. The trousers lost their crease and became rumpled as soon as I put them on. After a time I gave up wearing them and wore instead a pair of khaki shorts and long stockings, which with jacket and tie made me reasonably presentable. However, my jacket then began to disintegrate. Frequent wear and washing caused the collar and lapels to fray badly. Bit by bit I had to have the whole collar replaced by pieces of material cut out from the lining. Later I had another jacket made locally at great expense, which seemed passable when I first tried it on but soon showed up the limitations of the tailor's craftsmanship when, after being washed for the first time, it resolved itself into a shapeless mass of creases.

Problems of this kind were never accepted as excuses for falling down on the job, at least not in the provincial administration, to which I still belonged although I was devoting the whole of my time to judicial work. There was a huge volume of cases to be dealt with every day and I had to sit for long hours to prevent myself being swamped. The majority of them were charges of illicit diamond mining, the main economic activity of the district. Shortly before my arrival in Kono the situation had got out of hand and the government had been forced to bring in hastily drafted legislation restricting the entry of Africans into the district from other parts of Sierra Leone. Hitherto the only residential restrictions had been on 'native strangers' — something of an oxymoron — from neighbouring Guinea and Liberia.

Under the new legislation no one who was not a native of the district could enter the area declared as a diamond protection area without a permit issued, in the case of a native, by the tribal authority of the chiefdom in question, or in the case of a non-native by the DC. At the same time the Alluvial Mining Ordinance was amended, providing a *minimum* sentence of one year in gaol for anyone convicted of the offence of illicit diamond mining (IDM). This was draconian legislation indeed and I was sent to Kono to administer it. Hugh Beattie had explained all this to me when I was his guest at Kenema, and he made it clear that he expected me to toe the line and convict and hand out appropriate sentences in the interests of improving the security situation in the district. When I pointed out that I would be independent when sitting as magistrate he was obviously not pleased and told me that this was arguable. I replied that so far as I was concerned there was no argument. No one could tell me how to judge cases that came before me in a judicial capacity and my only master was the law.

IDM cases were long and tedious and it was not long before I came to the conclusion that I could easily have had printed sheets produced with a standard form of testimony on them for prosecution and defence witnesses, leaving blank spaces for names to be filled in. The evidence of a police witness usually read as follows in the record:

> At 2.00 a.m. on the morning of 9 January I was on patrol with Sergeant Turay. Police Constable Yawai Number 582 was also in the patrol. We went near Jowahun swamp where we came upon a dozen men working with shovels and sieves. These are the tools people normally use when they are engaged in illicit diamond mining and I believe that that is what they were all doing. We surrounded the men, then Sergeant Turay blew his whistle and we all ran into the swamp. I saw the second accused holding a shovel. When he saw me running towards him he dropped the shovel and ran away. I caught him, brought him back to where the shovel was and told him to pick it up. This is the shovel [identified, tendered and marked Exhibit A]. I cautioned the accused and he said, 'it is all right; I admit I was digging diamonds. I was hard up.'

A typical statement by the accused in his own defence might read thus:

> I never saw this policeman before. I do not know why he arrested me. I was suffering from dysentery and went to Jowahun swamp to relieve myself late at night.

Suddenly I saw some policemen running through the swamp. This policeman came up to me, grabbed me by the shoulder and said, 'I am arresting you for digging diamonds.' I replied, 'I have not been digging diamonds, I came here only to relieve myself.' The policeman made me go with him to where there were some shovels lying on the ground. He made me pick up one of them and carry it back to the police post. There were a lot of other men at the police post who had also been arrested, but I had never seen any of them before. The evidence against me is all lies.

There was a certain amount of fabrication of evidence and perjury on both sides, but on the whole the police presented their cases well, and the defence evidence was usually too ridiculous and flimsy to be taken seriously. Police prosecutors were not very good at cross-examination, but even so were often able, with a few skilful questions, to show up the transparent falsity of the statements made by the accused and their witnesses. It was not difficult to do justice, but some of the cases were unconscionably long. The police would often arrest as many as 20 men in a single raid and put all their names on the same charge sheet. Few of the accused pleaded guilty, knowing what heavy penalties they were liable to incur, and in consequence I would have to record over 20 statements on each side. Everything had to be interpreted, since most of the accused were illiterate and spoke no English, and this doubled the length of the proceedings. A case of this kind would often take up to 12 hours of court time and I felt a sense of relief when I finally passed judgment and sentenced those whom I had found guilty. This relief was, however, tempered by the realization that many more such cases were on my list awaiting disposal.

Once or twice a week, as a form of relaxation, I would deal with traffic offences. The accused in these cases were lorry drivers who did not want to lose money by spending time in court and who felt in any case that no great moral stigma was involved in being convicted of having a vehicle on the road in a mechanically unsound condition or not licensed for the current year. They would plead guilty, pay their fines and go back to work. I felt an almost pathological gratitude to these men for providing light relief in this way and enabling me to dispose of a few cases so speedily. I was envious of the Bow Street magistrates, whom I had seen in action for a few days during the Devonshire Course, disposing nonchalantly of cases against drunks, prostitutes and petty thieves at great speed.

Legend had it that one of Sierra Leone's puisne judges, a Mancunian, was in the habit when taking criminal sessions of advising prisoners on how to plead to the charges against them in the following fatherly way: 'Now if you plead not guilty and make me sit here for hours on end writing down evidence I shall be bloody annoyed and give you a heavy sentence. So if you are sensible, plead guilty, save me a lot of time and bother and I won't be too hard on you.' Advice cast in this form is hardly consonant with the rules of natural justice, but I could sympathize with the judge's feelings if he did say that. Recording evidence is drudgery, particularly when there are no court stenographers and the judge or magistrate has to bear the entire burden of keeping a verbatim record. At the end of each day my fingers were cramped from holding a pen and I was bored and exhausted by having had to listen to the same monotonous evidence from so many different mouths.

In spite of the tedium, the work had some consolations. It gave me more sophisticated contacts than I was accustomed to in the course of daily work in a district office, where so much of the time was taken up with listening to illiterate complainants. I now had before me every day educated police inspectors and sometimes officers of the rank of assistant superintendent and above, as well as a stream of lawyers from Freetown, who had no trouble finding prosperous clients to defend in Kono District. The quality of their advocacy was not high and I never found myself over-whelmed by their superior knowledge of the law. It some-times happened that I acquitted a defendant on grounds that his counsel had failed to argue. In one case the police failed to give any evidence to show what the defendant had been doing, which caused them to arrest him and put into the witness box only the constable who had subsequently taken down a written statement at the police station. This was a glaring omission and defence counsel ought to have been on his feet as soon as the police prosecutor had closed his case, submitting to me that there was no case to answer. How-ever, the lawyer concerned had not even noticed this patent defect and was about to put his client into the witness box. I saved him the trouble by acquitting and discharging the defendant forthwith. It grieved me to think that counsel was earning much kudos and substantial fees but doing nothing at all to deserve them.

Occasionally a case came up that involved consideration of a point of law and gave me a break from the dreary routine of sending illicit diamond miners to gaol. I had no law books to refer to other than the Sierra Leone ordinances and my outdated copy of Archbold, but relying on these and on fad-ing recollections of the law tripos at Cambridge I blithely went ahead and gave judgment in a rough-and-ready manner.

The laws governing diamond mining and restrictions on the entry of persons into the diamond protection areas were complicated and understood by few people. They illustrated the pragmatic but sometimes haphazard methods of British colonial administration and can be quoted in support of the thesis I adumbrated earlier, that when the theory was put into practice literally it produced some ludicrous results that would have astonished Lugard. At the end of 1958, when there had been an almost complete breakdown of law and order in the district and illicit mining was taking place on an unprecedented scale, government rushed through emergency legislation as part of an attempt to reassert its increasingly discredited authority. At this point I beg the reader's indulgence for going into slightly technical legal detail.

Since most illicit mining was being done by hordes of fortune-seeking Africans from districts other than Kono, as well as others from Liberia and Guinea, Sierra Leone's two neighbours, there was a pressing need to devise a way of restricting entry to the diamond protection areas. Diamond dealing was in the hands of wealthy Mandingoes and Lebanese. The government already had powers to exclude non-'natives' (a term that covered Creoles from Freetown as well as Europeans, Syrians, Lebanese, people of mixed race and others who did not belong to protectorate tribes) unless they held a permit from the district commissioner. Permits were issued for a limited period and could be revoked at any time.

Starting from first principles, the logical extension of this particular law would have been an amendment requiring everyone who was not by birth a member of the Kono tribe to show that he or she had been long resident in the diamond protection area, also to obtain a residential permit from the DC. A solution of such simplicity, however, did not meet the demands of Sierra Leone politics, according to which the paramount chiefs and the tribal authorities were the real rulers and therefore must have control over the movements of Africans within their jurisdiction. This was dogma, and it was pointless to argue that it took no account of the turbulent state of the district or that it was no way for the government to protect the rights it had granted to the mining company, which had invested a large amount of capital in its operations in the country and was making a huge contribution to the country's revenues by the taxes and royalties it paid.

The tribal authorities certainly in theory had a vital part to play in the maintenance of law and order within their chiefdoms, but the events of recent months had shown that they had made no effort to perform this duty; even had the will been there, the situation had gone beyond their effective power of control. The government would have been fully justified in arrogating to itself maximum powers for dealing with the emergency, but it preferred to stick to the theory of indirect rule rather than risk offending the paramount chiefs.

Rules to regulate the movement of 'native strangers' in the six chiefdoms within the diamond protection area were drafted in the secretariat. I am certain that no paramount chief or member of a tribal authority had any hand in the process and it is unlikely that they would have had any constructive ideas to offer if their comments had been invited. These rules, which were identical in all respects save for the name of the chiefdom and were to be promulgated under rule-making powers contained in the Tribal Authorities' Ordinance, were then placed before each of the six tribal authorities concerned and their general significance explained to them by the DC. After the usual debating and hanging of heads, each of the tribal authorities approved the rules, which thus became law. The rules defined a 'native stranger' as one who did not belong to or was not ordinarily resident in a particular chiefdom. No 'native stranger' was allowed to remain in a chiefdom without a permit from the tribal authority and anyone arrested in the chiefdom who did not hold a permit was committing an offence and liable to a prison sentence.

Ostensibly these were local by-laws made by a tribal authority and enforceable by that authority in the native court. In practice, they were an attempt to implement a new government policy, which was very necessary for the security of the country, through a circuitous and clumsy procedure. It was impossible to make them work as intended

because the tribal authorities were reluctant to drive strangers out of their chiefdoms. The strangers were a source of
additional taxes for the African administration and other less
lawful payments levied by individual members of the tribal
authority who were not averse to lining their own pockets,
and their earnings from illicit mining created unwonted
prosperity. Furthermore, even if they had been willing to
make the by-laws work, they were not equipped to do so,
not having any police forces of their own and having to rely
on government police. This was local government gone mad.

It was up to the police to enforce the by-laws and their
usual method of doing so was to surround larger towns and
villages just before daybreak, search all the houses and arrest
any non-Konos who had no permits. The men arrested were
then taken before the native court, which was requested to
try the men arrested on charges under the by-laws. Sometimes they cooperated and imposed fines or prison sentences,
but on one occasion the court sitting in one of the chiefdom
headquarters towns flatly refused to convict anyone the
police brought before it. Over 100 men had been arrested
and there was a danger of the whole operation being a complete failure. To avert this the assistant district commissioner
who had accompanied the police intervened and ordered
that all the cases still outstanding be transferred to the magistrate's court, which he had power to do under the 'Native
Courts Ordinance'.

This bizarre legislation illustrates a maxim that used to be
quoted: 'under direct rule you decide what you want to do
and do it. Under indirect rule you decide what you want to
do, try to persuade the local rulers that that is what they also
want to do, give them the powers to do it, then do it yourself!'

It fell to me to hear the cases against these men, a daunting
prospect since each of them had to be tried individually.
Another element in this topsy-turvy situation was that senior
members of the tribal authority concerned, in theory the

prosecutors, hired one of Freetown's best lawyers to come to Kono and conduct the defence. He was Berthan Macauley, noted for his ability to find loopholes in local legislation. His main defence in the first of the cases to come before me was that the by-laws under which the accused had been charged were invalid. In the by-laws a 'stranger' was defined as a person who did not belong to or was not ordinarily resident in the chiefdom. However, in the diamond protection ordinance a 'stranger' was defined as any person other than a native of the protectorate. This meant that there was a conflict, for the by-laws defined a stranger much more narrowly and purported to make strangers requiring permits out of people who were natives of other parts of the protectorate. Since the ordinance was primary legislation it must prevail and the by-law was invalid. I gave myself half an hour to think about this submission, came to the conclusion that it was unanswerable, wrote out a hasty judgment in which I found the by-law invalid and went back to court to deliver it and acquit the accused.

In these proceedings the forces were unequal. Having found out beforehand that Berthan Macauley intended to raise this issue, I agreed with him that it would be appropriate to mount a test case. When I warned the police about this, they sent a European assistant superintendent to conduct the prosecution, a duty that would normally fall to an inspector or sergeant. However, even senior police officers are not skilled in the law. Later my provincial commissioner told me that I ought to have adjourned the hearing, since the prosecutors were obviously not skilled at arguing legal points of this kind and should have been given an opportunity to bring counsel up from Freetown to act for them and ensure that the case was properly argued for the crown. To this I replied that if the police had asked for an adjournment for this purpose I would certainly have granted one, but they had not done so and it was not appropriate for me to suggest one.

May I not be accused of immodesty when I relate that this decision of mine upset the governor, prime minister, attorney general, provincial commissioner, ministers and others as much as a major riot. I appeared to have toppled the clumsy edifice of legislation. Retribution was soon under way. The attorney general immediately lodged an appeal, which was heard a few weeks later in the Supreme Court. The attorney general himself appeared for the crown and Berthan Macauley for the accused. My decision was overruled on the point of the invalidity of the by-laws, though the acquittal of the accused was upheld on a different ground, namely that the prosecution had failed to prove that the accused was a stranger as defined. The effect of this judgment of the Supreme Court was that the by-laws, though now held to be valid, were in any case unworkable, for it would be impossible to prove that a man did not belong to or was not ordinarily resident in any particular chiefdom. The police were therefore forced to withdraw the charges against the 100 plus men who had been arrested.

I took what some might think was a perverse satisfaction in the brief moment of fame or notoriety the case brought me. I often thought about it afterwards and concluded that I ought to have spent more time writing such an important judgment. I did it in a hurry because I knew that Berthan Macauley was leaving for Freetown that same day and because I felt sure of my reasoning. I should of course have borne in mind the possibility of an appeal and have written a more cogently argued order. In his judgment, the learned Supreme Court judge admitted that he found Berthan Macauley's submission attractive, but nevertheless was able to give reasons for rejecting it. Had my order been less slapdash he might have been convinced. As it was, in quoting one paragraph he said, 'With respect, I am unable to follow the learned magistrate's reasoning.' This was hardly surprising.

Later I discussed the case with Sir Milton Margai, Sierra

239

Leone's first prime minister, when he was visiting the district. He spoke of the consternation I had caused in Freetown, but added that he had been very happy to point out to his fellow ministers that this was a decision *against the government* by an administrative officer sitting in a judicial capacity. There was much feeling among politicians that administrative officers ought no longer to be empowered to sit as magistrates, as they were thought to be incapable of distinguishing between their executive and judicial functions and were suspected of allowing political and administrative considerations to influence their judgements. Here was a clear disproof of that theory.

This and a few other cases involving the interpretation of controversial portions of the same by-laws brightened a few days in court, but otherwise I had to face the same daily drudgery and wanted to get back to administrative work. There was some improvement in the security situation and a reduction in the volume of arrests being made by the police, and I took advantage of this lull to ask to be relieved of full time magisterial work.

16

Finale

The Sierra Leone Selection Trust, an enigmatically named and British owned company, dominated Kono District. It carried on opencast mining in all those parts of the district in which it had concessions. This process involved the sifting of diamondiferous alluvial gravel in special jigs and the use of bulldozers, dragline excavators, giant dumpers and elaborate pan plants where the sifting was done. Its headquarters were at Yengema, seven miles from Sefadu. It employed large numbers of Europeans as plant foremen, geologists, engineers, accountants, security staff and even a pilot for the light aircraft it operated from its own small airfield. Most of them lived in beautiful bungalows on the company's estate, though a few were scattered around the district away from Yengema, looking after outlying pan plants.

The club at Yengema was the centre of social life and government officers were welcome as guests. It had a huge bar, a snooker room, tennis court, open-air swimming pool and nine-hole golf course. To someone like myself, accustomed to remote stations, such amenities were a rare delight. We all went to Yengema frequently, especially on Sundays when there was always a large gathering in the bar at lunchtime and a free film show in the evening. The *barri*, which I used as a court, was on the road from Sefadu to Yengema, and often I would go straight from court into the swimming pool, glad to get rid of the dust and sweat and meta-phorically purge myself of all the stuffy formality of the day's wearisome proceedings.

While I was there the company celebrated the 25th anniversary of its operations in Sierra Leone. There was much junketing, with sports days, dances, parties and a beauty queen contest. The Sierra Leone police band was brought up from Freetown and gave a concert on the company's football pitch. The highlight of the performance was 'Beating the Retreat', in the same routine as the Royal Marines, ending with the moving and nostalgic 'Sunset Call' on the bugles.

We were sometimes envious of the affluence the company's European staff enjoyed. They were paid salaries beyond our wildest dreams and occupied beautifully furnished bungalows rent free, plus all the other facilities I have described. On the other hand, they had to lead circumscribed lives, seeing nothing other than their places of work and getting to know nothing of Africa. They lived a cocooned existence at Yengema and formed a thoroughly inbred community whose members never saw anything of outsiders either at work or in their leisure hours. As government officers living at Sefadu we were poor relations, but we led more interesting lives.

After much lobbying, I was able to cease sitting full time as a magistrate in June 1959. The government needed a development officer for the district and, being on the spot, I was appointed to the position when I indicated an interest. For years Kono had been neglected and little public money had been spent there, although it had contributed a substantial slice of the country's wealth and taxes. Two years previously a survey of the district's needs had been undertaken and a development plan had been produced, covering roads, electricity supplies, telephones, agriculture, forestry, social development and so on. Unfortunately, there had been a financial crisis in 1958 and the government was hard pressed to find the funds to keep essential services going, so there was little left for financing new capital projects. The most important schemes, especially the improvement and surfacing of the district's main roads, had to be shelved. In spite of these financial constraints, £80,000 of public money was provided to be divided among all the departments that had an interest in Kono, and it was a major part of my responsibilities to ensure that this was made to go as far as possible. In addition, all six African administrations within the diamond protection areas were prosperous and had thousands of pounds to spend on capital works, but they had neither the energy nor the skilled staff to make sure that the money was put to good use. All of them were keen to spend large sums on enormous new *barris* for prestige purposes. I tried unsuccessfully to dissuade them, but once one chiefdom had had a *barri* built on an impressive scale, costing £4000, the others had to follow suit.

This was a constructive and beneficial task, all the more welcome to me after the endless and depressing routine of sending illicit miners to gaol. These attempts at development had of course a political motive, in that the government realized that it was not enough merely to control security and prevent disorder. In the best colonial tradition, money was somehow found for a few capital schemes in order to appease the critics who made the well-justified complaint that the district had been neglected. These schemes would bring the extra benefit of providing a certain amount of employment for young men who would receive wages that were at least regular, if not as spectacular as the potential earnings from illicit mining. This belated provision of funds and my appointment as development officer illustrated a well-known colonial aphorism; 'there is nothing like a riot for the roads.'

I was doing the kind of work the more idealistic administrative cadets of my generation used to dream of, and with far more money under my control than they would normally have been able to expect. I set about establishing a small works organization by collecting contributions from the more prosperous chiefdoms. I helped the Kono district council recruit a European inspector of works to take charge of maintenance of the council's roads. I had discussions with the Posts and Telegraphs Department about setting up a telephone exchange in Koidu, toured all the new public works schemes in progress in the district and supervised the improvement of a native administration water supply. I called on the general manager of SLST whose company, as a special contribution to the welfare of the district, had undertaken to spend £10,000 annually on development and at this time all the money was being spent on primary schools.

I enjoyed the job. I toured the district much more than I had been able to do previously and became acquainted with the paramount chiefs and other personalities. Nevertheless, I felt that it was time for me to be moving. I was almost 29 and it seemed doubtful whether there would be much of an empire left to govern within a few years. I was rooted and happy and had no wish to leave. I had never worked in the United Kingdom and most of my friends and acquaintances were now in Sierra Leone. I am able, however, to face unpleasant decisions, even though I may reach them only after much internal agony. At the beginning of July 1959 I wrote out my resignation and asked to be released in October. It was not well received. No one tried to dissuade me, but an attempt was made to keep me until the following spring. In the end I had my way and a sea passage home in October was booked for me.

I began the melancholy task of selling possessions and winding up my affairs. I sold my car for less than I still owed the government on the loan I had received to buy it three years earlier. Cars had a very low resale value because of the punishment they took on Sierra Leone's atrocious roads. I felt pangs at parting with my camp equipment, the bed, trek boxes and other battered items, which had been my constant companions, providing a modicum of comfort on trek.

I spent the last few weeks saying goodbye to friends and to a job that meant a great deal to me. I often wondered whether I had made the right decision, though looking back I have no doubts. If I could have felt that there was any prospect of a career in Sierra Leone or in any other territory to which I might have been transferred, I would not have resigned. But Colonial Office policies gave little assurance to young men in my position. We had the option of continuing in the service of newly independent governments, but few of us were enthusiastic about that. It would have meant working under very different conditions from those to which we were accustomed and poor promotion prospects, since preference would obviously be given to African officers.

Transfers to one or other of the remaining colonies were possible but often meant accepting a reduction in salary, and serving officers in the receiving colonies resented them because they upset the local balance of seniority. I had seen this happen in Sierra Leone, to which some officers were transferred from Ghana following independence. They were older men and came into more senior positions, which reduced the promotion prospects for men my age. Men who stayed on to the end when the Union Jack was finally hauled down and then left were given lump sums by way of compensation and pensions based on length of service. For men of my age and length of service the benefits were modest and I concluded that they were not worth waiting for.

The British government's policies on this matter came under fire in 1961, and criticisms were levelled at the Commonwealth Relations Office (CRO) (later merged into the Foreign Office). The department was expanding rapidly as a result of the number of territories gaining independence; though hard pressed to find staff to man its new missions abroad, it nevertheless resolutely refused to give preference to former members of the service on the grounds that they were tainted with colonialism and were therefore unacceptable to the governments of the newer members of the Commonwealth. For some reasons that are not immediately apparent, the civil servants from the contracting Colonial Office in London, who belonged to the home civil service and were the ultimate policy makers, were not considered to be tainted in this way and were regarded as readily acceptable recruits by the CRO — and this was in spite of the fact that most of them had no overseas experience at all.

A member of the government at the time went so far as to say in public that the overseas civil service was an embarrassment. It was deplorable that the masters of this body of dedicated people could find no better epithet for them. This attitude is reminiscent of that often complained of by returning ex-servicemen after the Second World War. Once the heroes of the hour, many of them found themselves unwelcome in the civilian community, which they had helped to save but which when the danger was past found them to be of no better value than a fireplace in a heat wave. Many of us felt that the British government was callous and indifferent in its treatment of members of the overseas civil service who had to face redundancy and the painful search for a new career when their territories became independent.

On the positive side there were gains to be listed. I, who from my youngest days had grown up to a bookish and solitary life, convinced that the rough and tumble of practical affairs were not for me, had astonished myself by falling into — and making a success of — a career and manner of living that posed major practical challenges daily. I had found a modest ability to deal with human beings and exercise power over them in a judicious manner that left no rancour in the hearts of those who had to accept decisions that were against their interests. I had learned to be a reasonably competent administrator and had even acquired a practical outlook in relation to motor vehicles and other essential pieces of machinery. I could not claim to have learned to build houses and roads as men in my position often had to do 20 years earlier, but I was able to discuss the practical problems of construction with engineers in a knowledgeable fashion and to supervise the work of contractors engaged on small projects without allowing them to swindle on too large a scale.

Above all, I had learned to be self-reliant. I could exercise judgement and make decisions without trepidation and without always feeling the need to consult someone else, since normally there *was* no one else to consult. I could run my own household and manage contentedly with the minimum of the trappings of civilization. I doubt whether any other initial career would ever have wrought such changes in me, transforming me from a nervous and timorous cadet into a confident administrative officer who in earlier days could reasonably have looked forward to a successful working lifetime in the service.

The chance to assume responsibility at an early age was the most valuable thing the service could offer, particularly as it was linked sometimes with an imperative necessity to cope with almost impossible conditions on an inadequate salary.

> This chance is now denied to young men from British universities and the country is the poorer for it. Part of the price of giving up an empire is the loss of opportunities for adventure, condemning us all to narrow horizons.

So, on 9 October 1959 I stood on the deck of the *Apapa* as it cleared Freetown harbour, the ship half empty because this was the slack season for travelling between West Africa and Europe. I watched the hills of the colony peninsula slip behind us until they were out of sight and reflected that I would probably never see them again. As the result of a perhaps perverse but necessary decision I was leaving behind this frustrating but at the same time delightful country and work I knew and loved in order to plunge into I knew not what. It might be said that because of the final necessity for this drastic decision, the five years had been wasted. I could not agree with this; in those five years I had added cubits to my stature. I had had enough wealth and range of experience to enable a more gifted man to write volumes and to move me to write this one volume of modest dimensions. The service had given me much to look back on that was worthwhile, and not the least of its consolations was that I could now truthfully say,

> But today I leave the galley,
> Shall I curse her service then?
> God be thanked — whate'er comes after,
> I have lived and toiled with men.

Index

249

Index

Index

Index

Index